Taya the Tortoise
Activity Book for Children who Bottle Up,
Retreat, or Disconnect

By the same author

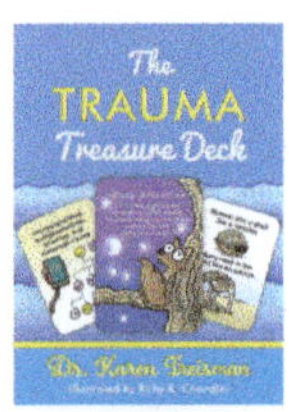

The Trauma Treasure Deck
A Creative Tool for Assessments, Interventions, and Learning for Work with Adversity and Stress in Children and Adults
Dr Karen Treisman
Illustrated by Richy K. Chandler
ISBN 978 1 83997 137 2

A Therapeutic Treasure Deck of Sentence Completion and Feelings Cards
Dr Karen Treisman
ISBN 978 1 78592 398 2

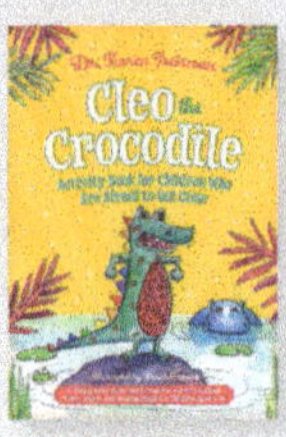

Cleo the Crocodile Activity Book for Children Who Are Afraid to Get Close
A Therapeutic Story with Creative Activities About Trust, Anger, and Relationships for Children Aged 5–10
Dr Karen Treisman
Illustrated by Sarah Peacock
ISBN 978 1 78592 551 1
eISBN 978 1 78775 078 4

Therapeutic Treasures Collection

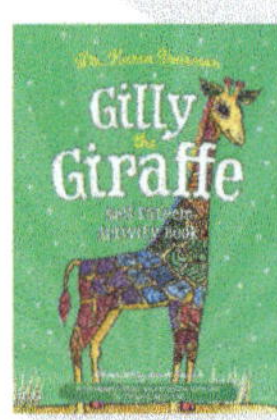

Gilly the Giraffe Self-Esteem Activity Book
A Therapeutic Story with Creative Activities for Children Aged 5–10
Dr Karen Treisman
Illustrated by Sarah Peacock
ISBN 978 1 78592 552 8
eISBN 978 1 78775 003 6

Taya the Tortoise

Activity Book for Children who Bottle Up, Retreat, or Disconnect

A Therapeutic Story with Creative Activities About Trauma and Dissociation for Children Aged 5–10, with Advice for Adults

Dr. Karen Treisman

Illustrated by Emma Paxton and Sarah Peacock

Jessica Kingsley Publishers
London and Philadelphia

First published in Great Britain in 2026 by Jessica Kingsley Publishers
An imprint of John Murray Press

1

A CIP catalogue record for this title is available from the British Library and the Library of Congress

ISBN 978 1 80501 795 0
eISBN 978 1 80501 796 7

Printed and bound in Great Britain by Ashford Colour Ltd

Jessica Kingsley Publishers' policy is to use papers that are natural, renewable and recyclable products and made from wood grown in sustainable forests. The logging and manufacturing processes are expected to conform to the environmental regulations of the country of origin.

Jessica Kingsley Publishers
Carmelite House
50 Victoria Embankment
London EC4Y 0DZ

www.jkp.com

John Murray Press
Part of Hodder & Stoughton Limited
An Hachette UK Company

The authorised representative in the EEA is Hachette Ireland, 8 Castlecourt Centre, Dublin 15, D15 XTP3, Ireland (email: info@hbgi.ie)

Contents

Understanding Trauma, Dissociation, and Retreating Behaviours 195

Therapeutic Re-parenting Skills, Tools, and Ways of Being 217

Resources 241

Acknowledgements

This book has been inspired by hundreds of children and teenagers, and their parents, carers, and professionals who support them. It is for those who have felt silenced, unseen, misunderstood, ignored; those who have fallen through the net or under the radar; those who have had to retreat, go inwards, disconnect; those who have been given labels such as 'quiet', 'shy', 'numb', 'hollow', 'empty', 'not fussed', 'fine'. I want to thank you for trusting me with your experiences, hopes, worries, and needs. I hope this book is a gift to you.

Thanks to the many amazing social workers, foster carers, kinship carers, children homes workers, teachers, adopters, and therapists along my way for their suggestions and questions in training and in consultations which help me form the content and make it as relevant and real to the audience as possible. And a special thanks to two of my best friends and brilliant therapists, Sue Hollingsworth and Carlotta Raby, for their ongoing support and powerful reflections during the process of writing.

I also want to thank my niece, Taya, for the inspiration of the name! And to my sister, Nicky, who took me on the most incredible trip to Ethiopia, which inspired this book's location.

I want to thank my wonderful and appreciated editor, Stephen Jones, for believing in me, for supporting me, and for giving me a platform to talk about this important topic. And all the wonderful team at Jessica Kingsley Publishers, including Jenny Edwards, who make this possible, from editing, to marketing, to formatting, to the front cover design, to printing, and beyond!

I also want to do a huge shout out to my incredible illustrators, Sarah Peacock, who did all the illustrations for the children's story and for all of my children's workbooks, and to the amazing Emma Paxton from Imagistical, for doing the majority of the worksheets and interactive activities. You are both a joy to work with and your talent and creativity are so appreciated and so enrich these resources. I am so grateful to you both!

About this Workbook

Hello, my name is Karen, I am a clinical psychologist, and I am also the author of this activity book, alongside the fantastic and colourful Taya the Tortoise.

You are not alone! The ideas in this book have helped lots of other children all around the world, who have sadly been hurt and let down and who have understandably had to learn to keep themselves safe by retreating into their shell, by disconnecting, distancing themselves, going quiet, or bottling-up their emotions. This activity book is here to help you and the grown-ups around you to:

- find ways to understand some of your feelings, sensations, and responses a bit more, in a way that feels safe and helpful to you
- find ways for you to show and communicate how you might be feeling, and to have people to be there to listen and to help you make sense of those feelings
- understand where the bottling-up, disconnecting, and retreating might have come from, and why they are there
- find ways to be able to come out of your shell (while understanding that you still might need to retreat for a bit)
- start to let some of the good, fun, positive things, feelings, and people back into your heart
- learn about some of the advantages of trusting some people and of being part of a team.

What is inside this workbook

- First, there is the illustrated story of Taya the Tortoise.
- Then there are lots of fun activities for you to do around Taya the Tortoise, such as colouring-in pages, a word search, a quiz, and some Taya-inspired arts and crafts ideas.
- These are followed by anchoring, regulating, grounding, soothing, and coping ideas. These are things which you can do before, during, or after going through parts of the story, activities, or other things in your day. These can be helpful when things might feel a bit overwhelming, a bit too much, a bit stingy, scary, or thorny. They might also give you a little brain break or a bit of a boost or reset, or support when you are gearing up to do something. This includes some things to help you to discover your different senses and to start to create or add to your treasure box of sensory, cognitive, and movement ideas that support you.
- Next, there are some activities to learn a bit more about your feelings – how to recognize them, how to understand them a bit more, how to show or express them, and how to respond to them.
- The last part is focused on different ways of letting in the possible magic, joy, and good things about life and relationships, including what makes us smile, laugh, and feel good, and what the benefits are of making connections with other people.
- After your sections, there is a whole section for the adults who are supporting you with this activity book to read, which gives them lots more ideas, games, and activities to help you. They will read their part first, so that they can help you along the way.

Things to remember when reading this workbook

- Take your time, there is no rush. It can be one step at a time, slow and steady, like a tortoise. It is a journey and we can go at our own pace and revisit at different times.
- The adults reading the activity book with you are there to help you along the way. Remember you are not alone, this is a team effort.
- Different activities and ideas will work and fit differently. We are all unique in our own way. There is no right or wrong. So, you and the adults helping you can choose which ideas and activities you want to try, and which suit you.
- The most important bit is that you make the ideas fit for you – you know what works best for you.

We are here believing in you and rooting for you, sending heart prints.

From Karen and Taya

Copies of the activities can be downloaded from https://digitalhub.jkp.com/redeem using the voucher code DXRWQMD

The Story of Taya the Tortoise

In the lush mountains and the desert lands of Ethiopia in Africa lived a colourful, beautifully patterned tortoise named Taya.

Taya loved to bask in the sun on the warm sand. She would slowly glide from place to place, digging muddy holes and pushing pebbles around the soil.

She loved to climb over the smooth stones and the crunchy branches.

Taya would spend her day at Baobab school.

Her favourite thing to do when she was there was art. She also really liked the obstacle course in the playground with its maze and tunnel.

Her teacher, Miss Daisy the Donkey, wore a garland of beautiful flowers and was very kind, patient, and caring. Taya liked how Miss Daisy would read the class poems and stories with all of the different voices.

Miss Daisy was so excited every morning when the children arrived to class, and she greeted them with a big smile on her face.

There were lots of other animals in Taya's class.

Taya's favourite friends were Cosmo the Camel and Harley the Hyena.

She liked how creative and imaginative Cosmo was – they both liked painting and colouring, so they could do it together.

Harley the Hyena was also great to be around as he was bubbly, funny, and confident.

Taya lived with grown-up tortoises, Tristan and Tillie.

They looked after Taya and really cared about her.

Taya's favourite thing to do with Tristan and Tillie was to go on nature treasure hunts. She would smell the wild jasmine, hunt for different plants, and climb on the rocks.

Tillie loved to sing to her and sometimes they would dance together while baking.

Taya hadn't always lived with Tristan and Tillie.

Before she moved to live with them, she was living with her mum and dad, and had been at a different school.

Living with Tillie and Tristan and being at Baobab school was all quite new. Taya was still getting used to it. There were some bits she liked and some that felt strange and different.

When she had lived with her mum and dad, Taya couldn't bask in the sun, or dig holes, or push pebbles. Her world and her life had looked and felt different.

Taya had lived through a lot of hurtful, thorny, stingy, and painful twists and turns.

Bumps and bashes...

Whirlwinds and stormy feeling seas...

Ups and downs...

She had been hurt, scared, and let down many times by her parents, in lots of different ways. There had been a galaxy of times when she had not felt protected and had not been kept safe.

In the past, Taya's world had sometimes felt too scary: too heavy, too big, and too much. She felt this way when painful things were happening to her.

Even when they were not, Taya would feel worried. She had a sense of dread about them happening again.

Taya had a whole mixture and tidal wave of feelings.

Back then it was often hard for Taya to find the words to say how she felt.

She felt scared to share what she was feeling or thinking.

She didn't know what would happen if she shared how she felt – she worried about:

- getting into trouble
- being ignored
- nobody believing her
- being told to keep quiet.

So, Taya would keep these feelings deep inside, locked away and hidden.

To protect Taya, her body and her mind would sometimes become numb and feel nothing at all. This was to avoid and push away the feelings, to protect her from more hurt.

She often felt alone.

She didn't think there was anyone to share her problems with.

Sometimes other people were the reason for her feeling scared, so she didn't know who she could trust to help.

She didn't know who could explain what was happening when she faced the whirlwinds and stormy waters of her feelings.

Because she didn't know anyone who could help her in these scary times, Taya's own body created shielding tools to help protect her.

Taya's mind was able to defend her using her thoughts, memories, and feelings.

Taya's gut defended her by drawing on her senses, intuition, and strong feelings – including those 'uh-oh' feelings.

Taya's reflexes defended her using the automatic things her body or mind could do when they sensed danger.

These shielding tools were like having her very own 'spidey senses'. Like Spider-Man, her body could detect possible danger, give her warnings, and try to keep her safe. Sometimes she didn't even know that her body was doing it!

Here are some of the shielding tools that Taya's mind, gut, and reflexes created.

She could...

Fly away in her mind to a different place, to a fantasy world.

Retreat into her shell so things outside felt a bit more distant, fuzzy, and foggy.

Shrink from the world by making herself smaller or less visible.

Become very quiet, clam-up, or shut down.

Imagine that she was someone else.

Put up an 'emotional shield' to try to bounce feelings away from her.

Avoid or block her feelings.

Camouflage, mask, and hide her feelings, so that nobody could see her inside feelings from the outside.

Put a locked fence around her heart.

Go into a protective bubble.

Float away.

Leave her body and watch her life happen, as if it were someone else or a movie.

Bottle up her feelings and keep them to herself.

Taya's body had to survive and protect her many, many, many times. Its shielding tools and spidey senses had been her friend and her protector through thorny times.

Through practice, they had become strong and powerful.

In fact, they would often detect danger and spring into action even if they were not needed – a false alarm!

She would worry when other animals tried to get close, even if they were being friendly. Her shielding tools and spidey senses would go on high alert!

For example, when she was with caring Tristan and Tillie, Taya would still feel unsafe. She would sense danger – even though Taya knew that Tristan and Tillie were not a threat.

'Will they hurt me?'

'Can I trust them?'

'I don't want to get into danger, like before.'

Taya's body stayed on guard and set up its defences: retreating, clamming-up, numbing, and bottling-up her feelings.

She didn't know when her shielding tools and spidey senses would go into high alert. For example, it happened when she was...

- at school, enjoying some creative art, and she spotted a drawing that reminded her of a painful memory...
- cooking with Tillie, and she smelt something that made her brain and body scared...

- chatting with Cosmo and Harley, and she heard a loud noise that made the panic visit...

- crawling through the tunnel in the school playground and she suddenly felt trapped and stuck...

Sometimes, Taya didn't know why she found these smells, tastes, sounds, sights, and feelings scary. She'd just get a horrible unsafe feeling.

In these moments, it felt like travelling back in time. Like being catapulted down a memory time hole, back to when she was being hurt or felt scared.

Quick as a flash, Taya would make a speedy retreat into her shell, safe away from others and the outside world.

Once she was tucked away in her shell it felt safer and quieter. She was far too scared to stretch out her neck – just think what might happen.

When Taya hid inside her shell, her body would be there, but her mind would sometimes seem as if it had travelled to a faraway place.

In the playground, when others were running around and having fun, Taya would retreat in her shell. She might just daydream, nod off, or zone out.

When asked a question in class, Taya might stare out from her shell, as if Miss Daisy wasn't even there, and stay very quiet.

When Taya was hiding, she wouldn't share or talk about things with others and just kept things to herself.

Usually, Cosmo enjoyed doing artwork with her, and chatty Harley loved to hang out and play, but when Taya was hiding inside, they didn't know what to do to help her come out.

Tristan and Tillie would find it difficult to know what Taya needed – when she wanted to go out for a walk, have a cuddle, or even when she needed to eat!

Miss Daisy could see Taya needed help but didn't know how to help her.

Sometimes, they all felt as if Taya didn't like them or didn't want to be with them.

This could make Taya feel alone and misunderstood and made it even harder for her to try to open up and let them in.

When her feelings were locked deep inside, it was harder for Taya to show her feelings – to get close to the other animals who did care about her.

Taya would lock up her painful, thorny feelings and memories deep inside to protect herself from feeling or remembering the horrible things.

Sometimes when she stayed in her shell and blocked out her feelings, Taya also ended up blocking out other things.

She'd find there were gaps in her memory, and she would lose track of time – it was as if time just seemed to slip away from her without her realizing.

Sometimes, she'd feel as if she had 'brain fog' – her head would feel fuzzy and she'd struggle to learn at school, do her homework, or hear what the other animals were saying or doing.

At other times, she'd feel as if her brain was too full and her feelings and worries were going to spill out.

When Taya locked herself away or retreated into her shell, sometimes this stopped and blocked out some of the good, sparkly, happy, exciting, amazing, and joyful things from coming in or being felt. All of the colours and magic of life! This could also lock away important parts of herself – the things that make her so brilliant – such as:

- her creativity and art
- her gentle nature
- her adventurous spirit
- her digging holes in mud skills
- her love of cooking and singing.

It was tiring having to be on guard all the time. Taya would sometimes feel that life was heavy and tough.

She thought about happier times – about the rocks she loved to climb over and push around from place to place, and how it now felt as if she was weighed down and carrying them on her back.

Taya had a lot of painful memories and experiences when she lived with her parents – but slowly she came to realize that now she was in a different place.

She loved Baobab school, and was surrounded by friends and helpers: Tillie, Tristan, Cosmo the Camel, Harley the Hyena, and Miss Daisy the Donkey.

They never gave up on her. They believed in her. They remembered the Taya who lay behind her hard shell, behind the quietness, behind the shields, and behind the locks.

EFFORT
AWARD

Tristan and Tillie would remind Taya how much they cared – they would make time for her, and invite her to cook, take nature walks, or just be together.

When she asked them to, they would massage her shell gently, and use comforting smells and sounds to help Taya to feel 'calm' enough to peek out of her shell – the smell of jasmine from their nature walks, or freshly baked bread from a busy kitchen.

They shared some ideas that could help, like repeating encouraging words: 'I am ok', 'Things are different now', 'I am not alone'.

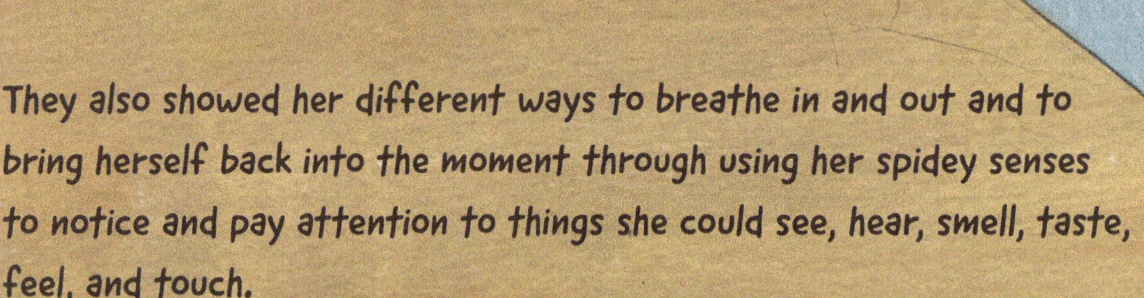

They also showed her different ways to breathe in and out and to bring herself back into the moment through using her spidey senses to notice and pay attention to things she could see, hear, smell, taste, feel, and touch.

They showed her how to move and 'relax' her body to make the big waves of 'uh-oh' feelings seem smaller, and so that she didn't feel stuck or trapped.

They told her that she could always take a few minutes and retreat into her shell if she needed to, until she felt ready to peek out again.

Each time Taya used one of these ideas, it became a little easier to do the next time.

Miss Daisy the Donkey would check in with Taya every morning – she'd ask what she might need. At the end of every day, she'd ask how her day had gone, and if there was anything they could do the next day to make it even better.

Miss Daisy helped Taya to find words to describe her feelings. If she couldn't find words she would paint her feelings, model them out of clay, or make a collage.

Miss Daisy told Taya that it was fine to say 'I don't know' if she was finding it hard in class. She said she was always happy to help, and she made Taya some communication cards to make this easier at school or home. They said things like 'I need to move around', 'My mind is wandering', 'I need some space'.

Each time Taya tried asking for help or said 'I don't know', and Miss Daisy was supportive and helped, she felt less worried and more confident about doing it next time.

At lunch, Cosmo the Camel would ask Taya if she'd like to spend time with her; Harley the Hyena would bounce up and down excitedly to see if Taya would like to go on an adventure.

They found moments to laugh, have fun, and play together: making dens, drawing in the sand, basking in the sun, digging holes, pushing pebbles around, and just hanging out!

Every time Taya joined in, she felt a little more comfortable. She found herself smiling and feeling more and more joyful!

Tillie and Tristan shared with Taya some more ideas which could help her – they explained how and why the spidey senses and shielding tools work and how they can give false high alerts, even when there is no real danger.

The more Taya understood her senses, and the more she came out of her shell, the less powerful they felt. Gradually, Taya started to create new memories and new adventures and she found she didn't need her spidey senses as often.

Her mind, gut, and reflexes started to learn new habits and would not go into high alert so often. She came to understand that it was ok to feel pain and to feel scared.

Through her own courage and the help of her friends, she knew she could get to a different place.

Together, Taya's friends showed her how much they loved her and how important she was. They wanted to hear what she had to say and how she felt.

By being kind and there for her, they showed Taya that they were a team and were in it together. Little by little, they left heart prints on her shell, each time brightening it a little more.

With the help of her friends, Taya started to find different ways to peek out of her shell – very very slowly, just like Taya's slow glide...

Glimmer by glimmer, peek by peek, moment by moment, heart print by heart print, Taya started to see how wonderful it could be to stretch her neck out a little.

She felt lighter, brighter, and more connected with the world. She was excited to see what she could see, hear, feel, touch, and notice when she was out of her shell.

Taya started to see the amazing shapes of the lush green Ethiopian mountains. The beautiful, big blue sky. The warming feeling on her shell from the beaming sun. The soft bouncy sand under her feet!

There were so many holes to be dug, dens to be made, and basking in the sun to happen – many more memories to create, heart prints to collect, and adventures to be had!

Activities

Introduction to the activities

This section features exercises and activities to explore the ideas covered in the story of Taya the Tortoise.

Before carrying out any of the exercises with your child, please first read the Guide for Adults – later in this activity book – to familiarize yourself with the ideas that lie behind the activities and how they can help your child. You and your child will get much more out of the activities if you first have a good understanding of what they are doing and how they work.

A huge part of working with children who retreat and dissociate is the responses of us as adults around them. With a subject like this, there is a lot of potential for the work to be misunderstood or misinterpreted, and even cause harm, so it's important that as responsible adults we do exercise care and ensure that our own knowledge and understanding of the topic are in place before we work through this book.

What is next?

I've grouped the activities in this section into three parts:

- Part 1: Anchoring, Regulating, Grounding, Soothing, and Coping Ideas
- Part 2: Exploring and Talking About Feelings
- Part 3: Letting Some Joy, Happiness, Fun, Lightness, and Connection In

Copies of the following activities can be downloaded from https://digitalhub.jkp.com/redeem using the voucher code DXRWQMD

Part 1

Anchoring, Regulating, Grounding, Soothing, and Coping Ideas

Activity 1

Fun Facts About Tortoises

Tortoises are so interesting.

Here are some facts which you might not know:

There are many different types and species of tortoises.

When tortoises are startled, they hide in their shell – they can hide their head, feet, and tail inside their shell.

A tortoise's shell is not a single shell, but rather is made up of multiple bony plates.

Tortoises can live for a very long time – sometimes over 100 years!

Tortoises are cold-blooded and get warmth from their environment. This is why they like sunbathing.

Most tortoises hibernate in the winter.

The largest tortoise species is the Galapagos tortoise, which can weigh up to 440 pounds and grow up to 1.2 metres long.

Shells have nerve endings, so tortoises can feel when they are rubbed, touched, or scratched.

Tortoises have no teeth, so they chew their food using ridges in their tough mouths.

Tortoises can have a sharp sense of smell and can be sensitive to bright light.

Females leave their eggs in deep burrows that they dig and let the eggs incubate for 90–120 days.

Tortoises are important symbols in some cultures: they can represent long life, wisdom, knowledge, protection, stability, strength, and perseverance. What do tortoises represent to you?

Female tortoises can lay up to 30 eggs at a time.

Tortoises have no ears, but they do have two tiny holes on the sides of their heads.

A group of tortoises is known as a creep.

Other things to do

- Find out more interesting tortoise facts to add to this list.
- Find out facts about the other animals in Taya the Tortoise's story and in Ethiopia.
- Find out facts about the country Ethiopia itself – things like its flag, traditions, food, history.

Activity 2

Thinking, Sharing, and Discussion Questions

Here are some questions or things you might like to discuss about the story of Taya the Tortoise and the themes within it.

You might like to talk with the adult supporting you with this workbook about these questions. You might like to pick just one or two questions.

You can skip, pass, or come back to some of the others. There is no rush, take your time to think about them.

There are no right or wrong answers.

You might find it useful to do some of the activities in this workbook to go into a bit more detail about the question and your answer. And you can add your own questions too!

1. Who is your favourite character from the story, and why?
2. If you were a tortoise, what colours or patterns would you have? (See Activity 7.)
3. Taya loved to climb over the smooth stones and the crunchy branches. She also liked baking, art, doing obstacle courses, and going on treasure hunts. What things do you like and enjoy doing?
4. Taya lived in Ethiopia. Can you find Ethiopia on a map? Are there some interesting facts you can discover about Ethiopia?
5. What was your favourite part of the story, and why?
6. What was your worst or most difficult part of the story, and why?
7. What feelings, thoughts, or sensations did you have when reading the story? What feelings, thoughts, or sensations do you think other people reading it might have? (If you want to, you can use several of the activities (such as 19–28) in the workbook to support you in this, and also other resources like my feelings cards or lists of feelings.)
8. What things, if any, in the story do you feel are similar to your own experiences?
9. What things do you think or feel are different?
10. What, if anything, would you add or change about the story?

11. Taya's world had sometimes felt too scary, too heavy, too big – have you felt this way?
12. What things do you think made Taya feel this way? What things do we think made her retreat into her shell? (See Activities 27–36.)
13. Taya had a whole mixture and tidal wave of feelings – what different feelings do you think she had? (See Activities 19–28 and 34.)
14. Taya sometimes found it hard to find the words and would retreat into her shell. What do you think we could do to support her to find the words or to come out of her shell sometimes?
15. If she is always in her shell, what might she miss out on or not get to do, see, and experience? (See Activities 38, 39, and 43.)
16. Taya sometimes felt unsafe, and her body and gut would tell her. Her spidey senses would spring into action. What do you think is happening for her and why? When are these spidey senses helpful and your friend, and when might they be tricky and get in the way? (See Activities 31–34.)
17. Sometimes, when Taya felt that things were scary or too much, she would do things like fly away in her mind to a different place, to a fantasy world. She would retreat into her shell so things outside felt a bit more distant, fuzzy, and foggy, or shrink from the world by making herself smaller or less visible. What would be helpful about doing this? What might be tricky about doing this? What do you do when you might feel things are scary or too much? (See Activities 27–30.)
18. If Taya puts a fence around her heart, locks it away, when is this helpful and important? And when does it stop her from enjoying the magic and joy of life? (See Activities 43–57.)
19. Every day Tristan, Tillie, Cosmo, Harley, and Daisy did little things to support Taya, glimmer by glimmer, peek by peek, heart print by heart print. What little things make a difference to you? What things have others around you done that make a difference? (See Activities 43–57.)
20. Tillie, Tristan, Cosmo, Harley, and Daisy did lots of things to help Taya and to support her to start to learn that some relationships can be caring, kind, and trustworthy. What things did they do? What would you

say to Taya to try to support her? What else might you do? (See Activities 43–57.)

21. What are some of the benefits that we can get when we let others who are kind and caring in? (See Activities 43–57.)
22. What do you think Taya learned by the end of the story? What do you think were the main messages of the story?
23. Taya is a tortoise. Which other animal or creature is your favourite, and why? If you were an animal, which would you be, and why? (You can do mix and match or choose more than one if you like.) What would you look like, sound like, and do? What colours would you be, or patterns would you have? Where would you live? What about other people in your life, like the people you live with, your teachers, friends? (You might like to draw, write about, sculpt, or make your animals.)
24. If you were going to add another character to the story, who would they be? What would they look like, say, and do?
25. At the end, we learned that Taya was ready to go on some new adventures. What adventures do you think Taya will go on? (You could write your own story, comic, or poem about this.)

What other questions would you ask?

Activity 3

Taya the Tortoise Colouring In

Activity 4

Taya the Tortoise Colouring In

Activity 5

Taya the Tortoise Colouring In

Activity 6

Taya the Tortoise Word Search

Find all the words hidden in the grid (across, down, and diagonally).

T	E	H	L	T	E	U	B	H	O	P	E
R	O	Y	A	M	N	E	E	F	E	O	T
E	I	E	S	T	L	W	C	E	P	N	H
T	T	N	T	I	D	T	N	E	Y	S	I
R	L	A	E	S	H	I	E	L	D	A	O
E	A	V	A	I	T	K	B	I	O	A	P
A	E	M	M	A	E	C	S	N	N	S	I
T	A	N	Y	E	A	P	T	G	K	H	A
H	E	A	L	M	I	R	S	S	E	E	P
B	R	N	E	D	U	U	T	A	Y	L	U
C	O	L	E	S	N	R	R	R	F	L	A
A	U	Y	T	O	R	T	O	I	S	E	D

TAYA
SUN
CAMEL
SHELL
DONKEY
RETREAT
HYENA

FEELINGS
PEEK
HEAL
TORTOISE
BELIEVE
SHIELD
HEART

SPIDEY
HOPE
ETHIOPIA
TRUST
SAFE
TEAM

Activity 7

Designing My Own Tortoise Shell

If you were going to be or design a tortoise, what pattern or design would you have on your shell? What would be your name? Where would you live? How would you spend your time? (You can draw, design, or colour on the image below, or you can make your own.)

Activity 8

Make Your Own Taya the Tortoise – Arts and Crafts Activities

If you want, you can keep your creations close to you, to remind you that Taya and her team are there cheerleading you on and supporting you. You can also use them to show others that you are having a Taya moment or that you need some support!

You can also put on a play, practise different scenarios, or make up stories of Taya using your own creations! You can also talk to Taya about some of your own experiences, thoughts, and worries, and tell her that she is ok now, things are different, and that what happened wasn't her fault and she is not alone (or whichever messages you want to share). The next few pages will show you some ideas for bringing Taya to life. You can be as creative as you like. These are just ideas – there are loads more ways and you can find others which you prefer. Also, you can mix and match. For example, you can use an egg box and buttons. I would love to see what you create! You could also make some of the other characters – Tristan, Tillie, Cosmo, Harley, and Daisy. Other materials you might like to use include an egg carton, pipe cleaners, bubble wrap, shells, dried beans and pasta, stickers.

Taya the tortoise using paper plates

These are two different versions of Taya using paper plates. The first is a whole paper plate decorated with tissue paper. This could be decorated with pens, stickers, buttons, or anything you like. Here, the legs, tail, and head shapes were cut out from card. The second one is a side view of Taya. It is a paper plate cut in half with a curvy edge at the base, then coloured in with felt pens. Again, you could paint this, or use tissue paper, stickers, or anything else you want. And then add the face, legs, and tail in card.

Taya the tortoise using stones

You can go looking for a large flat stone or you can buy one. Then you can decorate the stone using acrylic pens or paint it with Taya's different patterns, or you can choose your own pattern. Then you can add the feet, tail, and head using card.

Taya the tortoise using a cup

Get a paper cup and decorate it with pens or paint. Or if you prefer, you can use tissue paper or stickers. Then add the feet, head, and tail using card.

Taya the tortoise using a paper cupcake holder

Get a paper cupcake holder and decorate it with pens, paint, or something else like stickers. Then add the feet, head, and tail using card.

Taya the tortoise with buttons

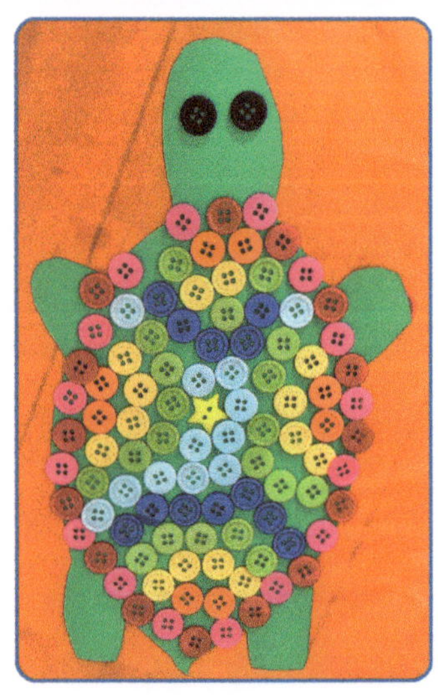

You can either use a plate as a base or cut out a tortoise shape using card. Then decorate the plate or card with different coloured buttons. You can also use shells, pipe cleaners, dried beans or pasta, or other materials if you prefer.

Part 1
Anchoring, Regulating, Grounding, Soothing, and Coping Ideas

Introduction to this activity book and what is coming next

This activity book is full of different ideas, possibilities, and activities. The adult supporting you can be alongside you while choosing which to do.

Remember this can be done over time. There is no rush. It can be one step at a time. Slow and steady, like a tortoise.

The first part of this activity book gives you some 'anchoring, regulating, grounding, soothing, and coping' ideas. These are things which you can do before, during, or after going through parts of the story, activities, or other things in your day. These can be helpful when things might feel a bit overwhelming, a bit too much, a bit stingy, scary, or thorny. They might also give you a little brain break or a bit of a boost or reset; or support you when you are gearing up to do or try something.

The second part provides some activities to learn a bit more about our feelings.

And the third part is focused on different ways of letting the possible magic, fun, joy, and good things about life and relationships in.

You can go back and forward and try things in your own time at your own pace. There are lots of gems infused throughout.

Next few pages and this first section

The next few pages (Activities 9–17) are all about our different senses – things we can see, hear, smell, taste, feel, touch, do. They are an opportunity to discover a bit more about your senses and find different tools and options for you to 'anchor, ground, soothe, relax, calm, get a boost', and so on. You can try these when you are feeling a bit overwhelmed, scared, and things are feeling too much, or thorny. They can give you a little brain break or make a change in how you might feel in your mind and body. Sometimes, you may need things which you can do to help ride the tidal wave of feelings or to take the ouch out a bit, so that it feels less intense or overwhelming. Sometimes, you may need to have some of these tools or strategies first, before you can go on to talk about feelings or the other bits. Sometimes, you may need something to help your mind, body, and nervous system to feel anchored, soothed, or rebalanced. These activities can help you stay connected and in the present. They can also show you things you can do which can provide you with choices and options, and which can help you feel less stuck.

There is no one-size-fits-all and different ones will work or be helpful for different people at different times. Sometimes, you won't know, so it is about discovering and exploring. You might change these along the way, learn new ones, or add ones which are not included here!

I hope you have fun exploring and discovering.

Activity 9

Grounding, Calming, Anchoring, Soothing – Things We Can Do

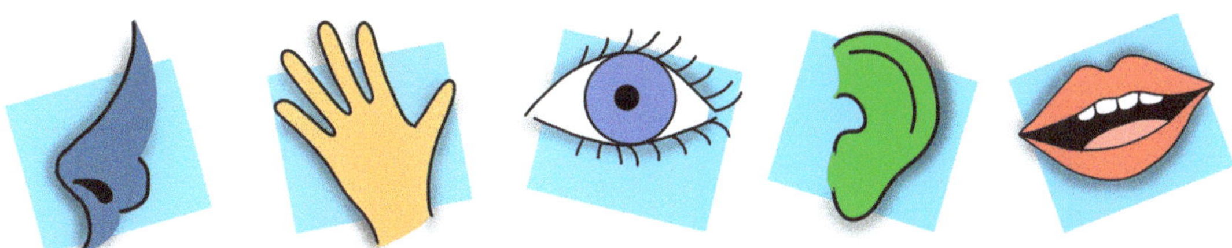

Our senses can be very important.

We use them every day to get to know, observe, discover, explore, and understand the world around us..

Sometimes, we can use our senses to bring different feelings or sensations. For example, sometimes, if we touch something or listen to something we like it and it can make us feel "happy", "excited", "calm" etc.. Other times there might be things we might touch, see, listen to, taste, smell which might make the worry, the anger, the sadness etc visit. So, we will spend some time discovering, thinking, and noticing about our senses.

If you don't know or can't think on the spot that is ok.. It means we can take our brain to the gym and be a senses explorer and try to pay attention and notice our senses and preferences over the next few days, weeks, and months.

The examples which follow might give you some ideas but there is no right or wrong! For example, one person might love touching velvet and another person it gives them the heebie jeebies; or one person might love the smell of a perfume, and another does not.

Different people have certain senses which they might pay attention or notice more. And some people might not be able to use a sense in the same way as someone else, such as due to a medical condition or for example, someone who is blind or deaf.

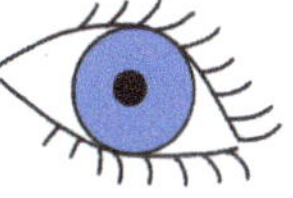

Smells I might like or not like:

If you would like to, you can use the next page for some ideas and inspiration around different smells. (Sometimes, smells can take us back to a beautiful place or memory and other times they can remind us of things we don't like).

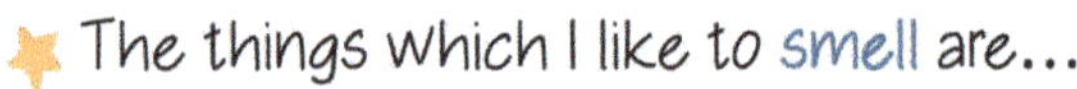

The things which I like to smell are...

The smell which makes me feel calm/relaxed/soothed/peaceful/mellow are...

The smells which make me feel excited/happy/uplifted/alert are...

The smell/s which I don't like are...

... smell reminds me of...

If I created my own special smell, it would smell like...

I would call it...

The things that I have or use which have a smell are...
(e.g., incense, candle, slime, playdoh, baking, a toy, pens, hand cream, shampoo etc).

Here are some ideas of different smells to get you started

- Flowers, plants, or trees–which ones?

- Fresh cut grass

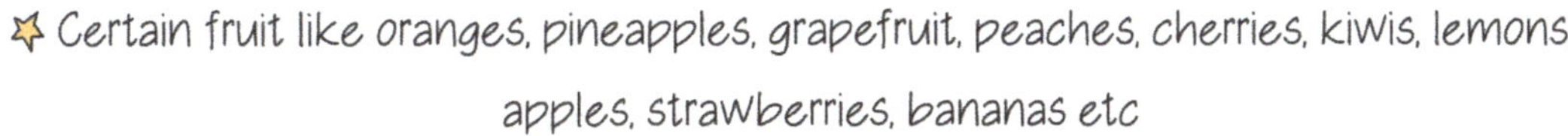

- Certain fruit like oranges, pineapples, grapefruit, peaches, cherries, kiwis, lemons, apples, strawberries, bananas etc
- Other foods e.g. bacon, onion, garlic, soup, curry, popcorn, fresh bread, chocolate, coconut
- Baking
- Jasmine

- Bubble gum

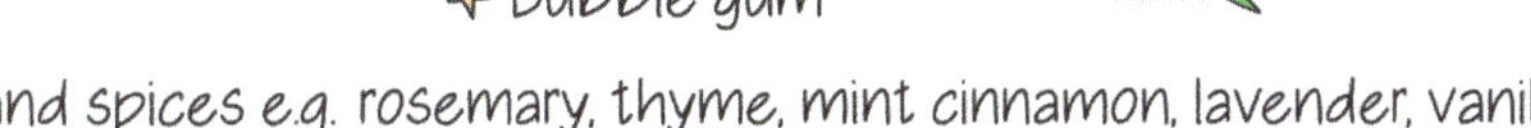

- Herbs and spices e.g. rosemary, thyme, mint cinnamon, lavender, vanilla

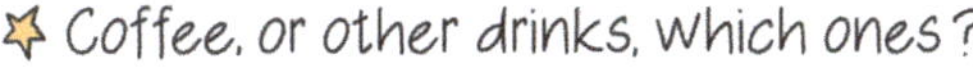

- Coffee, or other drinks, which ones?

- New books

- Clean clothes or bed sheets
- Perfume or aftershave

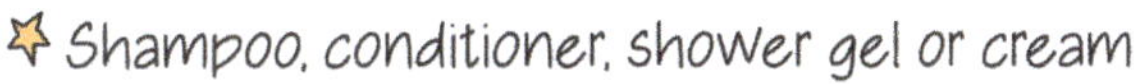

- Shampoo, conditioner, shower gel or cream

- Candles

- Fire, smoke, or a BBQ
- Rain or the sea

- Petrol
- Nail polish

- Glue
- Leather

- Poo
- Vomit
- Bins
- Mould

- Cleaning products

- Fish
- Cigarettes

What else would you add?

IMAGISTIC.CO.UK

Sounds, noises, and things I might like or not like to hear/listen to are:

If you would like to, you can use the next page for some ideas and inspiration.

★ The things which I like to listen to/hear are…

★ Some things I can listen to/hear which makes me feel calm/relaxed/soothed/peaceful/mellow are…

★ Some things I can listen to/hear which makes me feel excited/happy/uplifted/alert are…

★ Some things I can listen to/hear that might make me be able to concentrate more are…

★ Some things I don't like to listen to/hear are…

because…

IMAGISTIC.CO.UK

Here are some ideas of things you might listen to or hear:

- ☆ Birds

- ☆ Sea and waves
- ☆ Chime or bell
- ☆ Singing
- ☆ A drum

- ☆ A thunderstorm or lightning

- ☆ Rain
- ☆ Laughing
- ☆ The wind

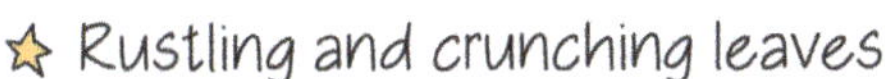

- ☆ Rustling and crunching leaves
- ☆ Crackling of a fire

- ☆ Music or TV– certain songs or programs
- ☆ Hairdryer

- ☆ Washing machine

- ☆ Clocks ticking

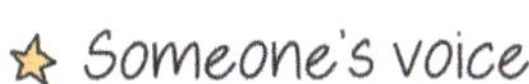

- ☆ Someone's voice
- ☆ Certain words
- ☆ A podcast
- ☆ Fireworks

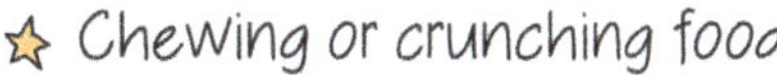

- ☆ Chewing or crunching food
- ☆ Buzzing of a bee or a fly
- ☆ Breathing sounds

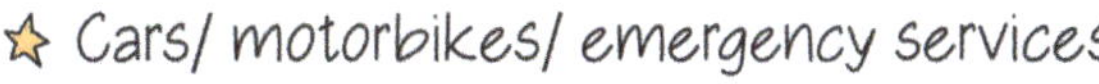

- ☆ Cars/ motorbikes/ emergency services
- ☆ Clinking or clanking of plates
- ☆ Clapping
- ☆ Scratching
- ☆ Farting
- ☆ Loud talking

- ☆ Screaming/shouting

- ☆ Whispering

- ☆ Chalk on a board

- ☆ Nail file
- ☆ Crying
- ☆ Alarms

- ☆ Barking

- ☆ Snoring
- ☆ Beeping

What else would you add?

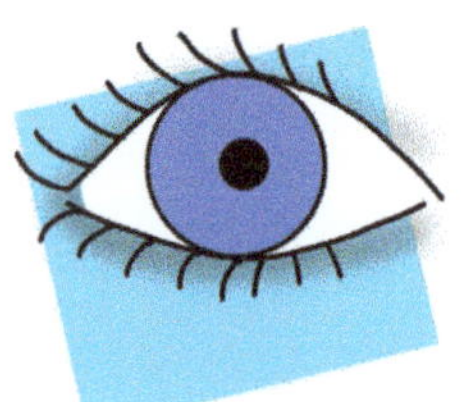

Things I might like or not like to see/look at/watch are:

If you would like to, you can use the next page for some ideas and inspiration.

- The things which I like to see/look at/watch are…

- Some things I can see/look at/watch which makes me feel "calm/relaxed/soothed/peaceful/mellow" are…

- Some things I can see/look at/watch which makes me feel "excited/happy/uplifted/alert" are…

- Some things I can see/look at/watch that might make me be able to concentrate more are…

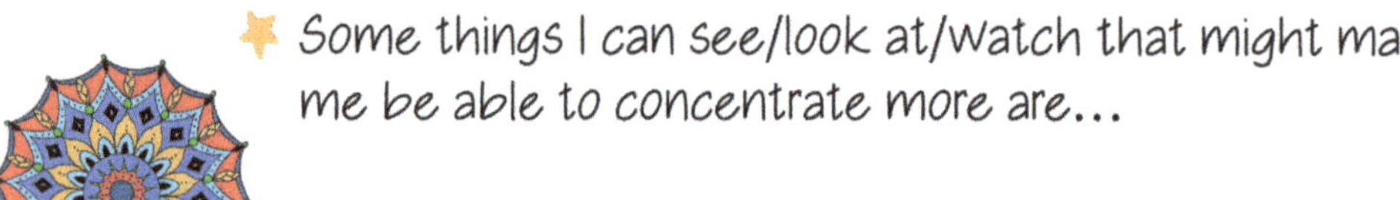

- Some things I don't like to see/look at/watch are…

  because…

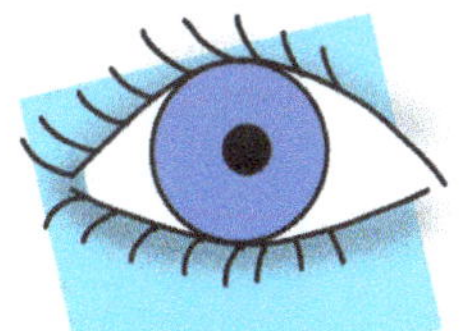

Here are some ideas of things you might like or not like to see/look at/watch:

- ☆ Certain colours or shapes
- ☆ Things in nature like the sky, stars, mountains, trees, sea, plants, flowers, sunsets, sunrises, waves, clouds etc

- ☆ Animals or pets
- ☆ Laughing/ something funny/ happiness
- ☆ Facial expressions- which ones?
- ☆ Certain people

- ☆ Certain photos/ drawings/ paintings/ postcards/ images/ posters etc
- ☆ Certain TV/ movies/ videos/ programmes/ the News etc

- ☆ Fireworks
- ☆ Puzzle or a game
- ☆ Certain toys or items
- ☆ Water moving or falling
- ☆ Glitter moving/ liquid timing/ aquarium/ lava lamp
- ☆ Snow falling

- ☆ Fire

- ☆ Certain scenery/ view
- ☆ Sensory box or bottle
- ☆ Darkness
- ☆ Optical illusion/ kaleidoscope
- ☆ Flags

What else would you add?

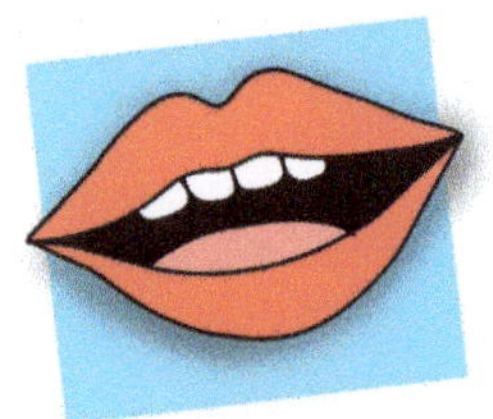

Tastes and things with my mouth I might like or not like are...

If you would like to, you can use the next page for some ideas and inspiration.

The things which I like to taste and do with my mouth are...

Some things I can taste and do with my mouth which makes me feel "calm/relaxed/soothed/peaceful/mellow" are...

Some things I can taste and do with my mouth which makes me feel "excited/happy/uplifted/alert" are...

Some things I can taste and do with my mouth that might make me be able to concentrate more are...

Some things I don't like to taste and do with my mouth ...

because...

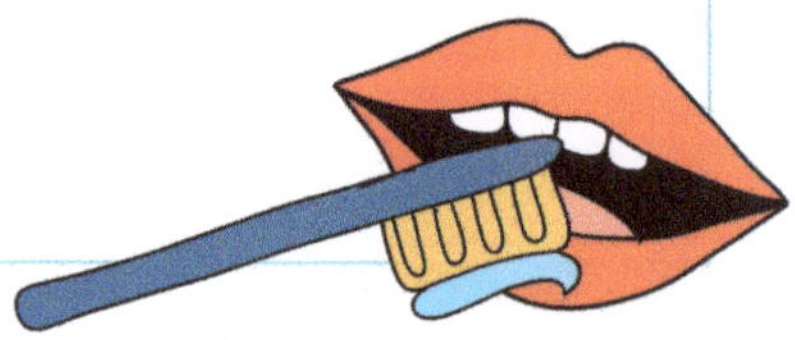

Here are some ideas of tastes and things with your mouth you might like or not like:

- Certain foods or textures including things that might be sweet, sour, bitter, or salty

- Certain drinks

- Lip balm/gloss

- Blowing bubbles
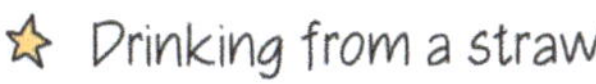
- Drinking from a straw
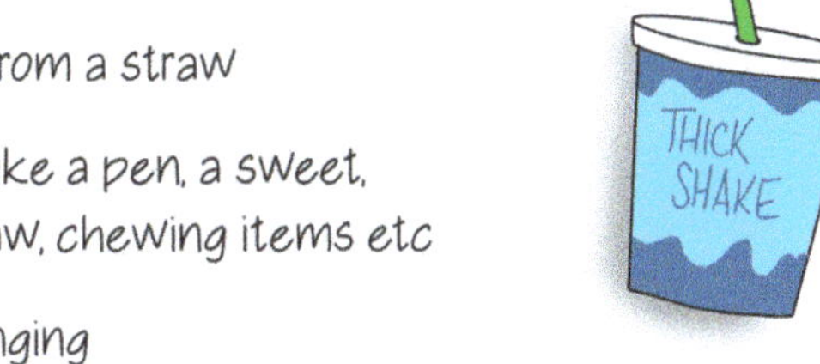
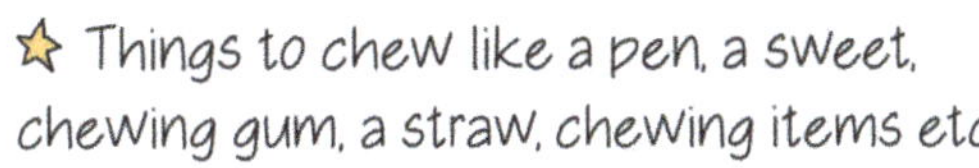
- Things to chew like a pen, a sweet, chewing gum, a straw, chewing items etc

- Singing
- Talking
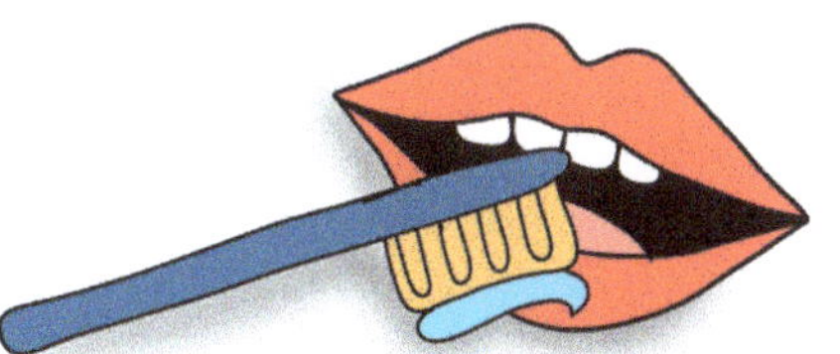
- Whistling
- Humming

- Whispering
- Reading

- Brushing teeth
- Licking
- Chewing
- Sucking
- Crunching
- Grinding teeth

What else would you add?

You might like to write these things you like or don't like on an outline of your hand, on a star, a flower, or a different image.

IMAGISTIC.CO.UK

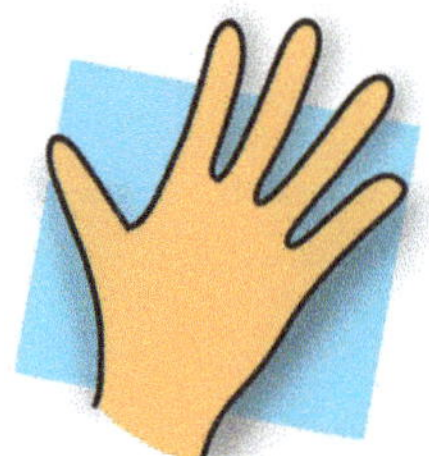

Things I might like or not like to touch/feel/do are:

If you would like to, you can use the next page for some ideas and inspiration.

The things which I like to touch/feel/do are…

Some things I can hold/ touch/ feel which makes me feel calm/relaxed/soothed/peaceful/mellow are…

Some things I can hold/ touch/ feel which makes me feel excited/happy/uplifted/alert are…

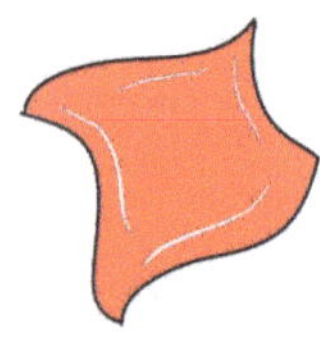

Some things I can hold/ touch/ feel that might make me be able to concentrate more are…

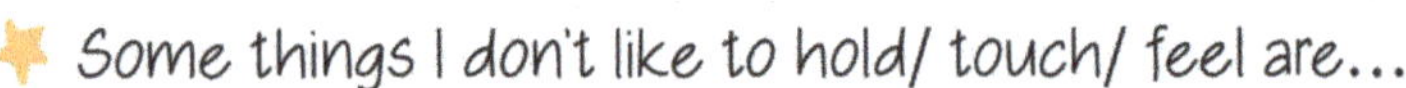

Some things I don't like to hold/ touch/ feel are…

because…

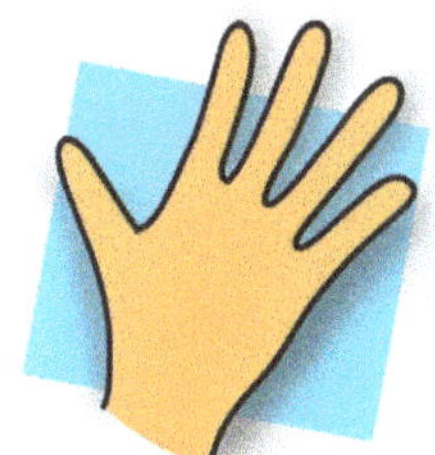

Here are some ideas of things you might touch, hold or be touched with:

- ☆ Pop-it/ bubble wrap

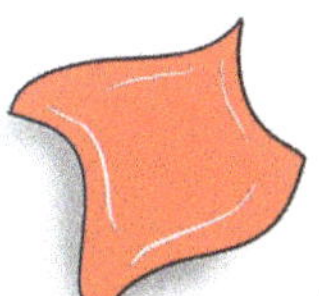

- ☆ Silk/satin
- ☆ Velvet
- ☆ Leather/suede
- ☆ Fluffy/furry
- ☆ An animal or a pet

- ☆ A teddy or toy
- ☆ A rubix cube
- ☆ A puzzle

- ☆ Building blocks/construction items/lego
- ☆ Skin/hugs
- ☆ Massage
- ☆ Stones, rocks, or pebbles
- ☆ Blanket, towel, or sheet

- ☆ Velcro
- ☆ Heat
- ☆ Cold
- ☆ Slime, clay or play-doh
- ☆ Stress or squishy ball
- ☆ Maze or labyrinth
- ☆ Vibrating items

- ☆ Heavy items like weighted blanket
- ☆ Tickling
- ☆ Sandpaper/things that are rough
- ☆ Cream/gel/soap
- ☆ Paint
- ☆ Glue
- ☆ Drumming
- ☆ Clapping

- ☆ Hair being touched/stroked/cleaned/brushed
- ☆ Feet on the grass/floor
- ☆ Certain clothing textures

- ☆ Glitter sticks/bottles/liquid timers

- ☆ Rubbing

- ☆ Scratching

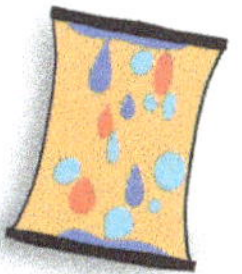

- ☆ Stretching
- ☆ Squeezing
- ☆ Crunching
- ☆ Water
- ☆ Sand
- ☆ Water beads
- ☆ Cooking/baking

What else would you add?

IMAGISTIC.CO.UK

Some things which I might want to do with my body and mind to anchor and ground myself:

Sometimes, there are things we can do with our bodies and our minds which can help to anchor and ground us. Especially if we are feeling overwhelmed, scared, trapped, worried, tired, stuck etc. These might also be little micro strategies we can use throughout the day to support us.

Some of these things might make us feel "calmer, more relaxed, happier, more connected", and others might make us feel more "awake, alert, energised" etc. So, we need to have a treasure box of options so that we can use different things at different times and for our different needs. Like certain smells, sounds, sights etc will either help us to energise and wake up or do the opposite and help us to "calm" down. It is about experimenting, being a detective, trying them out and noticing what works or doesn't work for us. There is no right or wrong.

Sometimes, also making small tweaks can really help us, such as by combining more than one sense at the same time. So, for example, if you like using a squishy stress ball- that uses your tactile sense. But it might be that you can make it even more effective by using "calming movements" such as moving it from our left hand to our right hand, or squeezing it in a rhythm etc. Or you add a visual sense like choosing a stress ball in a "calming" colour, or popping a drawing or sticker of something we like on it; or whilst using the stress ball to also look at a "calming" image, photo, or item like a glitter stick. Or you might add something for our auditory (our hearing) like listening to "calming" music whilst using it or singing or humming etc. Or if you like going for a walk, you might think about zoning in on the different senses. Like the crunching of the leaves, or the colour of the flowers, or the sounds of the birds etc. It might also make a difference making small tweaks like you might want to listen to music whilst walking, or wear a particular comforting jumper or jacket on your walk etc.

So, it is about not rushing and trying different things and then once we find what we like and find helpful, then it is about practicing it on a regular basis, so we are training our brains.

Possible bigger movements:

So, as shared, everyone is different and has different things that make them comfortable or fit for them and which make them feel a certain way, but it can make a big difference to change or choose a different position to be or to add in some movement. B an experimenter or detective and try them out and see if there are little things that you might adjust or do to make them even better for you. This might be things like (they are just ideas and there are many more to try if these don't suit):

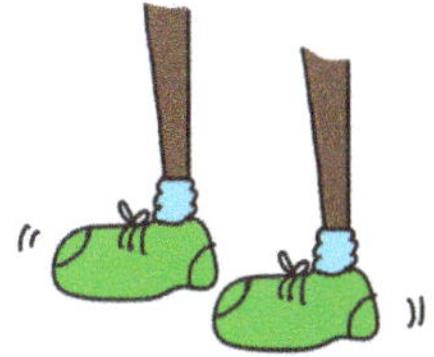

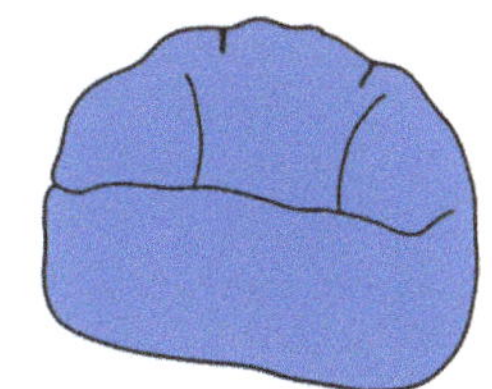

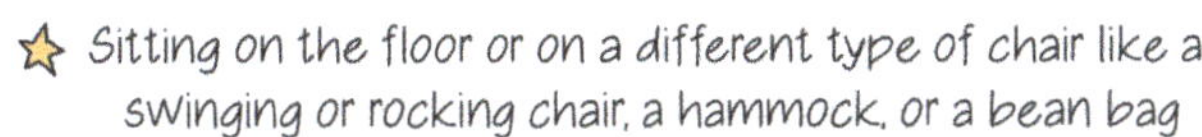

- Sitting on the floor or on a different type of chair like a swinging or rocking chair, a hammock, or a bean bag

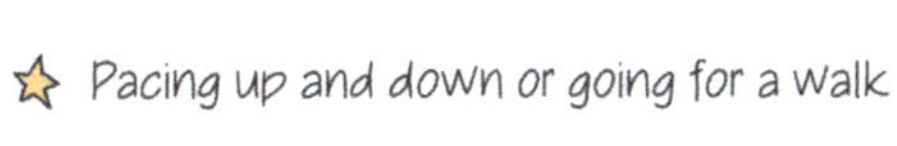

- Pacing up and down or going for a walk
- Standing up
- Pushing against a wall

- Stretching

- Tensing and releasing your muscles

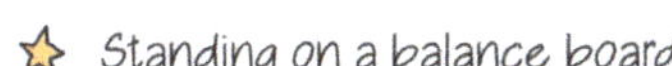

- Standing on a balance board

- Shaking it out

- Dancing

- Drumming, clapping, or doing a rhythm

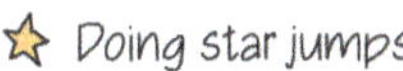

- Doing star jumps

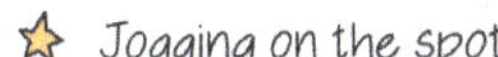

- Jogging on the spot

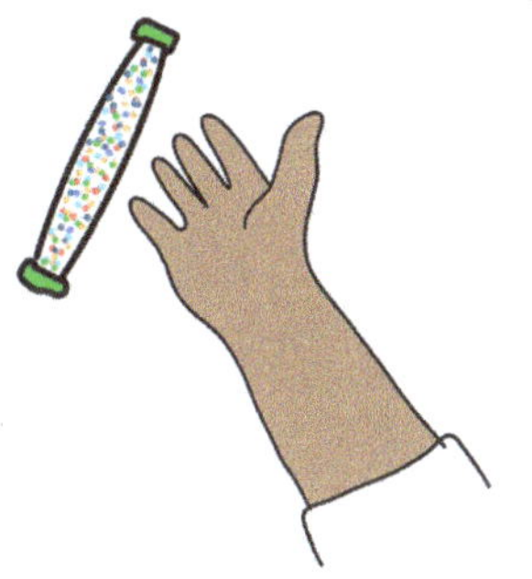

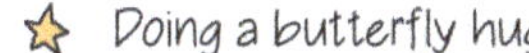

- Doing a butterfly hug

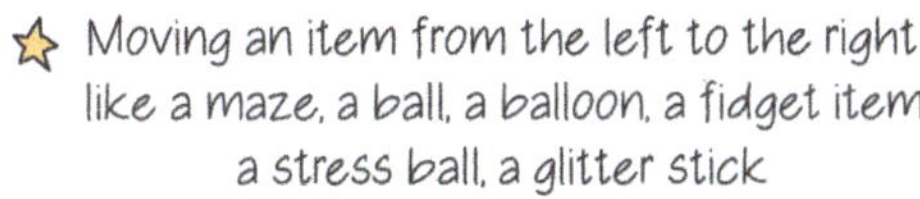

- Moving an item from the left to the right like a maze, a ball, a balloon, a fidget item, a stress ball, a glitter stick

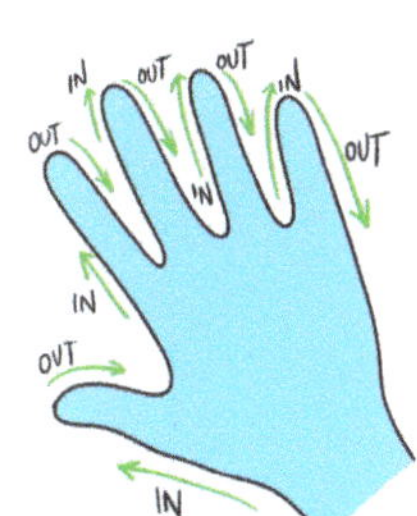

- Breathing tools (there are so many different ones, but for example, hand breathing, figure of eight breathing, star breathing, rainbow breathing, tower or ladder breathing etc).

What else would you add?

Some examples of smaller micro movements you might like to try are:

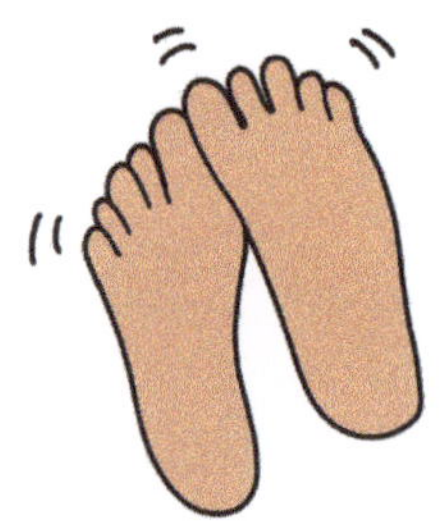

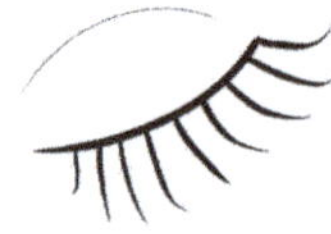

- Blinking
- Tapping
- wiggling your fingers or toes
- Rubbing your hands together
- Feeling your feet on the floor
- Putting on hand cream with a scent that helps you to feel the feeling you are trying to move towards
- Squeezing an item
- Hold on to a grounding item or stone
- Ripping paper
- Using a stretchy
- Drink water or put water on your face

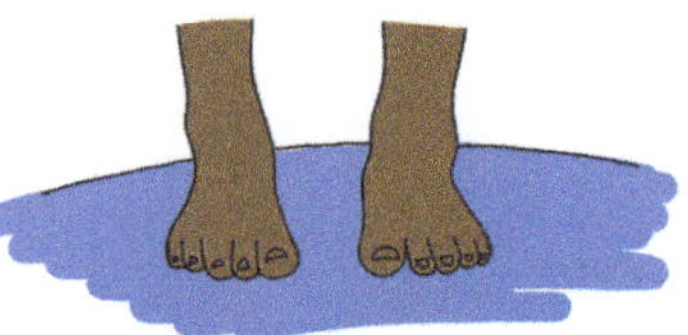

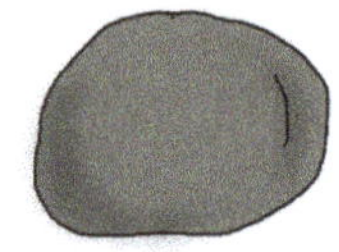

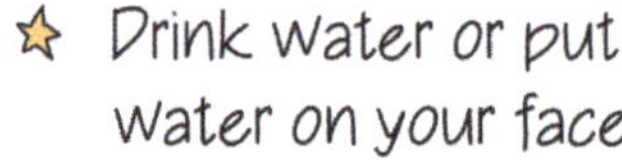

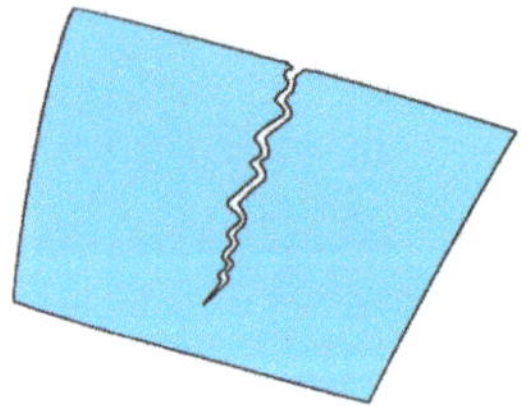

What else would you add?

IMAGISTIC.CO.UK

You might also do ones with your mind to ground or anchor

For example:

- ☆ Play cognitive games like I went shopping and bought, I spy, alphabet games etc

- ☆ You might have an affirmation, a rhyme, a chant, or a mantra you want to say and repeat

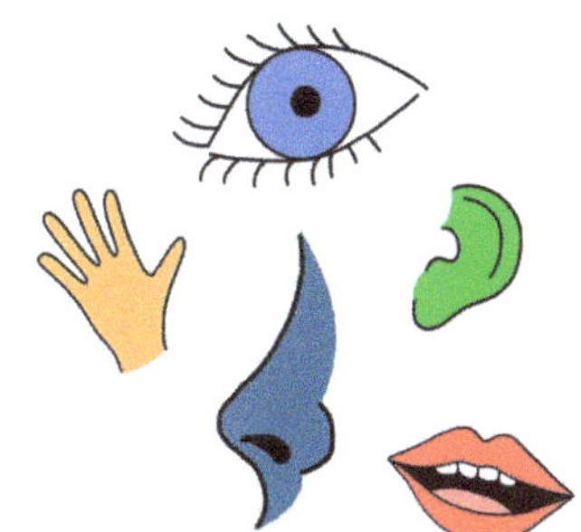

- ☆ You might focus on things you can see, hear, smell, taste, and feel around you. Or do a sensory treasure hunt

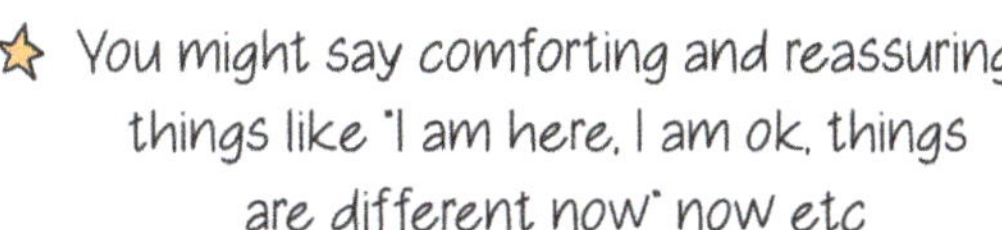

- ☆ You might say comforting and reassuring things like "I am here, I am ok, things are different now" now etc

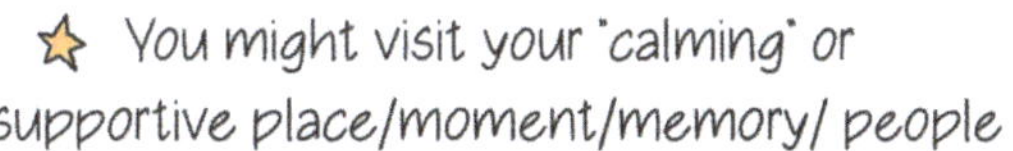

- ☆ You might visit your "calming" or supportive place/moment/memory/ people

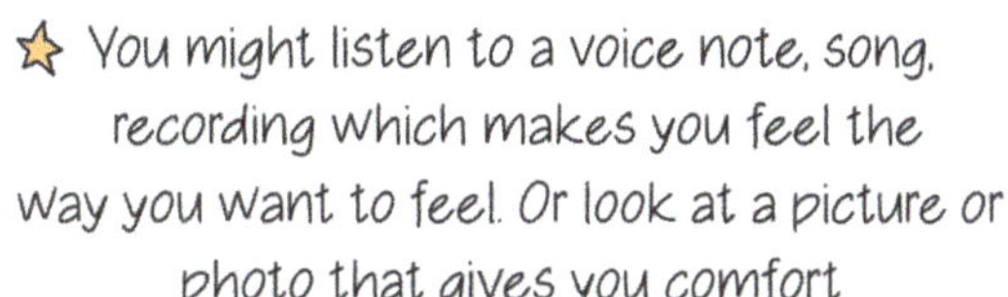

- ☆ You might listen to a voice note, song, recording which makes you feel the way you want to feel. Or look at a picture or photo that gives you comfort

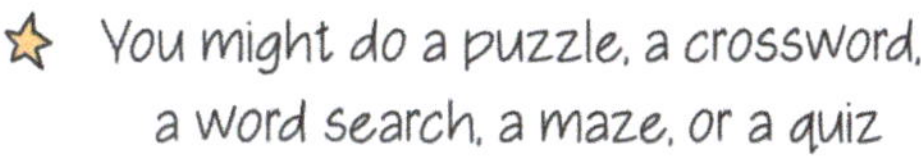

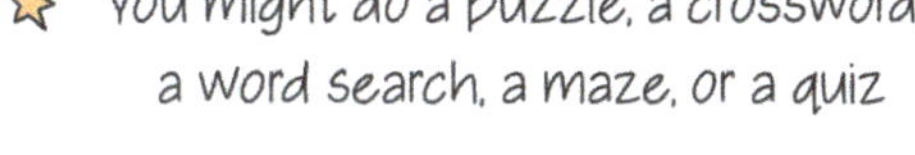

- ☆ You might do a puzzle, a crossword, a word search, a maze, or a quiz

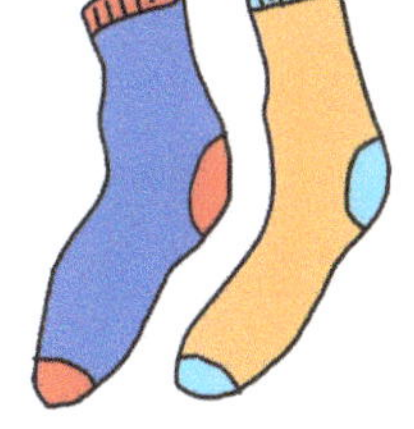

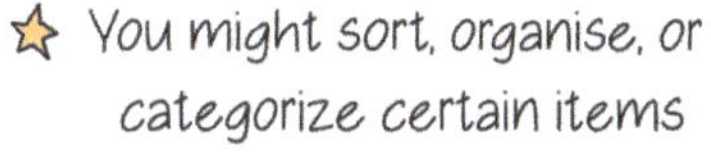

- ☆ You might sort, organise, or categorize certain items

Which do you do already/ like/ not like/ notice/ want to try?

Which would you add?

IMAGISTIC.CO.UK

Activity 10

Sensory Treasure Hunt and Discovery Adventure

You may not know this, but a cool fact is that the more we look for something and pay attention to it, the more we see it! Think about a treasure hunt – the harder you look for the treasure, the more places you look, and the more time you spend looking for clues, the more likely it is that you will be able to find it! This can be the same for things like our strengths, things that make the happiness visit, and much more. Also, when our mind is wandering or it is harder to stay in the present or connected, zooming-in and noticing our surroundings and focusing on our different senses and what is around us can help. You might also just look around and think about what you can see, hear, smell, feel, taste, and do – this can help to anchor and ground us to being in the here and now (the present). This can sometimes be helpful if your mind is wandering or you are finding it hard to stay in the moment.

Below are some ideas for carrying out your very own indoor and outdoor treasure hunts. This can help you to focus on something else and be in the moment. You can also design your own. When you find the items, try and really look at and notice them. What colour are they? What shape are they? Are they soft/hard/shiny/smooth? What temperature are they?

Possible ideas for an outdoor treasure hunt – can you find or see:

- a leaf
- a pinecone
- some bark
- some grass
- an insect
- a stick or twig
- a rock
- a flower
- a feather
- a bird
- a cloud
- something blue
- some mud
- a surprise?

Ideas for an indoor treasure hunt – can you find or see:

- a book or magazine or newspaper
- a blanket
- a teddy or soft toy
- a shoe
- a pen or pencil
- a spoon
- something soft/hard/hot/cold/shiny/round/square/colourful
- something the colour../shape...
- What else?

Activity 11

Calmness, Peacefulness, Safety, and Relaxation

This activity is in addition to the possible tools in Activities 9 and 10. Sometimes, when the world feels too big, too loud, too overwhelming, or too much, it can be helpful to think about and connect to things that make the 'calm, peace, safety, relaxation' visit. You might like to choose a different word or term (whatever fits for you or make up your own words); for example, 'mellow, chilled, soothed, anchored'. Some people can think of this, but for others it takes some time and they need some ideas and examples to be offered. So, these questions and the image that follows are to support you to think about some of those things. Once you know what it might be, for example a hot air balloon, you can then find ways to bring this into your life and mind a bit more (e.g. imagining for a few moments that you are floating in a hot air balloon, or having images of hot air balloons on your pencil case, or on your notebooks). Also, the more you know what 'calm' means, feels like, or looks like to you, the more you can notice it, pay attention to it, and have some ideas of how to get there. This can look and feel different for different people. There is no right or wrong.

It might be helpful for you to think about these statements below (or if you prefer, you can think about them for other people/characters. You can also come back to them and use Activity 9 to support as well).

- The word I would use and choose is...
- 'Calmness, peacefulness, safety, and relaxation' for me feels like... (Choose an image below or choose your own.)
- If I gave the feelings of 'calmness, peacefulness, safety, and relaxation' a name it would be...

- If I described the feelings or sensations of 'calmness, peacefulness, safety, and relaxation' I would say...

- A specific time or example when the 'calmness, peacefulness, safety, and relaxation' visited was when... (Can you describe this time in more detail if possible, for example where, when, what, and how? Maybe you could write it as a story, a poem, a rap, or in a few sentences. If you have a few examples, that's great, as you can create a whole list or write about all of these different examples. Use another piece of paper if you need more space.)

- The things, smells, sounds, people, sensations, and places that make the 'calmness, peacefulness, safety, and relaxation' visit more are... (Use Activities 9, 28, and 44 to support you.)

- The things, smells, sounds, people, sensations, and places that make the 'calmness, peacefulness, safety, and relaxation' go away are... (What is the opposite of these feelings? Use Activities 27–34 to support you.)

- If the 'calmness, peacefulness, safety, and relaxation' was an animal/item/something in nature/colour/sound/texture/type of weather (whatever you choose), what might it be? Look like? Sound like? Do?

- How do you know when you are feeling 'calm, relaxed, safe, and peaceful?' (What do you feel in your body, on your face, in your heart, in your mind? What signs and clues are there? Use Activity 21 to support you.)

Being a joey in a kangaroo's pouch
Floating on a cloud
Being wrapped in a blanket / bed
Floating in a hot air balloon
Being hugged
Being filled with love
Feeling grounded like a tree
Being in a safe bubble
Held up by a safety net
Protected by a life jacket
Being a tortoise in its shell
Being in a cosy cave
Surrounded by loving people
Feeling warmed by sunlight
Feeling protected by a guardian angel/ shield
Protected by an umbrella
Taking a deep breath
Being free like a bird
Smiling inside
What else?

Activity 12

Calming, Anchoring, Relaxing, Soothing – Place, Time, Memory, or Moment

Sometimes, in addition to the other things we have suggested, we might also need or want a little brain break or a reset. Even more so when things are feeling a bit thorny, stingy, or too much. This can be a place or, if you prefer, a memory or a moment.

For some of us when we need this, we can go to an actual place that we might like and that makes us feel good. But some of us don't have that place, or we can't go there because we are at school, or it is far away, or it is raining. So instead, it can be great to have a place that is in our mind and in our hearts and heads that we can go to for a few moments without having to actually travel there, a place that is always with us, a place that makes the 'calm, happiness, peace' (whatever word or term you want) to visit.

This isn't a place to spend hours or lots of time in, it is a place to go for a few minutes – maybe for the length of a song. It is supposed to give us a little boost or gentle retreat so that then we can come back into ourselves and our surroundings.

If you can't think of a place, that's ok, don't worry, it can be tricky, and it can take some time. There is no pressure. The adult with you is here to support you on your discovery journey. Activities 9 and 11 might also be helpful, or you might like to look at some pictures or photos. Here are some useful questions if you are finding it hard to think of a place:

- If you could click your fingers and travel back to a place, a moment, or a memory, where and when would it be?
- If you could travel back in a time machine to a place, a moment, or a memory, where and when would it be?

- If you could click your fingers and be anywhere, where would you be? What would you like to see, hear, smell, taste, touch, feel?

And if you still can't think about it, it's ok, give yourself some time and come back to it. Alternatively, if you want to, you can make up your own magical, fantasy, and imaginary place. You might also like to consider that if you were going to make this place for an animal or for a favourite friend, what might it be like?

Just remember, if you do make up a place, it can be harder to travel back to it, so it is important to really describe it, write it down, record it, and make a creative reminder of it. (See Activity 16.)

You can also choose if or how you want to share your place or moment – you don't have to if it doesn't feel right.

You can have more than one place or memory, but maybe start with one!

And sometimes, we think of one, and then realize we don't really like it, or it doesn't quite work for us, so make sure you test it out and see that it works for you and is the best fit – otherwise, you can choose another!

Here is an image of some of the steps to think about your place, memory, or moment. These will be expanded on and explained more in Activities 13, 14, and 15.

Activity 13

Safe, Calming, Happy, Relaxing, and Soothing Places

Below are some common places which people have said they use and visit as their safe, calming, happy, relaxing, and soothing places.

The 'What else?' box is important – remember that you can add or create your own, and this sheet is just to provide some ideas.

Activity 14

My Very Own Safe and Calming Place, Moment, or Memory

Can you think of a place where you have been, seen, or visited where you felt really happy, calm, safe, peaceful, and relaxed? (You might want to use the image from Activity 11 or Activity 13 to help you with some ideas.) This might be:

- your favourite place
- a place where you felt at peace, safe, relaxed, and calm
- a place where your brain had a little break
- a place that makes you feel warm inside, and that makes you smile
- a place that, if you could click your fingers and travel back to, or pop into a travel machine and travel back to, you would love to visit.

Remember or revisit what we said earlier about taking your time to think about your place. And if it isn't a place, it can be a moment, a time, or a memory.

____

____

____

If so, what was this place called? Or, if you were to choose a name or a title for this place, what would you choose? This could be a real name like Radfield Park or a name we like that captures the place, like My Zen Zone.

____

____

____

Imagine you are an author of a descriptive story or a director in a movie – we want to focus in on the detail (you can use Activity 9 to build on this). When in this place, what can you (or would like to):

- see/notice; look at?

- hear/listen to?

- smell?

- touch/feel/do?

- taste?

When you think about or visit in your mind this place, what do you feel in your body? If your body could talk, what might it say?

What feeling do you have when you are in this place?

If you had to choose a reminder or a cue word or phrase to help you to remember your place, what might it be (e.g. mellow or breezy sky)?

Some people find it helpful to imagine entering and exiting their place – like having a journey in, a way to get there, a bridge. This might be through a door, using a magic key, flying there, swimming there, and so on. Use Activity 15 for some ideas.

I would travel to my...by...

It can be super helpful to have tangible and visual reminders of our place/ moment/memory. Lots of ideas are shared in activities...

The reminder I would like of my...is...

Questions, worries, thoughts, hope I have around this place, moment, memory.

Activity 15

Travelling to Your Calming, Safe, and Magical Place

This might give you some more time and space to travel there and to make the journey feel a bit more special. It can help to imagine us entering and exiting our place – and to travel and transtion from one place to another.

How might you like to travel to your calming, safe, and magical place? Circle or colour in any that you feel apply to you, but remember that these are just ideas, and you can add your own.

Activity 16

Creative Extensions on the Place/Moment/Memory

Sometimes, when we are feeling full up, overwhelmed, stressed, or worried, it can be hard to remember or to travel back to our 'special' place. This is one of the reasons why it can be helpful to choose a reminder word, to describe your place in lots of detail, and to practise going to your place loads of times on a regular basis – so that you train your brain. But also you can make your place even more special, alive, and memorable. If you like, you can also make a piece of art, or multiple pieces of art or visual items to remind you of your place. An adult can help you with this too.

There is no right or wrong way to do this, and you might make one, or loads of different ones. Below are some ideas of things which you can do, but the sky is your limit – be as creative as you wish. Other people in your life might have some great ideas too!

You can also have reminder cards in your diary, as stickers, in your pencil case, in your locker, and so on.

Draw/paint a picture, make a collage or sculpture, or write (e.g. a story, song, poem, or rap) to show:

- how you would like to travel to your place – the journey or entering in. Use Activity 15 for some inspiration and ideas
- yourself in your place
- the feelings, sensations, and thoughts you have when in that place. You could use any of the feeling's templates throughout this activity book.

 	Make a pillow of your place. Use fabric pens on a plain pillow cover; or use photos and get a photo company to make it. It doesn't need to be a pillow, it could also be on wallpaper, on a lamp made up of photos, or on pyjamas, a blanket, and so on.
 	Decorate a teddy bear with photos of your place, or put a photo of your place in the face of the bear, or on its t-shirt. You could also use fabric pens to draw your special place on a plain doll or on a doodle doll.
 	Put your place on a range of different items, such as a keyring, a snow globe, a pencil case, or on your diary.
 	Ask a photo company to make things like a cereal bowl, a mug, a plate using photographs of your safe place.
	Produce a painting, a collage, a poster, a picture, or a mosaic of your special place. You could then mount or photograph this piece of art, and put it in lots of different places, such as in your diary, next to your bed, in a keyring.

 	Make a three-dimensional model, a sculpture, or a mould of your special place using lots of different materials, such as clay, miniatures, sand, wood, shells.
	Do a picture or a painting or make a mould or sculpture of the way you plan to travel to your special place, showing the journey or the way you can enter it.

Activity 17
So What Might Help Me?

You have now learned from Activities 9–16 some sensory ideas, some big and small movement ideas, some cognitive ideas, the 'calm place or moment' exercise, and some other tools to try when the feelings of 'worry, fear, disconnect, and overwhelm' visit, or when you need a bit of a boost or to soothe your nervous systems and find some calm, relaxation, and peace.

It is important to have things we can do to ground, anchor, and soothe ourselves. These are sometimes called micro strategies or coping gems. Of course, there are no right or wrong options – we are all unique and different things will work for different people; this book is just a start. So, remember to keep adding, noticing, and discovering until you have a few strategies that are helpful to you (and these might change at different times and days). There are also lots more ideas peppered throughout this workbook, including using the word 'yet' (Activity 42), the life cheerleader exercise (Activity 59), and ways to connect to joy (Activities 43–56).

The more we practise these and take our brain to the gym, the better we remember these strategies – and if they aren't working, we can think with the adults around us about what else we might try or how we might enrich or supercharge these ideas to make them more helpful to us.

- Which is your favourite 'grounding, soothing, anchoring, calming' activity, and why? (It is ok if you can't think or haven't chosen ones yet, as you can keep on discovering, and there are so many more to try.)
- What, if anything, did you notice happened to your body and mind when you did it?
- Do you or the adult reading this with you have other ideas that you would like to try?
- Do you understand why something is or isn't helpful? Sometimes, it is useful to think about why something is working for us, and what might be happening in our brain, our body, and our nervous system.

- Think about when you might like to try or use an idea. How can you infuse it into your daily routine? What might you do to enhance and supercharge it even more? Who might you like to talk about it to, if anyone? What might you do instead if you can't do the thing you like or if it isn't helping in that moment?

You might like to make your own 'wellbeing/options/coping/healing' (or whatever you want to call it) plan! This should be doable and tailored to you.

You might also like to create a visual or tangible reminder of these things (you can have more than one and keep adding to and tweaking it). There is no right or wrong way to do this. If, for example, you like rugby, you might write or draw the things you can do or try on a rugby ball, a picture of a rugby ball, or a rugby shirt. Or if you like the beach, you might do it on different shells. Here are some pictures to inspire you – but please feel free to do whatever you feel would work best for you!

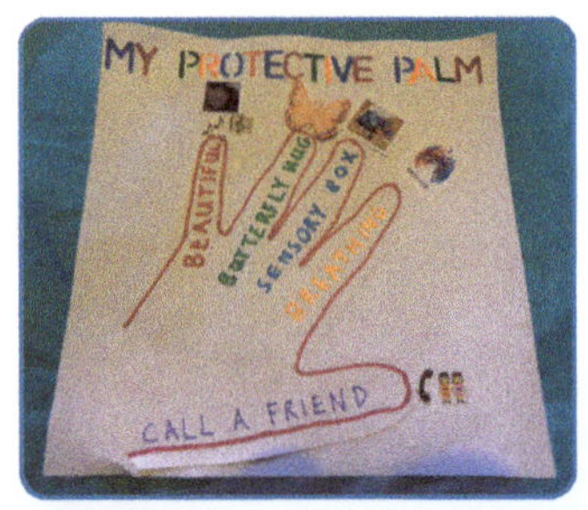

Other tools we will talk about throughout the workbook which can also be helpful and infused with the above are ways to express or name our feelings, reflecting on the advantages and disadvantages of retreating and connecting, different ways of letting the beauty and magic in, noticing the relational gems in our lives, and much more!

Activity 18

Communication and What I Need/What I Want Cards

Throughout this activity book and in other situations, it can sometimes be hard to find the words to express ourselves. This is particularly true if we feel that our needs haven't been met or listened to or respected, or when we feel stuck or overwhelmed or not sure what to say. Sometimes, it is hard for the other person to know what we might need or what might be helpful, as they don't have emotional x-rays, and we are all learning about each other. It is important that our voice is heard and we have some choice. So, this is another communication, anchoring, and coping tool.

I have made some communication cards for you. They are just ideas, and you can add your own to suit you, or change the existing ones. You might just like to choose two or three, or more. You don't need to use all of them or any of them if you don't want to.

You can laminate them, turn them into labels, a poster, pretend buttons – whatever works for you.

They are here for you to use if you think they might be helpful, and the adult with you might like to use them too. You can also use them for your favourite toy or a character on TV or in a book!

There are ones to say things like 'I need a break', or 'I need to move around', or to tell us what might be happening: 'You are saying too many things at one time', or 'My mind is wandering off'. These can be very helpful while doing the activities in this book but also in all sorts of other situations.

There are also ones for us to say things like 'yes', 'no', 'always', 'agree', 'disagree'. So, you might like to use these to express feelings about things that are happening, things you are experiencing.

There are so many different possibilities – you can play around with them and discover what works for you.

Take some time to look at them and think about which ones you do like, don't like, would add to. Think about when you might use them. It might be helpful to choose a few and have a practice.

Activity 18 Communication cards 1

Activity 18 Communication cards 2

Activity 18 Communication cards 3

Activity 18 Communication cards 4

Activity 18 Communication cards 5

Part 2
Exploring and Talking About Feelings

Activity 19

Messages About Feelings

Having thought a little bit about some of the things you can do to anchor and ground yourself when things feel a bit much or you feel a bit overwhelmed, we are now going to spend a little time exploring more about our own and others' feelings. This might include the feelings of characters in books and movies, or on TV.

Of course, as with this whole activity book, you can skip these pages or come back to them at a different time if you prefer. Taya sometimes felt scared of her feelings or overwhelmed by them. She learned to retreat into her shell, to distance or unplug herself from her feelings, to protect and numb herself.

She had experienced things that made feelings feel thorny or too much, and this was even worse when she felt alone at these times and hadn't had adults supporting her in these feelings, or they had done things or responded in ways that made things seem worse or unsafe.

As the story progressed, Taya started to learn a bit more about why feelings can be helpful and important, and also what some of the disadvantages and hazards of blocking our feelings and shutting them away can be. We go into more detail about this in Activities 38 and 39.

When we talk about feelings, there are so many different important messages. Take your time with the adult supporting you to look at some of these messages about feelings in the worksheets that follow over the next few pages.

- Which do you agree with or disagree with?
- Which make sense or don't make sense to you?
- Which are new or different?
- Which ones do you want to think a bit more about?
- Can you think of an example of how these might show themselves?
- These might be different from what you have been taught or experienced before. Which would you add?
- Which do you think we are missing?

Note to the adults supporting – please refer to the Guide for Adults for a range of tips and tools around talking about feelings.

SOME MORE KEY MESSAGES ABOUT FEELINGS

Dr Karen Treisman
SafeHands
ThinkingMinds

☆ WE DO NOT HAVE EMOTIONAL OR FEELING X-RAYS OR MIND READERS

☆ SOMETIMES, WHAT WE SEE ON THE OUTSIDE CAN BE DIFFERENT TO WHAT WE MIGHT FEEL ON THE INSIDE. FEELINGS CAN BE BODY GUARDED, CAMOUFLAGED & MASKED

☆ SOME FEELINGS CAN REMIND US OF OTHER TIMES THAT WE HAVE FELT THAT FEELING - THEY CAN BE ACTIVATING, RESURFACING & SEND US DOWN A MEMORY TIME HOLE

☆ FEELINGS CAN VISIT US- THEY CAN COME & GO LIKE A WAVE OR A CLOUD - WE CAN GO IN & OUT OF THEM

☆ WE EACH HAVE HAD UNIQUE FAMILY, CULTURAL & COMMUNITY EXPERIENCES ABOUT OUR FEELINGS. ARE THEY OK TO SHARE? WHAT MESSAGES HAVE WE HAD AROUND THEM? WHAT HAVE WE LEARNED ABOUT THEM?

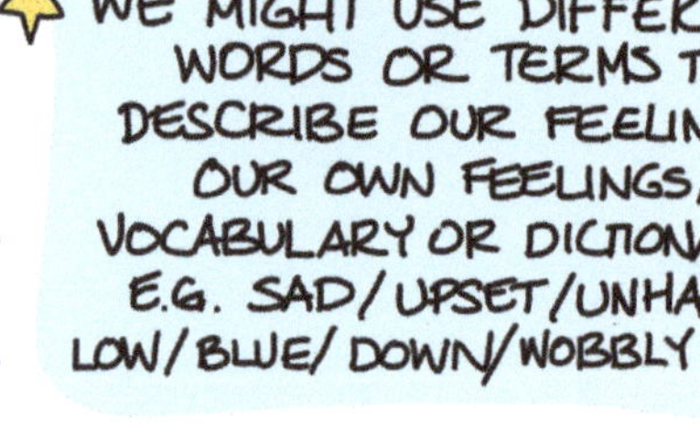

☆ WE MIGHT USE DIFFERENT WORDS OR TERMS TO DESCRIBE OUR FEELINGS- OUR OWN FEELINGS, VOCABULARY OR DICTIONARY E.G. SAD/UPSET/UNHAPPY/ LOW/BLUE/DOWN/WOBBLY ETC

☆ SOMETIMES WE MIGHT NOT KNOW HOW WE FEEL, WE MIGHT BE CONFUSED OR OVERWHELMED BY OUR FEELINGS

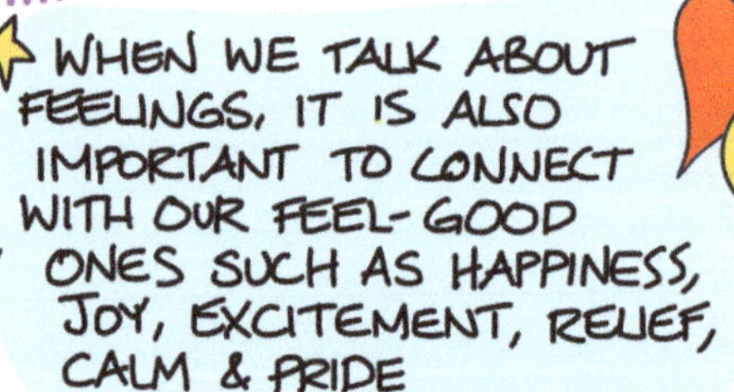

☆ OUR FEELINGS CAN BE DESCRIBED DIFFERENTLY, FOR EXAMPLE, SOME PEOPLE MIGHT LIKE TO DESCRIBE A FEELING USING A COLOR, A SHAPE, A TYPE OF WEATHER, A TEXTURE, AN ANIMAL, A SONG, A BODY SENSATION & MUCH MORE

☆ WHEN WE TALK ABOUT FEELINGS, IT IS ALSO IMPORTANT TO CONNECT WITH OUR FEEL-GOOD ONES SUCH AS HAPPINESS, JOY, EXCITEMENT, RELIEF, CALM & PRIDE

☆ THERE IS A DIFFERENCE BETWEEN BEING & FEELING E.G. BEING LOVED & FEELING LOVED

☆ WE OFTEN REMEMBER HOW PEOPLE LEAVE US FEELING - IF THE FEELING COULD TALK OR GIVE US A MESSAGE WHAT MIGHT IT SAY?

WHAT ELSE ???

IMAGISTIC.CO.UK

Building on the previous messages about feelings, another really important aspect and something that can be useful to understand and explore a bit more is that feelings (our own and others) can be mixed, blended, fused, and entangled. You can have multiple different feelings all at the same time, and one feeling doesn't take away from another feeling. The worksheet at the end of this activity shares some messages about mixed, blended, fused, and entangled feelings. The adult supporting you can go through and give you some examples and talk these through a bit more.

You might like to use my other feelings or trauma deck of cards or images throughout this workbook to think about which feelings can overlap, or draw these with overlapping circles (like below), or you can draw your own. This might be things like excited and nervous.

There are many examples of mixed and blended feelings. I might be sometimes scared of my parent who hurt me, and at the same time love them or parts of them; I might feel loyalty towards them, and miss them, and might also fear them at the same time. Or my body might have felt hurt, controlled, or in pain, but also might have felt special, or may have responded with pleasure. I might be excited and also worried. I might be proud and also have regrets and doubts. I might be in a place of pain, hurt, and overwhelm and also have hope and things I feel confident in. I might be smiling and also be sad or struggling. I might be kind and still need to set boundaries, and so on.

We can be both, and we can integrate and hold these different parts, layers, and feelings together.

As previously, you might like to think about these feelings and maybe write, draw, or make a collage about them. Which do you agree with or disagree with? Which make sense or don't make sense to you? Which are new or different? Which ones do you want to think a bit more about? Can you think of an example of how these might show themselves? These might be different from what you have been taught or experienced before. What would you add? What do you think we are missing?

Throughout this activity book, you might like to come back to these messages as anchors, for example if you are talking about how Taya might have felt, or how you or someone else might feel about a situation, a person, an activity. It is okay and valid to have mixed, blended, fused, and entangled feelings – there is no right or wrong way and you can feel however you feel.

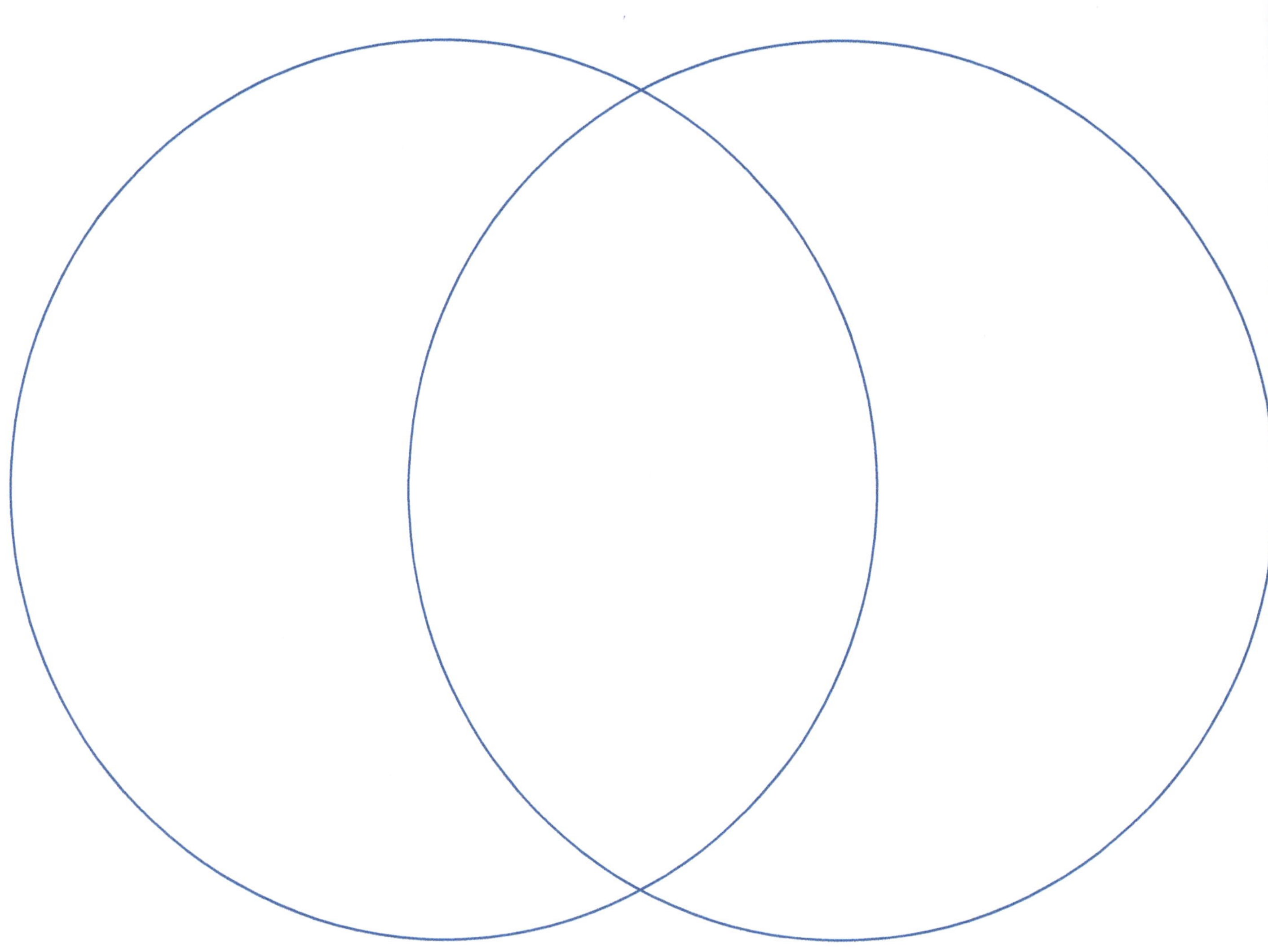

MIXED BLENDED FUSED "JUMBLED" & ENTANGLED FEELINGS

Dr Karen Treisman SafeHands ThinkingMinds

OUR FEELINGS CAN COME IN ALL SHAPES & SIZES IN OUR BODIES IN OUR SENSATIONS & IN OUR MINDS

FEELINGS CAN BE MIXED, BLENDED, FUSED, JUMBLED & ENTANGLED TOGETHER

A BIT LIKE A RAINBOW, SPAGHETTI, PAINTS, A MOSAIC, A TAPESTRY, A SMOOTHIE A PATCHWORK, A PUZZLE & MANY MORE

WE CAN HAVE, EXPERIENCE, & HOLD MORE THAN ONE FEELING AT THE SAME TIME, & THESE CAN ALSO CHANGE & MOVE

ONE FEELING DOESN'T TAKE AWAY FROM THE OTHER FEELINGS. THEY ARE ALL VALID.

FOR EXAMPLE, WE MIGHT BE A BIT EXCITED, A BIT WORRIED & A BIT SAD ALL AT THE SAME TIME; OR WE MIGHT FEEL CURIOUS & INTERESTED & ALSO FEEL UNSURE & OVERWHELMED, OR WE MIGHT FEEL IRRITABLE OR ANGRY WHEN WE'RE HUNGRY (EG. HANGRY) ETC

WE MIGHT HAVE DIFFERENT & CHANGING FEELINGS ABOUT SITUATIONS, PEOPLE, MEMORIES & EXPERIENCES. FOR EXAMPLE, WE MIGHT LOVE PARTS OF A PERSON & WE MIGHT ALSO BE SCARED OR SAD ABOUT OTHER PARTS OF THAT SAME PERSON

WE MIGHT HAVE SOME MEMORIES WITH THAT PERSON WE TREASURE & OTHERS WE WOULD LIKE TO FORGET ETC.

OUR BODIES & MINDS MIGHT HAVE FELT A RANGE OF FEELINGS WHICH MIGHT BE MISMATCHED & AT ODDS WITH EACH OTHER - THIS CAN BE CONFUSING, OVERWHELMING, PUZZLING & MORE.

OUR FEEINGS MIGHT ALSO BE HELPFUL & GIVE US CLUES & IMPORTANT MESSAGES. SOMETIMES WE MIGHT FEEL FULL-UP WITH FEEINGS & OTHER TIMES FIND THEM HARD TO CONNECT WITH. THERE CAN BE MANY DIFFERENT LAYERS OF FEELINGS, LIKE AN ONION, AN ICEBERG, & IN NESTING DOLLS.

IMAGISTIC.CO.UK

Activity 20

Different Ways to Express Our Feelings

In the previous pages, we have shared some key messages about feelings, and in the next few activities we will talk more about some of the thorny bits and hazards of keeping things in and of disconnecting from our feelings and the world around us. We will also explore some of the benefits of letting them out or sharing them, while acknowledging that this can be really hard to do, especially if we haven't been able to do this in the past or have been worried about what will happen if we do. It may take time to relearn and retrain our brains and bodies.

But if we feel it is ok and safe to do so, what are some of the ways we might show or express our feelings, needs, and thoughts to others? When might this be helpful? And who with?

Some people can say or show how they or others are feeling (in their heads, in their hearts, in their hands, or in their bodies). They might use a word like 'sad' or 'happy', or variations such as upset, low, down, blue. Or they can also choose their own word like 'icky', or mix and match words such as 'excited' and 'nervous' to make 'nervcited'.

Also, some people like to use words to express, describe, or label their feelings, but others find it easier to think about feelings or sensations in a more creative way, using different ways to describe them. See examples of different ways below.

Sometimes we can say out loud, use words, and talk about our feelings. And other times, we might like to express or show them in different ways. The worksheet below shows some different possible ways.

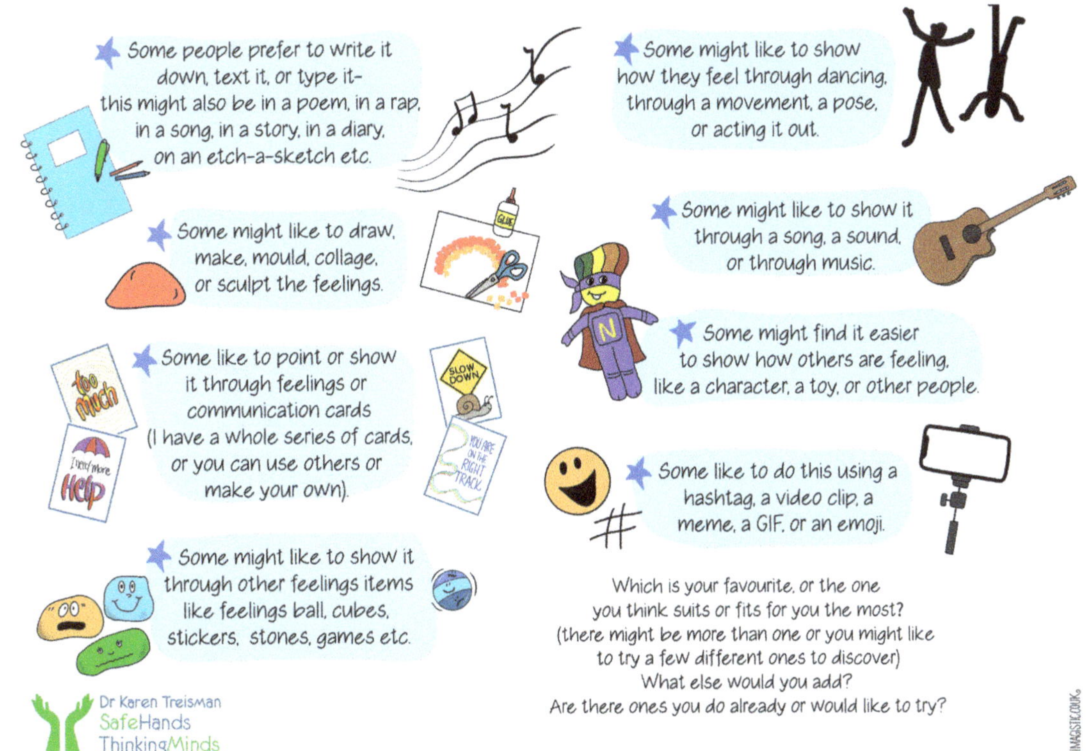

Which of the above fits and speaks to you the most? Which do you prefer? Which are easier/harder? Is anything missing? You might want to try some out and see. Different people prefer different ones at different times.

Some people like to show or express their feelings in different ways – for example, a feelings pizza (Activity 22), a feelings tortoise (Activity 23), a feelings football (Activity 24), feelings channels (Activity 25), a feelings patchwork (Activity 26), a feelings rainbow (Activity 55), a feelings puzzle (Activity 61). You can pick and choose. You might do one, you might do several different ones, or you might choose to make or find your own template. You can also use some of the other templates throughout this activity book. They can be photocopied and used for lots of different things. For example, the patchwork (Activity 26) could be a patchwork of feelings (about a particular time/situation/scenario, Taya's feelings or other characters' feelings, feelings in general, people in our lives' feelings) or it could be used however you like, for example as a patchwork of worries/thoughts/hopes/dreams/questions/coping tools/parts of your personality. (Adults – please check out the sections on feelings and enriching activities in the Guide for Adults.)

The next few pages have a few feelings worksheets you might like to use now, or in the future.

Activity 21

When I Am Feeling...

You might like to draw, talk about, write down, make a collage, and use stickers or play-doh to show the different feelings and sensations. This can be how you think this feeling looks like as a general feeling, or how it might look on another person or on Taya the Tortoise or one of the other characters in the story. It might also be about a specific thing or scenario.

It might be helpful to think about what sort of things might make these feelings visit? How might we explain or describe the feelings? What other words or terms might you use (e.g. sad/upset/down/low/blue)? You might use a feelings wheel or feelings cards to help you think about the whole range of feelings (you can mix and match). Sensations in your body might be things like butterflies in your tummy, headaches, skin rashes, tense muscles, dry mouth, and feeling shaky, hot, cold. You might like to use a larger piece of paper or keep noticing and adding to these.

When I am feeling…

(e.g. "Scared, full up, overwhelmed, angry, hurt, happy, relaxed" etc)
I show it through my… (Draw/sculpt/write/collage your answers).

It might also be helpful to think about how other people and characters show their different feelings through their body, words, facial expressions, and behaviours. You can add others too!

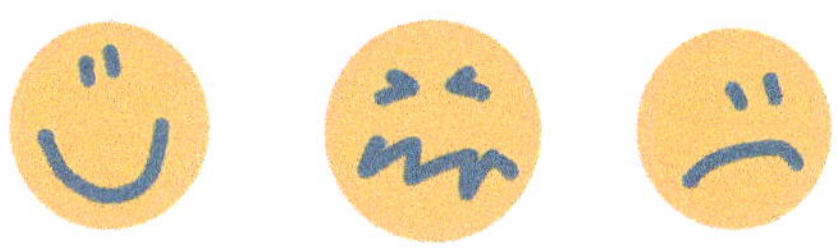

Body/senses	Words
Facial expressions	Behaviours/what do I do?

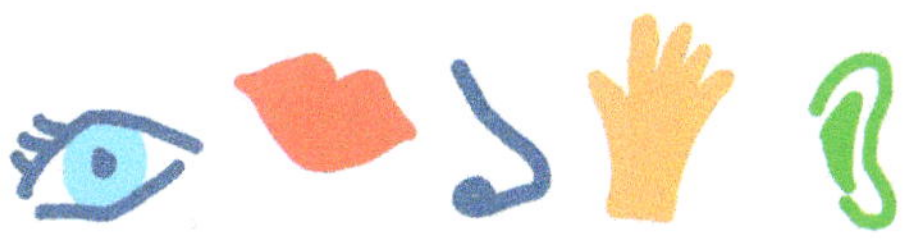

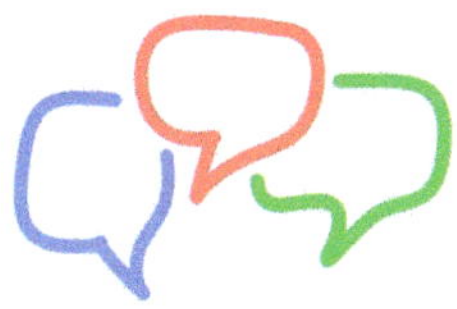

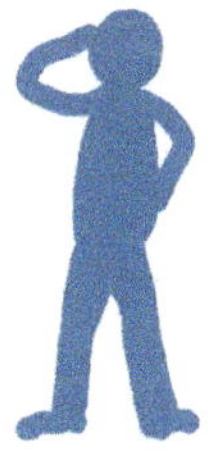

Activity 22

Feelings Pizza

You might prefer to call this a feelings pie, wheel, or cake – you choose. Split the circle into different slices, each slice representing a different feeling. The slice can be a different shape, size, colour, pattern. You can also decorate it with materials and items.

You might make a feelings wheel to show how you are feeling in general, for example 'Today I feel...', or it could be about something more specific, such as how you feel about starting school. It could also show how someone else, like Taya or your teacher, might feel. You can also use this pizza for other things, such as a worries/hopes/dreams pizza.

Activity 23

Tortoise of Feelings

You might like to decorate their shell with different feelings – words, pictures, or patterns.

Activity 24

Feelings (or whatever you want to fill or design it with) Football

Activity 25

Feelings TV Channels

If I turned the TV on to the...(angry, sad, happy, scared, fun etc.) channel, what would I see?

You can do a similar activity with rooms in a house or different feelings parts of an island if you prefer. This could also be for other things like wishes, dreams, hopes, goals, worries, and so on.

Activity 26

My Patchwork of Feelings

This can also be a patchwork of hopes, dreams, worries, experiences, sensations, memories, and so on.

My patchwork of ...

Activity 27

Taya's Different Experiences

We have looked at some of the different messages and some of the things to hold in our minds about feelings (Activities 19–26). What things do you think made Taya feel scared, overwhelmed, sad, hurt? What do you think might have made her retreat, clam-up, disconnect, and bottle-up her feelings?

What do you think this might have felt or looked like in her body, in her head, in her hands, and in her heart?

You can talk about, think about, write, show, or draw on the left-hand-side picture of Taya below. You can also use colouring-in activities 3, 4, and 5 to do this on.

What things do you think made Taya feel happier, more relaxed, safer, more supported, and more cared for? Where might she feel this in her body, heart, and head? You might like to write, draw, talk about, or show these on the right-hand side.

What advice, tips, or suggestions might we give to Taya? For example, we might want to remind her that what happened wasn't her fault, and that things are different now, and there are people who are there for her.

Activity 28

My Different Sides, Layers, and Feelings

Now that we have thought a bit about what makes Taya feel happy, loved, cared for, and calm (you might choose different words or terms), can you draw or write about yourself feeling the same?

On the left-sided box below, draw yourself feeling scared, clammed-up, worried, overwhelmed, unsafe, hurt; on the right-sided box, draw all of the things that make you smile, feel loved, cared for, calm, and safe. You might like to choose a name or a title for each of the different sides. This of course might change at different times and with different people and that is ok (you can do more than one, or revisit this activity at a later date).

Remember that feelings can be mixed, fused, blended, and entangled (Activity 19). For example, something might make us feel a bit happy and a bit sad, and that is ok. If you prefer, you can use a bigger piece of paper, or you can sculpt, write, or make a collage.

Activity 29

What Makes Me or Others Clam-Up, Retreat, or Shut Down

You can talk about, write, collage, and use items, music, or whatever you want to think about this. You can ask other people, go on a discovery journey, or come back to it. Try to take your brain to the gym and start noticing or being curious. You can also do this for others if you want to.

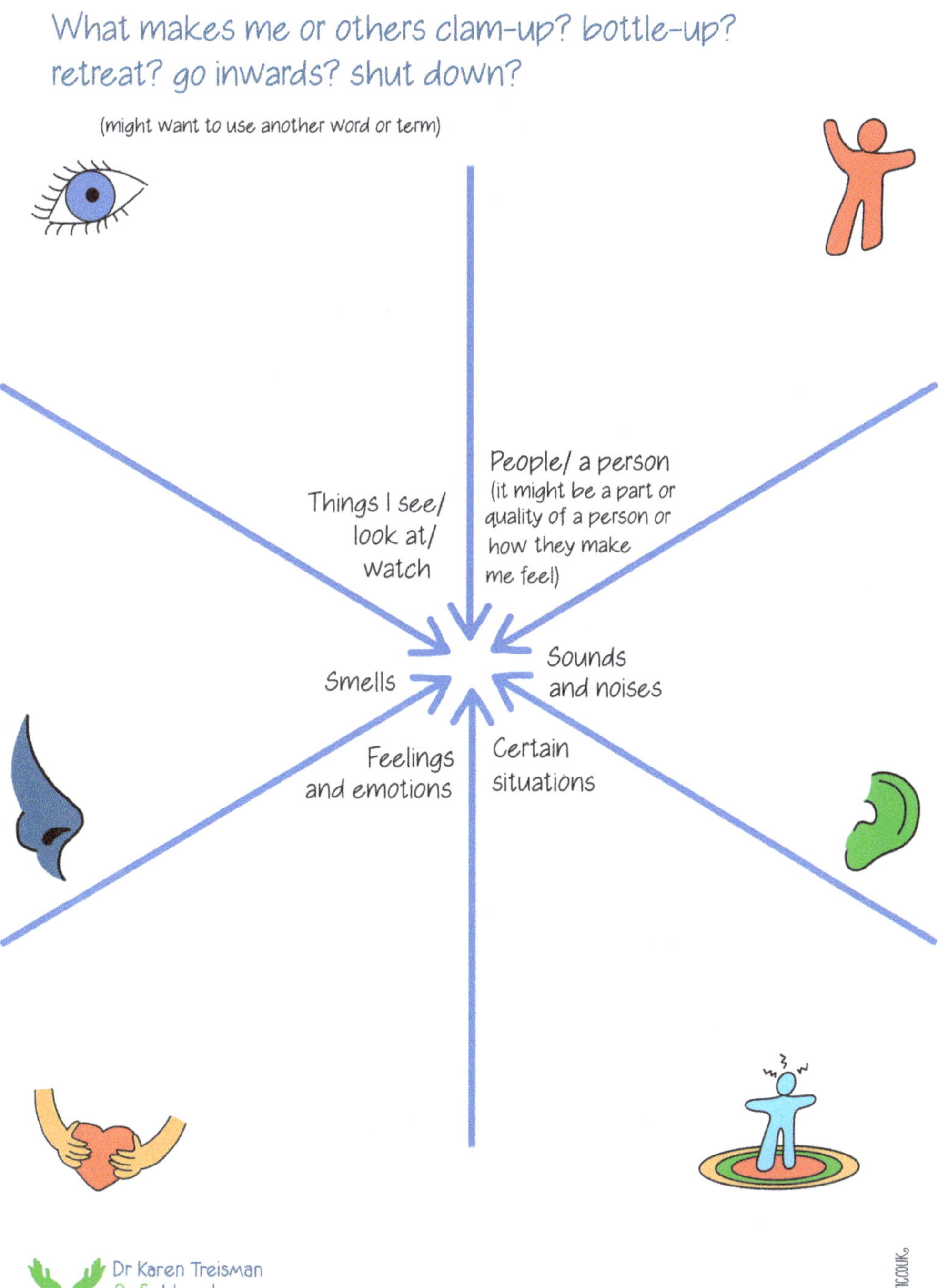

Dr Karen Treisman SafeHands ThinkingMinds

IMAGISTIC.CO.UK

What makes me or others clam-up? bottle-up? retreat? go inwards? shut down?

(might want to use another word or term)

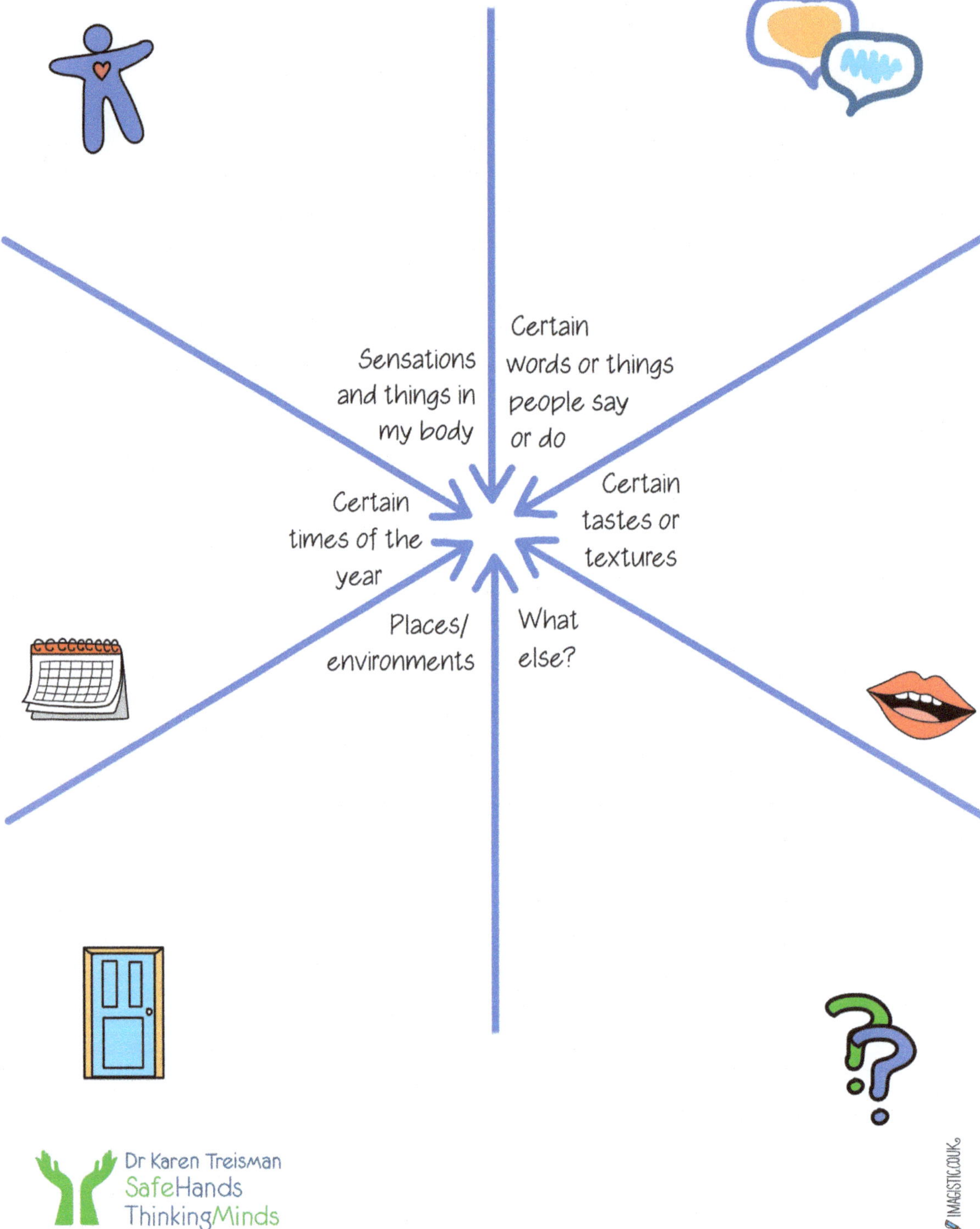

Activity 30

I Worry About...

This might give you an idea of some of the things that might make the worry, fear, and overwhelm visit, but remember that the 'what else?' is super important – what else would you add, what are we missing? You might like to expand on these or think about which you might experience and which you might not – and what they might mean, look like, and feel like.

Worry, Anxiety and Fear

The feeling of "worry/anxiety/fear" is like...

If I gave the "worry/anxiety/fear" a name I would call it...

I would describe the "worry/anxiety/fear" as being like...

Activity 31

Spidey Senses, Buttons, Bugs, and Tidal Wave Activities

What made Taya's spidey senses visit? Why did this happen? When can these spidey senses or warning sensors/detectors be useful and when can they get in the way? Are there things, smells, tastes, sights, noises, sensations, situations, sounds, people, and places that might make your or others' spidey senses visit? What might this look and feel like in your heart, head, and body?

You can talk about spidey senses or, if you prefer, you can do this activity to discuss things that might push your buttons (Activity 32), bug you (Activity 33), or visit like a tidal wave (Activity 34). You can choose which one you prefer or make your own. You might find Activities 9, 27, 28, 29, and 36 helpful with this too!

You can also use these for the opposite, which can be very helpful; for example, what pushes your happy, calm, safe buttons, or what brings a tidal wave of excitement, happiness, and calm.

Activity 32

What Pushes My Different Buttons?

Activity 33

Things That Bug Me...

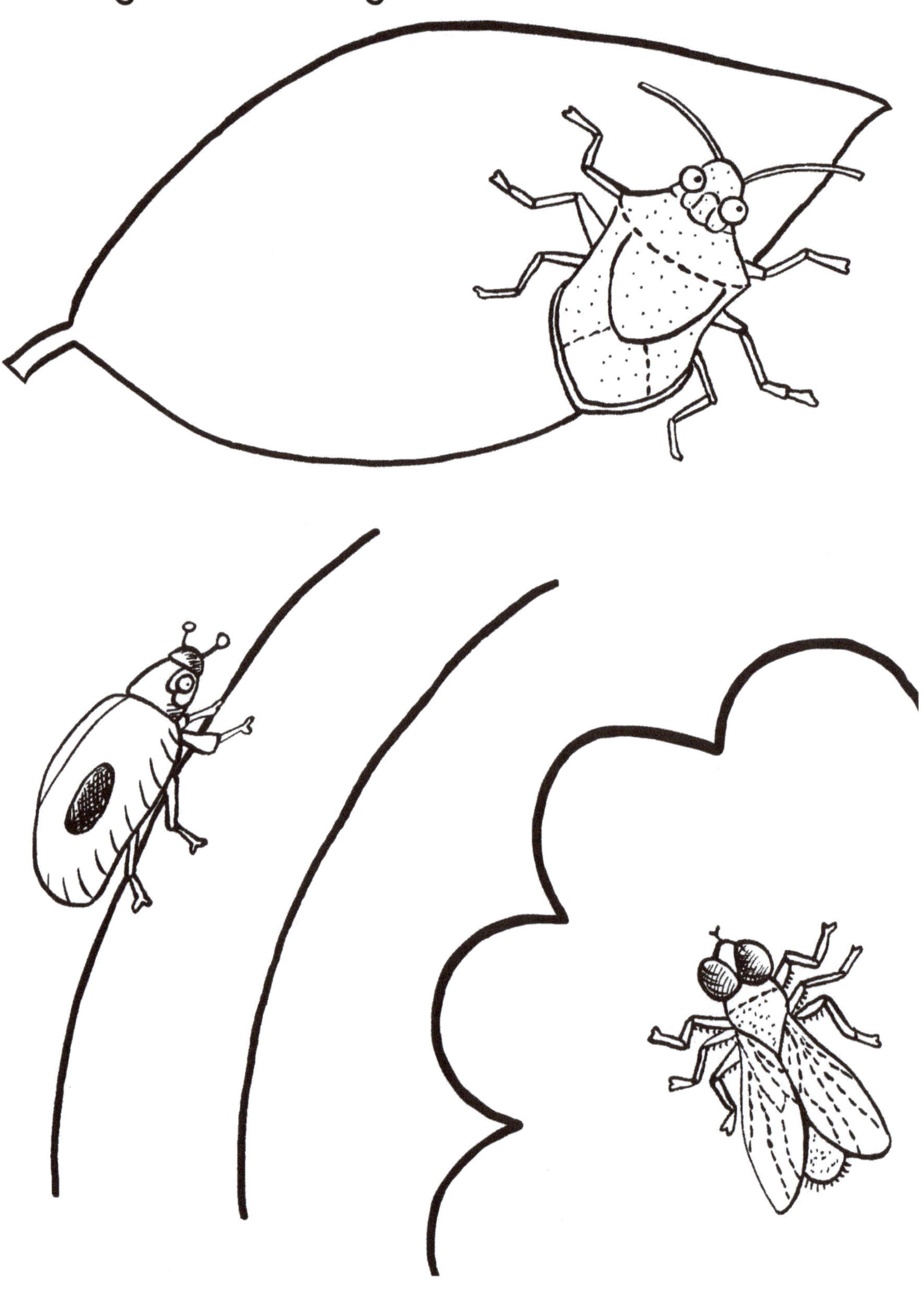

Activity 34

A Tidal Wave of Feelings/ Sensations/Memories

A tidal wave of feelings

Things making the worry or overwhelm visit, sensations, memories, hope (anything else you want to apply this to).

Activity 35

Travelling to a Different Place in Our Minds

Taya's mind sometimes flew off and escaped to a different place or zone. She sometimes understandably found it hard to stay in the moment and present. If you were to draw or describe where you go when you travel to a different place – and/or what it might feel or look like – what would this be?

Activity 36

Keeping Safe and Protected

As you read in the story, when scary things were happening to or around Taya, she understandably felt scared, unsafe, alone, and full up. To keep herself as safe as possible, and to avoid feeling and getting more hurt, her body, brain, heart, mind, and nervous system had found some ways to protect her. For example, she floated away, she locked away her heart, she retreated into her shell, she froze, and much more!

What do you do to keep yourself safe and protected? If you don't know or don't feel able to think about this for yourself, you can think about how some characters or other people you know keep themselves safe and protected in a range of different situations. Or you can take your time to notice this over time; there is no rush, and no good or bad, right or wrong way of doing it. We need to respect and honour the ways in which we protect ourselves, survive, and adapt in thorny times. We might have used multiple different strategies, at different times or with different people – sometimes, they can be similar to what other people around us do, and sometimes they can be different and can clash or be confusing. The 'what else?' box here is super important, as you might like to add your own!

Feeling Unsafe/Putting Up Defenses

When I am feeling "unsafe" and need to protect myself I ...

Surround myself with barbed wire 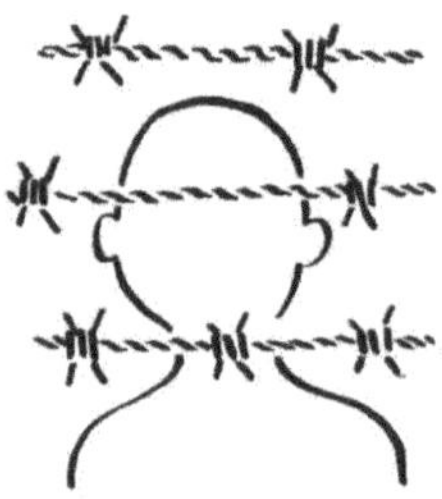	Go into attack mode like a hungry shark 	Go into my own protective bubble 	Put on my bulletproof vest 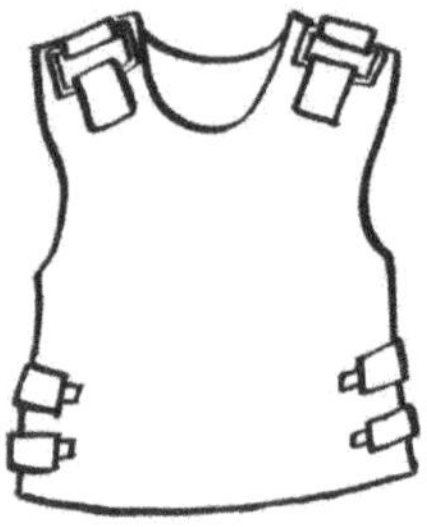	Retreat into my tortoise shell 
Make myself small/invisible 	Hide away in the fog 	Freeze on the spot 	Whizz around like a dart 	Paint on a smile like a clown 
Put up my spikes like a hedgehog 	Zoom away like a speeding car 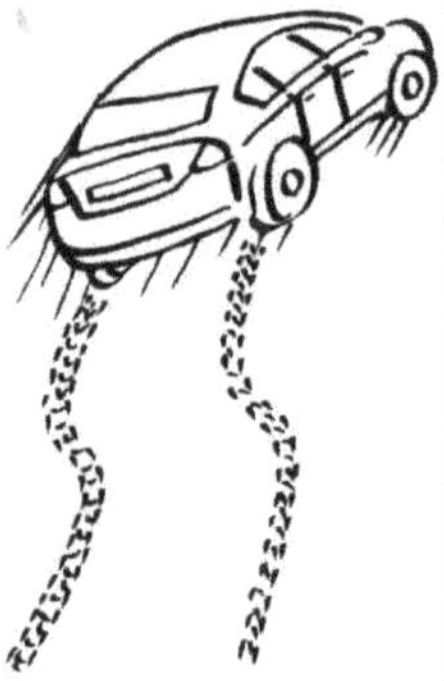	Push people away like an opposing magnet 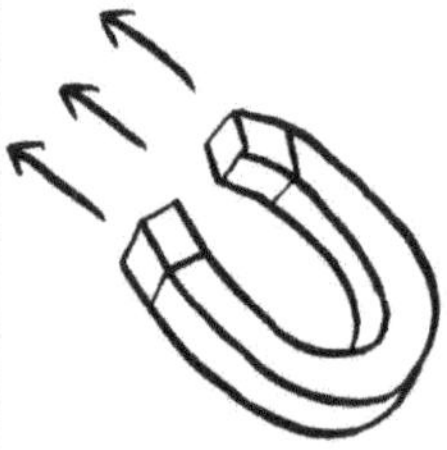	Think in black and white 	What else? 

Activity 37

Helpful Retreating, Unplugging, Disconnecting, and Bottling-Up

Building on Activity 36, think about when retreating, unplugging, disconnecting, and bottling-up feelings have been needed, been helpful, been your protector.

Taya often protected herself or kept herself as safe as possible by retreating, unplugging, going into her tortoise shell, making herself smaller, and staying quiet. Sometimes, retreating, unplugging, disconnecting, and bottling-up feelings can help and are needed. These ways of coping can be our friend, our helper, our protector, our shield.

When did Taya need to retreat or keep her feelings as protected as possible? When was this her friend, her helper, her shield, her protector? For you, when is or has it been helpful and needed? When has it been your friend? What might Taya or you miss or be worried about if you couldn't retreat, clam-up, or disconnect anymore?

Activity 38

Some of the hazards and thorny bits of keeping things inside, of bottling-up, of locking them away, or holding them in

This might be physical/body-based, emotional, spiritual, practical, relational/social, cognitively, etc.

Sometimes, if we hold things in, they can come out in other ways like how our body might feel or things we might say, do, or not do.

What might be some of the hazards, worries, and thorny bits of keeping things inside, of bottling them up, locking them away, or holding them in?

What things, feelings, opportunities, lessons, and experiences might we miss out on?

(Of course, sometimes this is needed and helpful, and we need to honour and respect that; but what are some of the times when it might hurt or harm us or make things trickier?)

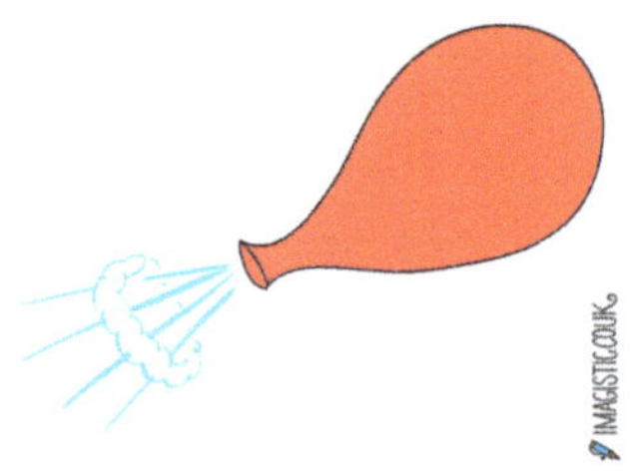

Activity 39

Helpful Things About Sharing and Expressing Our Needs, Feelings, or Worries

We might answer this for ourselves, for Taya, or for others, or the adults supporting us might give us some possible ways they think about this. You might like to revisit this also after doing Activities 43–57.

Dr Karen Treisman SafeHands ThinkingMinds

Activity 40

Giving Advice and Suggestions to Others

What would you say to or advise a friend/someone else/a character/a toy about sharing, expressing themselves, coming out of their shell, trying new things, believing in themselves?

You might like to do this on the head outline below or on the next page (Activity 41) around writing letters.

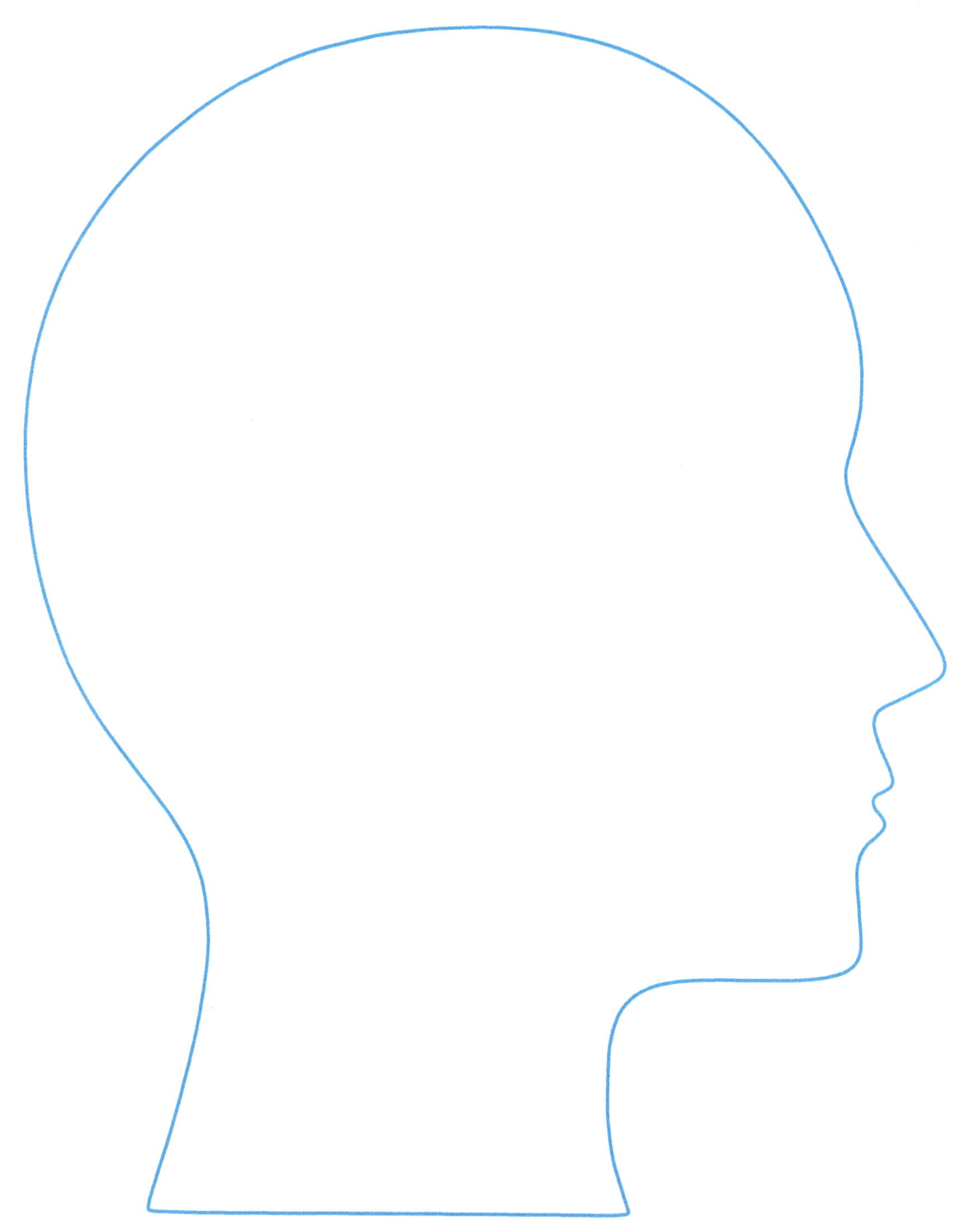

Activity 41

My Letter, Poem, Song, Rap, Postcard, Picture, or Collage

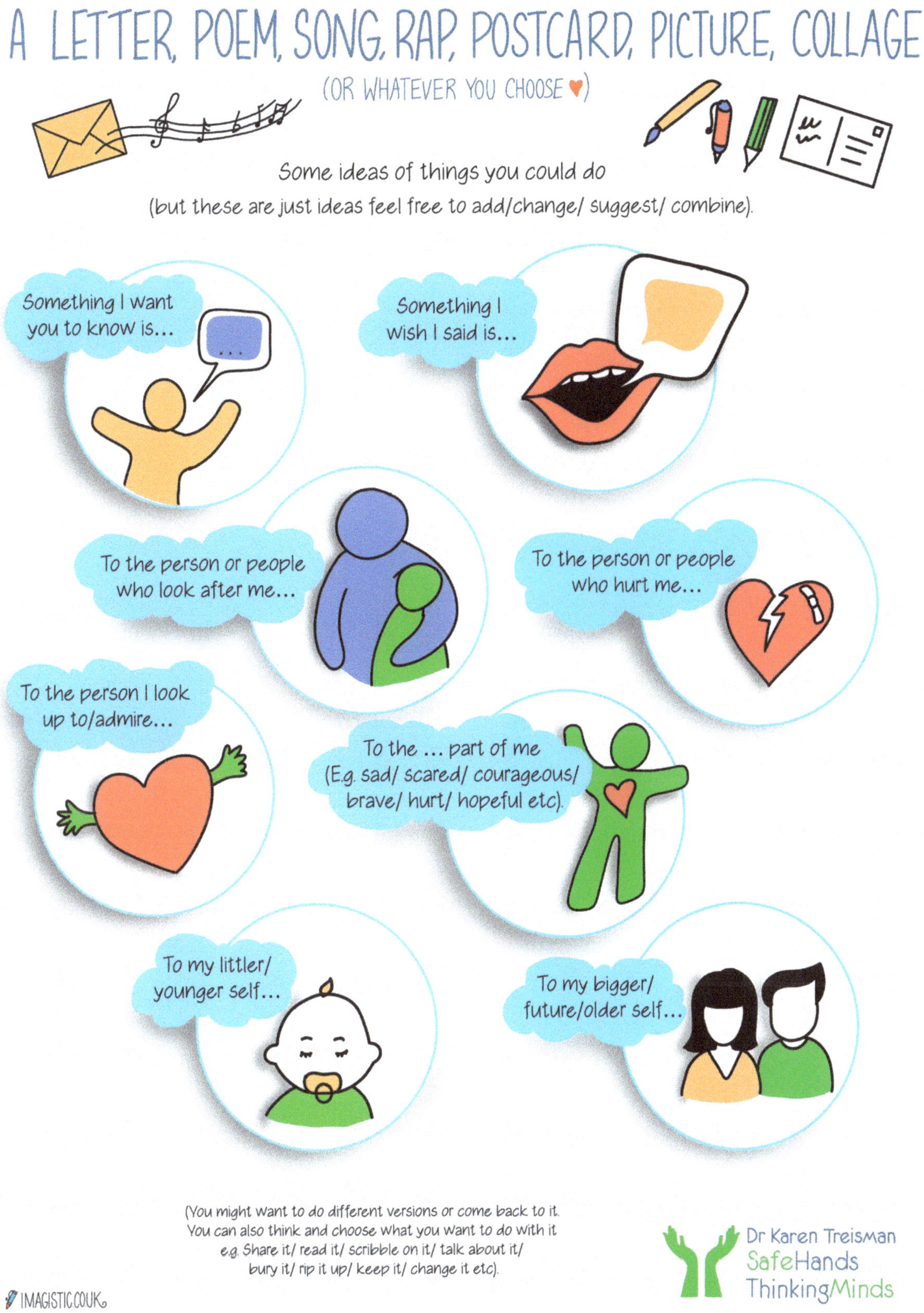

A LETTER, POEM, SONG, RAP, POSTCARD, PICTURE, COLLAGE
(OR WHATEVER YOU CHOOSE ♥)
Some ideas of things you could do
(but these are just ideas feel free to add/change/ suggest/ combine).
Something I want you to know is...
Something I wish I said is...
To the person or people who look after me...
To the person or people who hurt me...
To the person I look up to/admire...
To the ... part of me (E.g. sad/ scared/ courageous/ brave/ hurt/ hopeful etc).
To my littler/ younger self...
To my bigger/ future/older self...
(You might want to do different versions or come back to it. You can also think and choose what you want to do with it e.g. Share it/ read it/ scribble on it/ talk about it/ bury it/ rip it up/ keep it/ change it etc).
IMAGISTIC.CO.UK
Dr Karen Treisman
SafeHands
ThinkingMinds

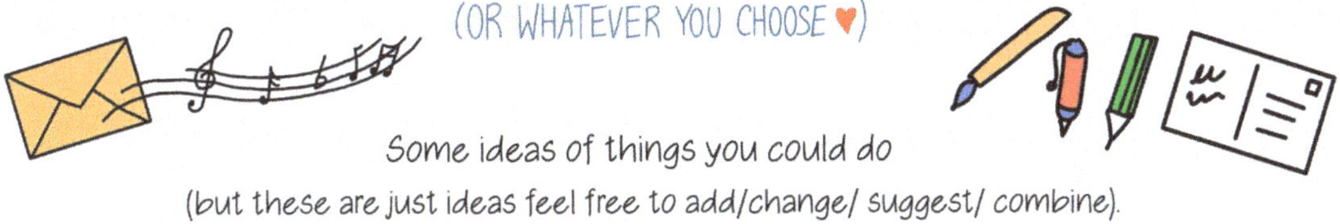

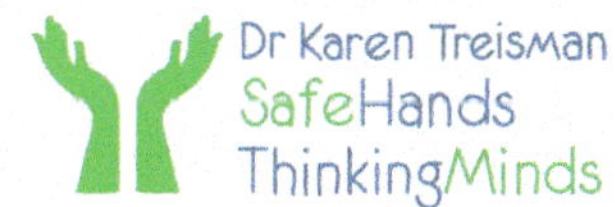

A LETTER, POEM, SONG, RAP, POSTCARD, PICTURE, COLLAGE

(OR WHATEVER YOU CHOOSE ♥)

(You might want to do different versions or come back to it.
You can also think and choose what you want to do with it
e.g. Share it/ read it/ scribble on it/ talk about it/
bury it/ rip it up/ keep it/ change it etc).

IMAGISTIC.CO.UK

Activity 42

The Magic Word, 'Yet'

Sometimes, we can doubt ourselves or talk negatively to ourselves. We can tell ourselves that we can't do things or that we aren't good enough. These words can be powerful, even more so if this is what we were told or how we have been treated has made us feel this way. So, it takes time to relearn and to train our brains.

It can be helpful to think here about the word 'yet' and to give ourselves grace, patience, and kindness: 'I can't do..yet' or 'I am struggling a little bit at the moment', or 'I am trying and these things take time to learn'.

- Are there things which you have found tricky or difficult or thought that you couldn't do and then discovered that you were able to do them (or start to be able to do them) after a bit of practice and time?
- Maybe you learned some ways to problem solve around them?
- What skills and strengths did you use?
- What things have you navigated through (a bit like snakes and ladders or an obstacle course)?

We will build on this throughout the activity workbook, so don't worry if these questions are a bit tricky to answer. We can come back to them and take our time.

Think about the things that you can do now, and the things that you are learning at the moment. You might like to keep a diary, or have a jar, a list, or another way of recording each time you try something or take a step forward. This can be helpful as a reminder of the journey you are travelling. It will also help you to think about the skills you use during difficult times, and what you learn. What would you say to a friend if they had done these things? (Note to practitioners doing this activity book: if you are qualified to do so, it might be helpful to interweave these with some cognitive behavioural ideas.)

What are some of the positive and encouraging words which you might be able to tell yourself when the self-doubt visits? (This needs to feel authentic to us, even if it is a bit gentler or a teeny tiny step.) This might be what your life cheerleaders say or what advice you would give to someone else. (See Activities 40, 41, and 59.)

If you were going to borrow some hope, courage, bravery, confidence (or whichever other thing you would like to borrow), who would you borrow it from? What would that person or part of that person tell you, advise you, or teach you? (See Activity 59.)

You could make a collage, poem, or drawing about these or add them to the head or letter templates in Activities 40 and 41. You could also pop them in the other templates found throughout the activity book such as the treasure box, the anchor, and the net.

Part 3
Letting Some Joy, Happiness, Fun, Lightness, and Connection In

Activity 43

Letting Some of the Joy, Happiness, Fun, Lightness, Connection, and Good In

Sometimes, when we protect ourselves (like Taya did by retreating in her shell, disconnecting, and putting her emotional armour on), we can keep the painful, stingy, and thorny bits out or a bit of a distance away from us. This can be very helpful and needed and can be important at the time of the hurt and when scary things are happening (see Activities 27–28 and 36–38). But unfortunately, this can also mean that sometimes the retreating, clamming-up, disconnecting, and blocking can also work the other way! It can stop the magic, joy, laughter, lightness, connection, and all the beautiful things from coming in and visiting us.

This is a bit like hiding in a cave or waiting for a storm to pass. It makes sense when there is threat, a storm, or danger and you might feel better, but if you stay in that cave or away from the outside world after the storm has passed, you might miss out on things and might not have opportunities to learn that parts of being outside can be ok and helpful.

- What do you think are some of the beautiful, magical, fun, connecting, and joyful things that might not be able to come in if we block them out?
- If you could choose, what good, joyful, magical things would you want to come and see you?
- What are some of the things that make the magic and happiness visit?
- What does 'happiness' look like, feel like, and mean to you?

Use the activities on the next few pages to explore these questions further. You might want to create a collage, a vision board, or a drawing, or write these down. As with the whole activity book, you can take your brain to the gym, notice what happens, and come back to it. You can ask others. You can take your time and dip in and out of these activities. You can add things as you discover them as part of your ongoing journey.

Activity 44

What Makes Me Happy, Smile, Laugh, Light Up?

Activity 45

Happiness, Joy, and Excitement are...

Happiness, Joy and Excitement

The feeling of "happiness/joy/excitement" is like...

If I gave the "happiness/joy/excitement" a name I would call it...

I would describe the "happiness/joy/excitement" as being like...

Rainbow	Sunshine	Fireworks	Hugs	Warm glow
Cosy blanket	Rollercoaster	Flying high	Music	King of the world
Opening a present	Warm bath	Carnival	Scoring a goal	What else?

- What do happiness, joy, excitement (or another word you choose) look, sound, and feel like to you?
- What makes them visit more? (People, places, smells, sounds, tastes, situations – you can use Activities 9 and 26.)
- If happiness, joy, and excitement could talk, what might they say to us?
- If happiness, joy, and excitement were a colour, shape, texture, type of weather, something in nature, an animal or creature, and so on, what might they be?
- When happiness, joy, and excitement visit, where might we feel them in our bodies? What might other people notice?
- What would you add in the 'what else?' box above? Which of the pictures do you agree with or disagree with? What is missing?

We might not know these answers on the spot but can notice and discover different things and keep coming back to this activity.

Activity 46

A Treasure Box of Relationship Gems and Qualities

You can also use this activity to support you over the next few activities, and you can come back to it.

A TREASURE BOX of RELATIONSHIP GEMS & QUALITIES

A TREASURE BOX of RELATIONSHIP GEMS & QUALITIES

Which do you have already?
(can you give examples of when they were felt – and can you notice the next time they visit).

Which do you think are important and would want more of?

Which ones do you look out for?

Which ones do you show to others?

What do these mean, feel like, and look like?

Why are these important?

These can be like our relationship feast! They can fill our bucket! They can give us a galaxy of new relationship opportunities! These will be built on in the next few activities.

Activity 47

Sentence Completions

This is about noticing and soaking in the possible colour, magic, lightness, fun, connection, and joy of trusted relationships.

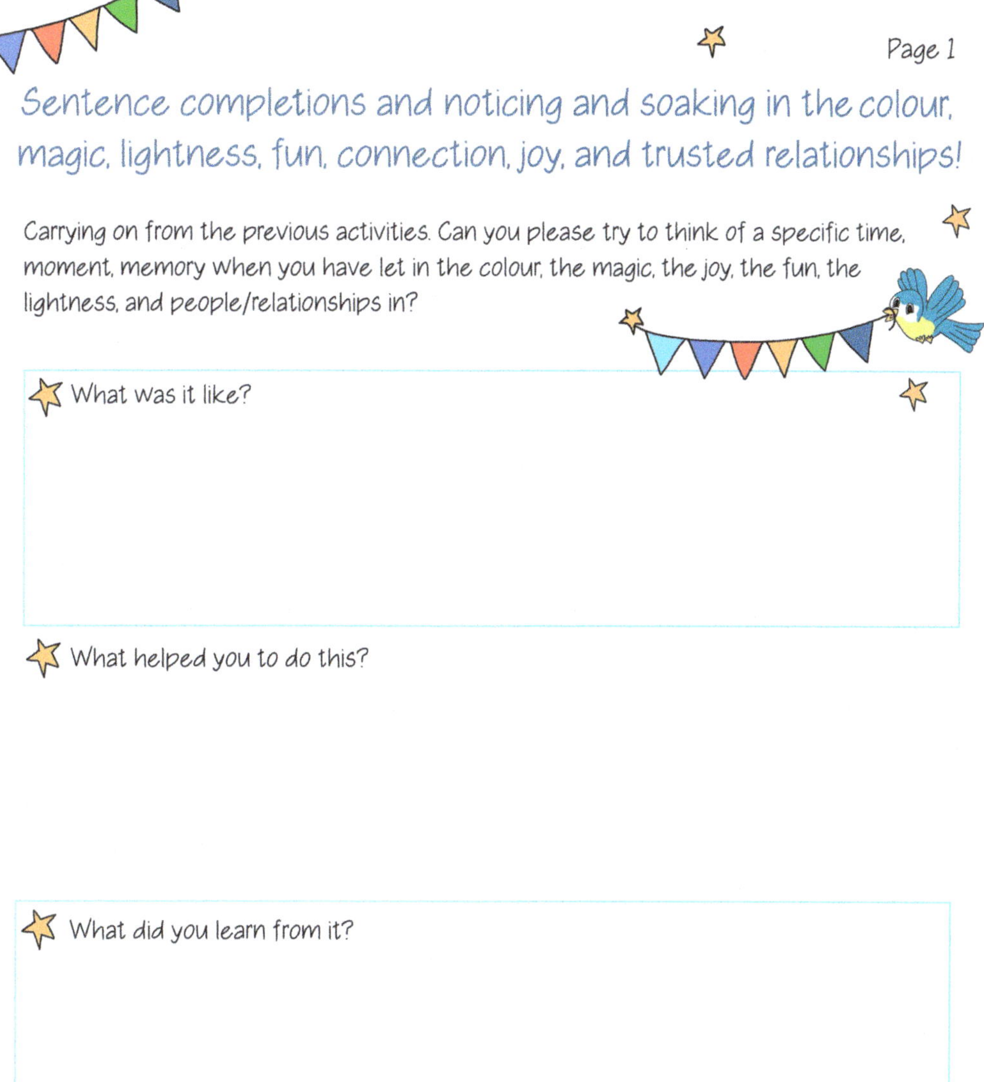

Page 1

Sentence completions and noticing and soaking in the colour, magic, lightness, fun, connection, joy, and trusted relationships!

Carrying on from the previous activities. Can you please try to think of a specific time, moment, memory when you have let in the colour, the magic, the joy, the fun, the lightness, and people/relationships in?

What was it like?

What helped you to do this?

What did you learn from it?

If it is tricky to think about yourself, that is ok. What about in movies, or on TV, or in books; can you think of a character who was positively helped and supported by an adult or others?

You can ask other people, take your time to think about, or just try to notice these things over time.

Sentence completions and noticing and soaking in the colour, magic, lightness, fun, connection, joy, and trusted relationships! Page 2

Now, see if you can complete these sentences. If you can't think of one, that is absolutely ok and understandable. You can always fill them out in future but remember to take your brain to the gym and be a detective. The more we pay attention, notice, and watch out for these moments and times, the more we are likely to see them.

A time/moment when I felt I could trust someone was...

A time/moment when someone helped me was...

A time/moment when I felt someone cared was...

A time/moment I shared a problem, and it was helped was...

A time/moment I trusted someone, and it was helpful was...

Dr Karen Treisman
SafeHands
ThinkingMinds

IMAGISTIC.CO.UK

Sentence completions and noticing and soaking in the colour, magic, lightness, fun, connection, joy, and trusted relationships! Page 3

A time/moment when I couldn't do something alone and I needed help, and it helped me was...

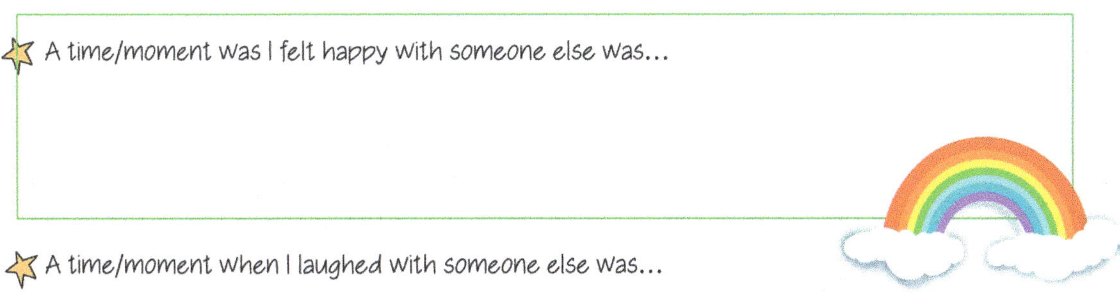

A time/moment was I felt happy with someone else was...

A time/moment when I laughed with someone else was...

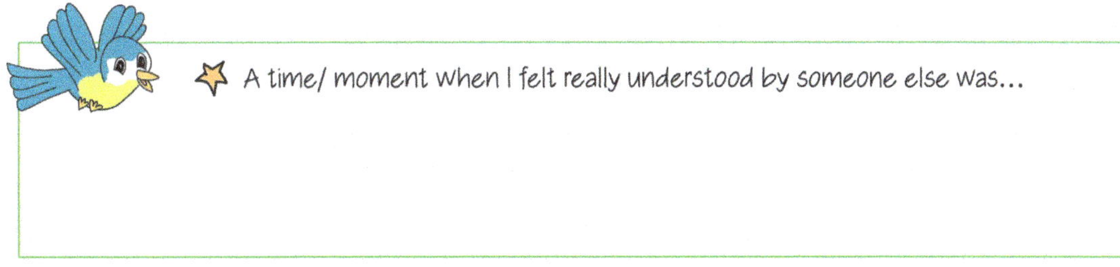

A time/ moment when I felt really understood by someone else was...

A time/ moment when I felt listened to was...

The things I want to say are...

What would you like to add?

IMAGISTIC.CO.UK

Sentence completions and noticing and soaking in the colour, magic, lightness, fun, connection, joy, and trusted relationships! Page 4

Think about some of these times, moments, and memories shared above.

- Who were these times with?

- What helped you at the time to let the "good" things in?

- What happened?

- What did the person/ people do?

- What did you do?

- What did it feel like?

- What could you learn from these moments?

Sentence completions and noticing and soaking in the colour, magic, lightness, fun, connection, joy, and trusted relationships! Page 5

You might like to draw, colour-in, collage, or write about all of the "positive" times you have had and/or also the "positive" times you have spent with an adult, had fun with them, trusted them, learned from them, asked for help, felt cared for, felt loved etc.

Sometimes, we need to train our brain and re-teach and re-learn! So, in the past, maybe if we cried, or asked for help, or said we were worried or struggling we might have been hurt, disappointed, let down, scared, and many other feelings. So now, we need to try to slowly notice and pay attention when there are times when we can cry, or ask for help, or show all of our parts to someone and be able to be our whole self and feel accepted and seen. Heartprint by heart print. Glimmer by glimmer.

You might like to add some of these moments and times to your treasure box, your net, your patchwork, your rainbow, your sparkle moment jar etc and keep taking your brain to the gym so that you might notice them even more on your ongoing discovery journey. You might like to imagine, draw, or write about yourself really absorbing and soaking these in! From your head to your toes!

You can keep adding to them! You can also use the following worksheets and ideas to really expand, and enrich these further.

IMAGISTIC.CO.UK

Activity 48

Capturing and Enriching those Moments and Experiences

You might want to draw and use Activities 43–47.

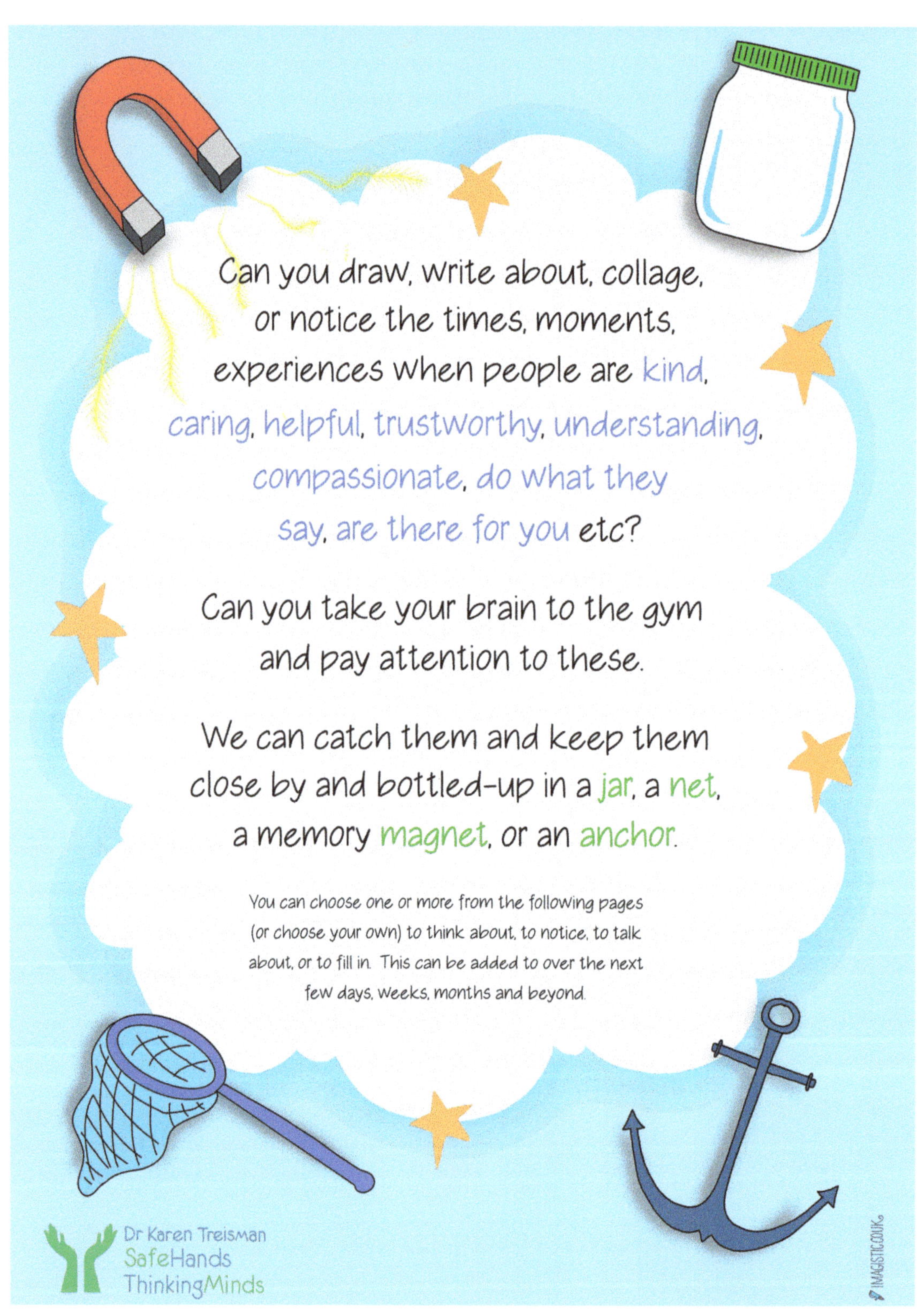

Activity 49

Bottling-Up Template

Activity 50

Catching them in a Net

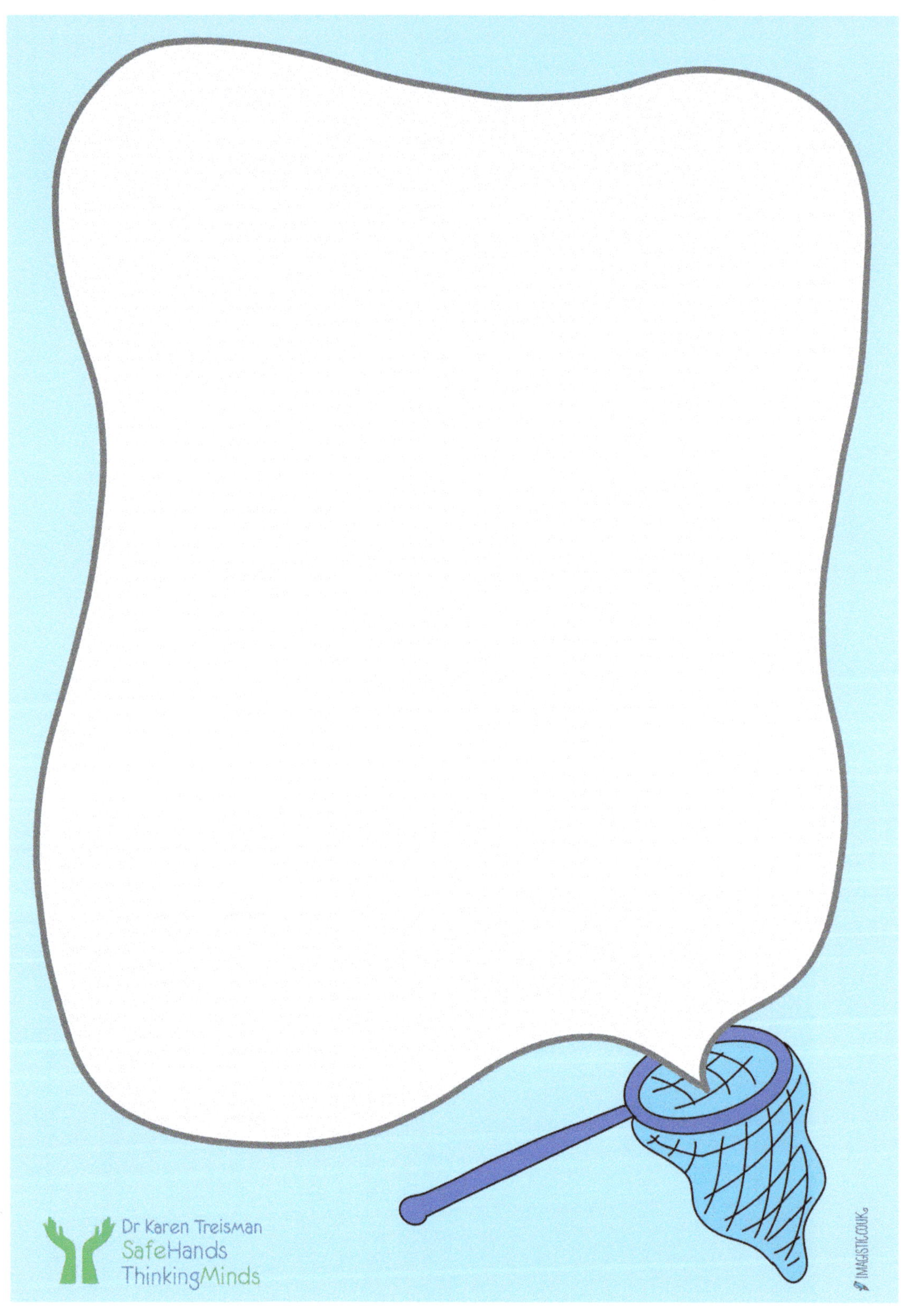

Activity 51

My Magical Magnet

These are things you want to remember and hold on to. (You could also do this with the concept of glue or Velcro.)

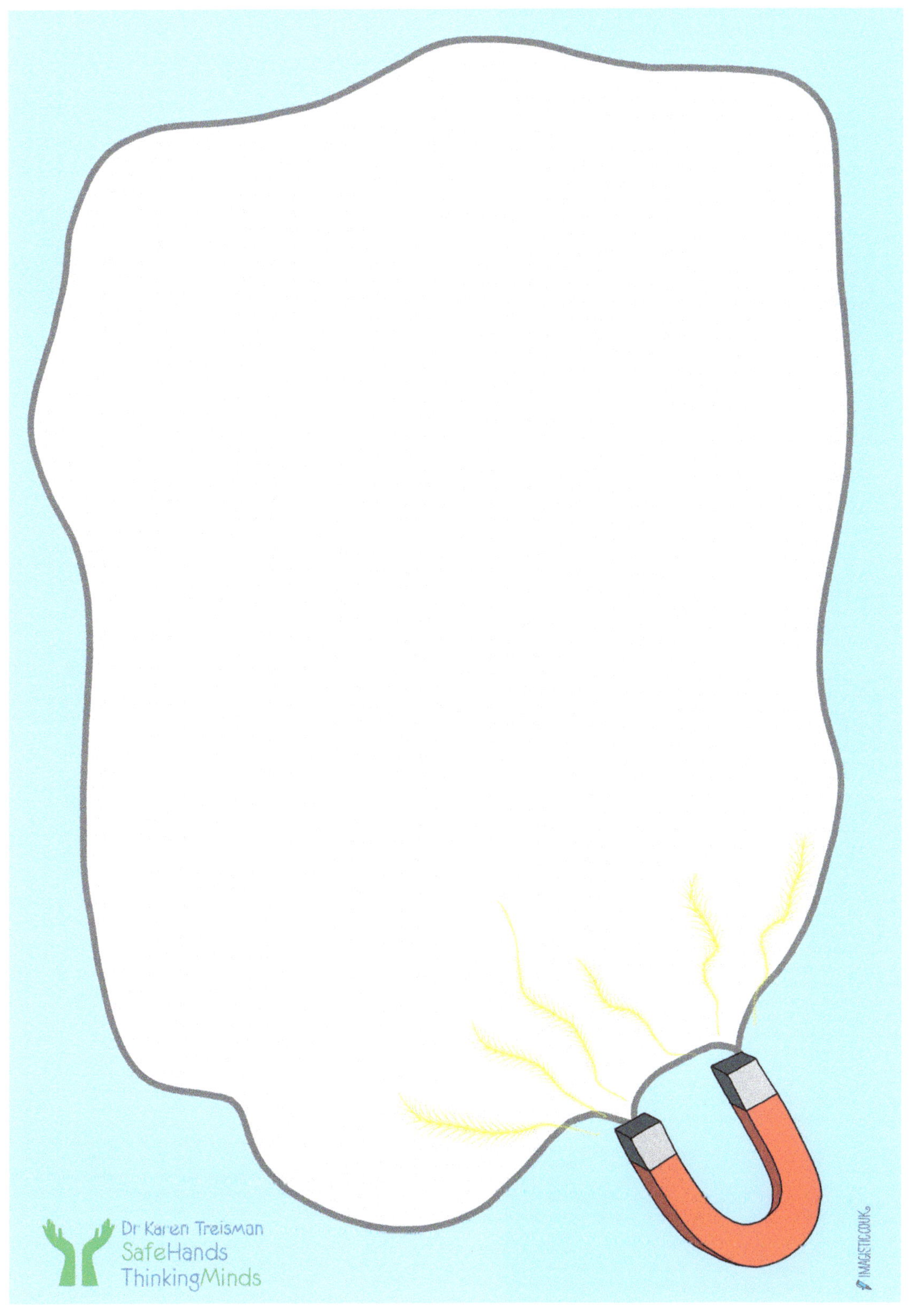

Activity 52

My Anchor

These are things you want to anchor on to, remember, and keep hold of.

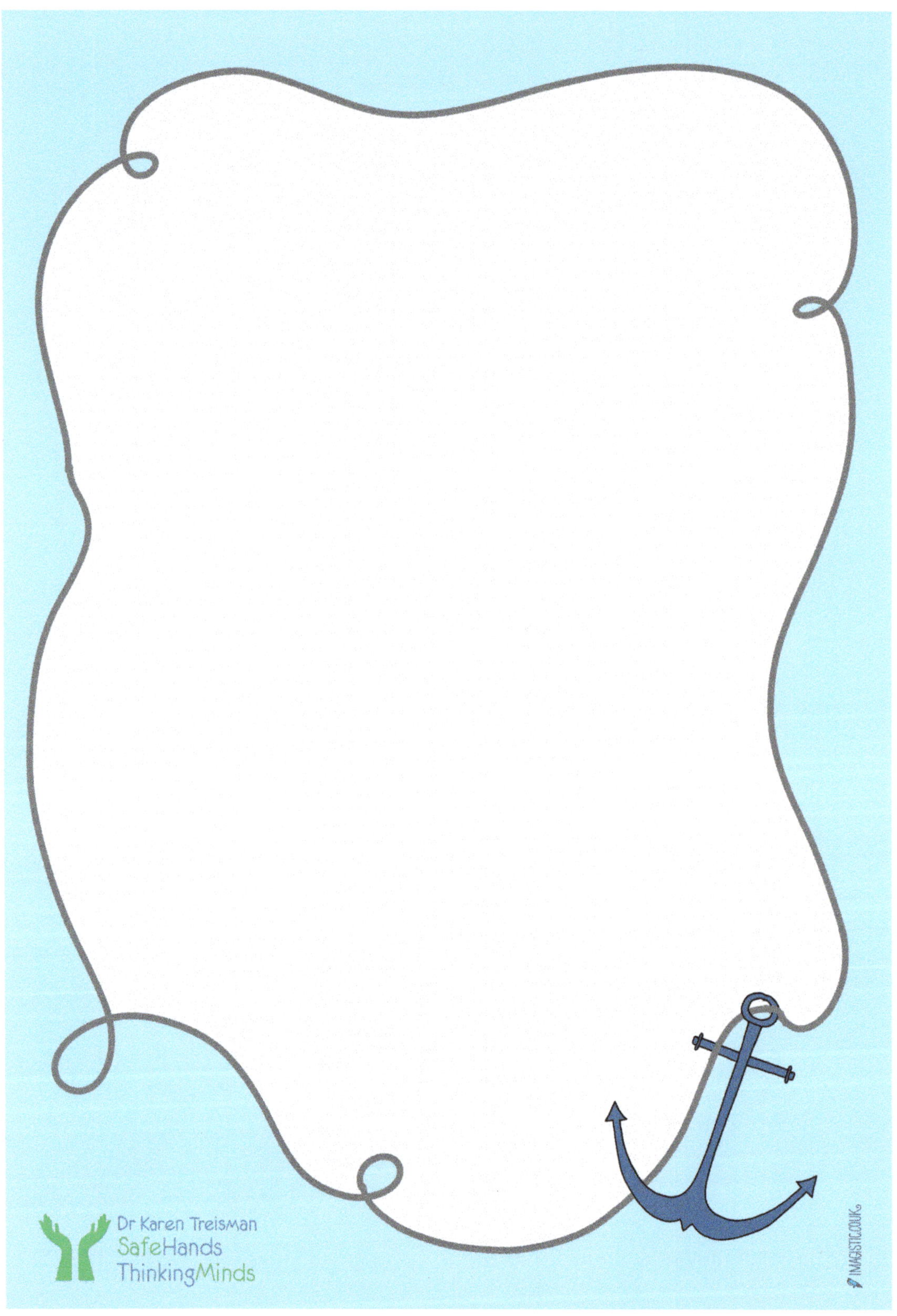

Activity 53

My Time Capsule of Memories, Moments, Experiences

Activity 54

My Treasure Box of...

Activity 55

My Rainbow of...

Activity 56

Expanding on and Enriching those Memories, Moments, and Experiences

In addition to the previous worksheet templates (a jar, net, anchor, magnet, time capsule, treasure box, and rainbow), here are some more ideas for you to try to make those experiences, times, memories, and moments sink in and be remembered and celebrated. There is no right or wrong way of doing them. You can design or choose your own; you can do a few different ones, and they can be a work in progress; you can keep on adding to them over time. (For the adults supporting, please read the sections in the adult guide about ways to expand and enrich these activities.)

You might like to write down, sculpt, draw, make a collage or scrapbook, or paint your answers. You could use a title or theme, for example 'My Best Parts', 'My..at Her Best', 'Us Surviving Being Stranded on a Desert Island', 'Twenty Reasons Why I Love..', 'I Appreciate My.., Because...', 'The Reason Why I Can Ask for Help or Trust..are..', 'Things We Have Done Together', or 'Our Best Moments'.

You can also make a voice recording or a video, or a letter, card, or comic book.

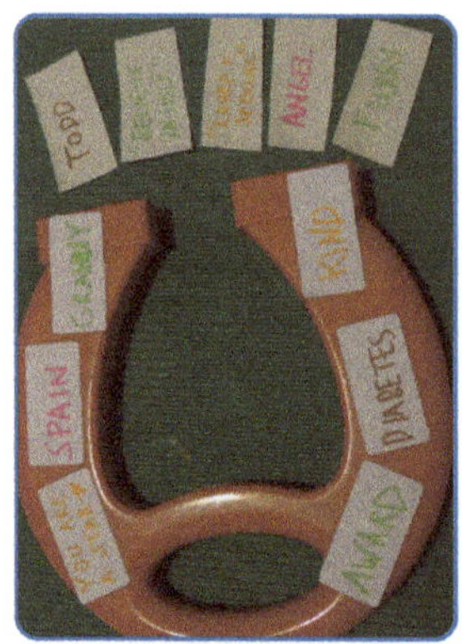

You might like to also capture and remember the special times, memories, or moments together or within relationships and friendships, like Taya started having with Tillie, Tristan, Daisy, Cosmo, and Harley.

Some people find it helpful to draw on some quotes and sayings about relationships, such as 'Sticks in a bundle cannot be broken' (African proverb) or 'I can do things that you can't, and you can do things that I can't, so together we can do great things' (Mother Teresa) – choose or make your own!

- A scrapbook, collage, album, personalized photo item. You could also keep a sparkle moments diary, journal, jar, a treasure box, or a board featuring cherished relational memories, photos, or post-it notes.
- A crest, cape, or shield of your strengths, positive memories, and things that you want to remember. You could also do this using different charms or beads.
- A tower or skyscraper of strengths. Write the positive memories, moments, and strengths of the relationship on different bricks of Lego, building blocks, or Jenga; or you could talk about them and make a pillow tower. You might also find it helpful to use my strengths cards (see the resources at the end of this book) and think about relational strengths and gifts. This is a great activity as you can visually see the height and strength of the tower, and this can lead to conversations about how you can maintain and strengthen the tower.
- A patchwork or puzzle of the relationship positives. Write the positive memories and strengths of the relationship on pieces of card, or on pieces of material; and then stick/sew them together to make a patchwork pattern or blanket. To make a personalized puzzle of positives, write or draw each strength, moment, or positive on a different piece of a tabletop or floor puzzle. You could also use the templates in Activities 26 and 61.
- A pillow of positives or a quilt of qualities. Use a blanket or a pillow to represent all the special moments, times, and qualities of your relationship and then draw or use fabric pens, photos, or quotes. Some people have taken this idea and applied it to make photo wallpaper or a photo lamp.
- A star, sun, or rainbow of strengths. Write down all of the positive memories and qualities of your relationship on the different stripes of a rainbow (Activity 55), rays of a sun, or corners of a star. This concept could be personalized, for example using carriages of a train, words on shells, hexagons on a football.

- **Hands of strengths.** Adult and child can print their handprints, or draw around their own, or each other's hands, and then write on the different fingers and thumb the different strengths, positives, and special moments from the relationship.
- **A chocolate box of positives, or gifts/presents of positives.** Write the strengths of your relationship and of each other, and put them into a chocolate box, or write them down and wrap them up as presents. You could also do this on stars, shells, pearls, beads, and so on.
- **An alphabet of strengths.** Different strengths and appreciated parts can also be written down in alphabet form. For example, Nate and his foster carer made an alphabet list of all the things they appreciated about each other. Such as 'A' for 'Artistic', 'B' for 'Great at baking', 'C' for 'Caring', and so on...This could also be inside the letters of their name or the first letter.

There are so many others – what else could you add?

Activity 57

Some of the Benefits and Positives of Being in a 'Healthy Relationship'

By the end of the story, Taya started to learn how much happier, safer, and more supported she could be with Tristan, Tillie, Daisy, Cosmo, and Harley by her side.

How do people show you that you can trust them? What might you like them to do? What do you notice? How is this different from other people and experiences? Why do you think it is important and helpful to have a team of people and life cheerleaders around us? What can we do when we have a team of people that we couldn't do if it was just us?

Activity 58

My 'Special' Person

If you were to create or design a 'special' person to look after you, help you, and support you, what would they be like? What would they say? What would they do? What would they be like with you? How would they make you feel? What would you do together? (Activities 44, 45, and 55 might support you with this.) This might be imaginary or based on a person or people you know in real life, on TV, or in books. It could also be different parts or qualities of different people added together, a bit like a mix-and-match person. You can draw or write on or around the person below – or you might prefer to make your own.

Activity 59

Life Cheerleaders and Supporters

Taya learned that not everyone is the same, we are all unique and different, and that Tillie, Tristan, Daisy, Cosmo, and Harley were different from the people who had hurt her – they cared for her and helped her. Of course, they are not superhuman, but the majority of the time, they believed in her.

Taya had often felt alone or disconnected. She had often had to navigate life without someone beside her. She had had so many missed opportunities and experiences. So, in the story she was starting to learn some of the advantages of letting some people, like Tristan, Tillie, Miss Daisy, Cosmo, and Harley, in. We can use these people or parts of people to remember that some people and relationships can be helpful and fun, and have a range of advantages (see Activities 43–58).

Life can be thorny and stingy and have twists and turns, but often it makes a real difference if we feel seen, heard, accepted, held, cared for, and believed in – if we have a team of people with us we can call our life cheerleaders and supporters.

When we feel alone, we can remind ourselves of these people, what they would say, how they make us feel. While we might be alone physically, emotionally we can be together. It is as if we are connected by an invisible string, energy, and force. Wherever we go or whatever we do, they can be in our heart and in our heads. When we feel alone, scared, or overwhelmed, we can soak in and breathe in these people and imagine they are there supporting us and cheering us on. We can feel their love, support, and energy all around us. They can be there to ride the storm and navigate the thorny times, but also to share the fun and to celebrate with us together! This also means that whatever worry, problem, or situation you are facing, there is a whole team supporting you!

You can keep on adding to your team throughout your life.

So, remembering some of the activities (43–58) in this book, take your time to think about your own team of life cheerleaders and supporters:

- Who are some of the people in your life who have been kind, caring, supportive, helpful, loving, honest, and compassionate to you? It can be different parts or qualities of people which you like or appreciate, it doesn't have to be a whole person. They can also be past, present, imaginary, or famous people, superheroes, pets, and creatures.

- What helpful or positive things might they say to you, or have said to or about you?

- How do they make you feel?

- If you asked them, what might they say that they like, appreciate, and enjoy about you?

You might like to show these people or parts of people in different creations. There is no right or wrong way to do this, but here are some ideas to give you some inspiration! You can choose what suits you best or do multiple different ones. For example, if you like trains, each person or part of a person can be represented by carriages on a train, or you could use hexagons on a football or rugby ball, or beads in a necklace or bracelet, or rays on a sunshine, or buttons on a control, or stars or planets representing different people, or petals or branches on a tree or flower.

Try drawing, making a collage, using stickers, and so on. You can also use some of the templates in this book.

Here are some examples of life cheerleaders displayed in:

- a blanket of love and support
- an image of life cheerleaders (e.g. a band, orchestra, sports team)
- keyrings of those people (e.g. muslin dolls, paper dolls, cutout people)
- a boat to ride the storm
- a safety net of cheerleaders (e.g. a shield, a parachute, an eco-map)
- a cape of cheerleaders.

What else could or would you like to do to suit your interests?

Activity 60

This is Me

Sometimes, we know we have had to camouflage, mask, hide, and not show some of our parts for a range of reasons. For example, we might have been hurt or shamed, or worried something bad might happen. We might have had to make ourselves less visible or smaller, or we might have needed to retreat from the world, like Taya did. (You might like to think about, draw, or share some of those reasons for wanting to be camouflaged.)

Sometimes, our pain, hurt, sadness, and fear can feel so big, as if it is who we are, or the biggest part of our story or life. But it is important to remember that while those parts of us are important, and we need to acknowledge them and give them space, they are just parts of us, just layers. There are so many other parts, textures, threads, and layers to us. There are so many other things that make us interesting, unique, and special. And so many more to discover still! No one can be reduced to be one thing, a label, or defined by what happened to us. We are like a tapestry, a kaleidoscope, a mosaic – there are so many different parts and layers to us!

With some people (Activities 37 and 41–57), it can be beautiful and helpful to show all (or more) of our different parts, threads, and layers – and people will be accepting and kind to them. This can take some time – glimmer by glimmer, peek by peek, heart print by heart print. The people around us can start to show us that all of our parts and layers can be seen, loved, and accepted!

- Can you talk about or fill in some of the different parts of you? This might be things you like doing and are interested in. It might be strengths, hobbies, or skills. It might be things you have done in the past. It might be things that are important to you, or things you might be looking forward to or are proud of. It might be what other people might see, say, or describe you as. It might be things that make you sparkle and things that bug you. (I have another workbook coming out which is all about this called This is Me!.)

- When might I show my different layers, parts, and colours? Who to? What are some of the advantages of this (while acknowledging it can be scary and a lot to do)?

You can take your time and add to this – it doesn't need to be all at once! I have popped a puzzle template on the next page, but it doesn't have to be a puzzle. It could be on anything – hexagons on a football, nesting dolls, masks, stones, badges, shells, patches on a patchwork (Activity 26), on a rainbow (Activity 55), on a tortoise shell (Activity 23).

Activity 61

Puzzle Template

Activity 62

Then, Now, and the Future

You might like to think about, write down, draw, or make a collage showing where you were then (at the start of this activity book or, for example, when you moved to live with new people, or when scary things were happening) and where you are now (what you are doing, what things look and feel like, what steps you have taken, what distance you have travelled, what lessons you have learned, what shifts have happened, however tiny). And finally, where you hope to be in the future (your dreams, wishes, goals, plans). You can keep on adding to and revisiting this throughout your journey. And we know sometimes it goes back and forth and ebbs and flows. If you prefer or in addition, you could also show your journey in another way, such as on a roadmap, a racetrack, a river, snakes and ladders, a maze.

Activity 63

Certificate of Completion

We have come to the end of this activity book. Thank you for being part of this journey with us. Thank you for everything you are. We hope that you continue to take us with you cheerleading you on and believing in you.

Copies of the activities can be downloaded from https://digitalhub.jkp.com/redeem using the voucher code DXRWQMD

Part 4
Guide for Adults

This adult guide is separated into three sections:

Introducing this Activity Book focuses on **important and foundational explanations and tips** and how to best use this book, including fears around it, practicalities, possible pitfalls, and ways of enriching the activities to be more meaningful and relational.

Understanding Trauma, Dissociation, and Retreating Behaviours provides psychoeducational explanations around why children might clam-up, bottle-up their feelings, disconnect, and withdraw. There is also a bit about dissociation, which again is crucial to understand if we are to optimize this workbook.

Therapeutic Re-parenting Skills, Tools, and Ways of Being focuses on adults' own wellbeing and regulation when supporting children who retreat, disconnect, and clam-up, and some of the core qualities of therapeutic re-parenting, and healing-infused, trauma-informed parenting.

Introducing this Activity Book

Who is this activity book for?

This Taya the Tortoise story and activity workbook is primarily written for those supporting and caring for children who have been hurt, violated, abused, or let down within their relationships, and who understandably can find it difficult to trust others, to let others close, and to express themselves. These adults include parents, relatives, caregivers, and helping professionals such as therapists, residential workers, social workers, key workers, nurses, and teachers.

Is the activity book specific to supporting children who have experienced trauma?

It is written for children who, in order to survive and to keep themselves shielded from further pain, trauma, and harm, have had to adapt and protect themselves by:

- retreating into their shell
- becoming smaller or shrinking themselves
- going inwards or shutting down
- blocking and numbing feelings
- shutting down, clamming-up, keeping things inside, or bottling-up their feelings
- locking feelings away or putting up a wall
- unplugging and disconnecting
- dissociating.

These children are often described as 'quiet', 'shy', 'withdrawn', 'avoidant', 'hard to reach emotionally', 'disconnected', and much more.

Within the story part of this workbook, Taya the Tortoise moves from living with her parents where she was hurt and felt scared, to living with her carers. Therefore, this book is particularly relevant to those children who are in foster care, a residential children's home, a kinship/connected person's home, or those who are adopted, or who have a special guardianship.

This book might also be particularly useful in supporting children who have experienced relational, attachment, developmental, and betrayal trauma, abuse, and loss.

However, some of the worksheets and activities can also be useful (with sensitive and adapted use) for those who are situationally mute or have experienced other forms of stress and hurt such as bullying, disability, health trauma, bereavement, and social exclusion.

Some aspects of this workbook might also be helpful for those children who often are quiet, clam-up, bottle-up their feelings, are less responsive, and say 'I don't know' or 'I'm not sure' for a range of other reasons (not always trauma-related). The activities and worksheets, if used in a non-trauma context, need to be selected to support and create opportunities for expression and identifying feelings, and some of the more focused information and story around abuse will not be appropriate.

Is it relevant for adults who have experienced trauma too?

This workbook is as much for the adults as for the children. It supports therapeutic re-parenting and healing-infused, trauma-informed parenting/caring, which is a core part of the relational healing and connecting with children who have been hurt.

It is psychoeducational and intends to give you (or the adults/parents/carers you are supporting) increased understanding and awareness, and lots of ways to strengthen the adult-child relationship, and a child's overall way of relating to others. As well as providing you, and the child, with strategies and ideas for further understanding and respecting their way of surviving and coping, it helps them to find ways to express their feelings and experiences in a safer way, and subsequently to reduce how much those fences are felt to be needed.

The majority of adults who are already caring for or supporting children who have been hurt will already be trying lots of relationship-based and trauma-informed strategies. This workbook is intended to complement those, and hopefully add some new ones.

This book is written primarily for children and the adults supporting them. However, many of the concepts and worksheets have been used in amazing and helpful ways by adults, in inner child and inner voice work, and for those who experienced similar trauma and abuse experiences as children.

We know that trauma often doesn't have a time stamp and can impact and interfere with our development. Our chronological age, stage, and needs often differ from our social, emotional, and developmental age, stage, and needs. Therefore, the concepts, explanations, and activities, when used with care and sensitivity, can be helpful across the lifespan.

Can this activity book be used instead of therapy?

This activity book is not a replacement for therapy or if more specialist support is required; however, it can be used with or as a support alongside such therapy. It is not offering a comprehensive explanation of dissociation, withdrawal, avoidance, emotional numbing, shyness, and so on, or the definitional or clinical differences between these, or trauma-specific interventions for them. However, it does aim to provide some psychoeducation, some reflections, and to increase awareness and understanding of, and sensitivity to, these ways of coping. There are also helpful suggestions for language, ideas, tools, and strategies to use.

It is hoped that this knowledge can support you to be more curious, informed, accepting, compassionate, and respectful of the child's needs and the way in which they might communicate and relate. It will help you to demystify some of their behaviours and ways of being, and to move away from pejorative or medicalizing discourses, and will provide grounding and key information to support others, such as family members, teachers, and other professionals. There are tangible ideas to support children in developing active anchoring and processing skills.

I am mindful that this activity book will be used differently by different people. How a qualified clinician will use it within therapy will differ from how a foster carer will interpret it in a therapeutic re-parenting context.

Some children and their supporting adults will still benefit from more formal therapeutic support or trauma-specific, dissociation-focused, or trauma-processing intervention by a qualified practitioner.

Why is shutting down, clamming-up, withdrawing, and retreating an important topic?

There are so many reasons why this book might be helpful and beneficial. There is so much focus and so many resources around anger, externalizing behaviours, and 'aggression', particularly in the area of trauma. However, those children who instead survive, cope, and show their feelings and experiences in a different way are often less well represented. Such children often fall off the radar, are unseen, and can be further neglected or less attended to within services and by others. They are often not given the same priority or support, and their needs can be less obvious or unmet. Moreover, foster carers and other supporting adults often will feel stuck, frustrated, and exhausted when they are on the receiving end of a child who is less responsive, very quiet, harder to connect with or reach, and who bottles-up feelings. I want this to be a book specifically for those children and their supporting adults. I want these children to be brought to the fore, held in mind, prioritized, and seen. So often, these children are silenced and voiceless – and I want this book to support adults to hear and connect with their voices.

Additionally, some of these children can be misunderstood. They can be viewed and unhelpfully labelled with words and phrases such as 'callous', 'aloof', 'disinterested', 'indifferent', 'cold', 'lacking in empathy', 'not feeling', 'uncaring', 'resilient', 'tough'. This means that their needs aren't seen or met and their way of surviving is not recognized or validated. So again, I want this book to highlight this, so that we have more understanding, empathy, and compassion for these children.

What about children who are happily quiet or introverted?

I am not saying that everyone needs to be a 'talker' and express their emotions. This workbook respects and acknowledges that different people express themselves in different ways, and some people might talk less or communicate in varied ways, and that there isn't a 'right way' of being or connecting. Many people are quiet or introverted. There are huge benefits for some around this, for example being deep thinkers, great listeners, calm under pressure, happy in their own space and company. But this workbook is not about those children who are content in that way of being and communicating. It is focused on children who are bottling-up their feelings or clamming-up because they feel scared, overwhelmed, and silenced, particularly those in a trauma or stress context where this is how they have had to survive and adapt to thorny circumstances. It is more about how it might be impacting their day-to-day life and interactions, like with Taya the Tortoise and the ripple effect of all she was missing by retreating, and the heaviness that it was causing for her.

Of course, it is a fine balance, and one which needs to be thought about for each child, but it is about supporting children to have the space and opportunities to share, name, identify, and express themselves – it is not about forcing or pushing or expecting them to be shouting how they feel from the rooftops. We want those children to feel seen and heard, and that they matter, and to avoid their feelings being unprocessed and spilling out in other ways.

How to read this book

Let's explore some questions about this book:

- **How important is the relationship, playfulness, and connectedness within these activities?**
- **Does an adult need to go through this workbook with the child?**
- **What difference can the adult make to the helpfulness of the activities?**

While some activities like the colouring-in pages or word search are quick and fun and might be used as one-offs in some contexts and by some people, the majority of the activities in this workbook are centred around relationships, connection, playfulness, fun, co-regulation, and relational regulation.

They are not intended to be tick-box or checklist activities which are rushed or crossed off, but rather it is hoped that they provide the child with a galaxy of experiences where they feel relationally held, listened to, accepted, connected, seen, supported, and soothed. They provide experiences where the child feels that the adult is empathetic, supportive, reflective, understanding, and curious, and the child is able to name, express, and be responsive to a range of feelings and sensations.

As Maya Angelou says, 'It is not what we say or what we do but how we make people feel.' It is how we make the child feel within and around these activities, and the enriching relational conversations that we have with them that provide the magic ingredients – we are the strategy, and we are our greatest tool and treasure. Where children have felt alone, unseen, silenced, and wounded, this shapes what they might expect from relationships, and how they might be in relationships or feel within or about them.

These activities and the conversations we have around them are intended to be a springboard for reparative and healing relationships. This fits with the concept that relational trauma requires relational repair and healing (Treisman 2016). How we make them feel and how we do the activities in a relational way is the invisible force and energy that children can sense, absorb, and be enveloped in. When doing these activities or having these conversations, we want the child to feel different from previous experiences and take their relationship, brain, and body to the gym. This means being mindful of our body language, our tone of voice, our energy and mood, the language and questions we use (being curious, interested, and not blaming or shaming), and the responses that we give.

They need to know that this time they are not alone and have someone beside them. This adult guide will show you lots of ways to enrich and expand on the activities in a more meaningful and relational way, so please take the time to read and reflect on this adult section *before undertaking any of the activities*.

This emphasis on relational strategies and taking the time to reflect, ground, anchor, and practise on ourselves is so important. The more we practise things, the more familiar, comfortable, and confident we will be, and this will cascade down to the child. Through practising, we can learn about possible pitfalls, questions, and apprehensions that might come up, and this will help us to support the child, to help them understand and make sense of the activities, to ask relevant, open, and exploratory questions, and to think about the topics that are presented. This also means that you can help guide them and select the activities which they and you feel fit best, and which the child is ready to do. Other activities might need to be skipped, adapted, or revisited at a later stage. If you are sensitive to the child's responses and needs, you can also adjust the pace and delivery accordingly. For example, if the child is finding things too much, noticing this, and offering them, for instance, a brain break, a regulating activity, or some additional adult support, will be very helpful.

You are also there to give them a positive experience of thinking about difficult topics, and offer them a place where you are both physically and emotionally present (there for them), fully listening, caring, and supporting them. This also sends the message that they are not alone, and that you are someone they can talk to about tricky areas. Ways to convey these messages are expanded on in the sections that follow.

Using the Activities section

STRUCTURE OF THE ACTIVITIES

The activity book starts with a section on anchoring, grounding, and coping tools and ideas. This is intentional, as we know that often we need to find ways to prioritize 'safety' and to balance and soothe the nervous systems first. As trauma specialist Bruce Perry (2014) says in his Neurosequential Model, we often need to regulate, before we can relate and then reason.

I also wanted there to be some tangible coping strategies and tools that might be supportive for the child who is navigating daily struggles and ups and downs, and that can be interwoven throughout the activities. They need to have things to do to anchor themselves amid thorny conversations, and to have some tools to support them while trying new things or when things feel a bit overwhelming.

Part 2 of the Activities section then goes on to explore a bit more about feelings, both in the story of Taya and the child's own experiences, and these conversations can be infused and interwoven throughout. The aim is to start to teach them key messages about feelings, support them to be able to name and express their feelings a bit more, to give them an opportunity to have their feelings validated and empathized with, and to enrich their emotional dictionary and vocabulary.

Part 3 then offers a wealth of activities for strengthening child-adult relationships, for increasing their capacity for joy and relational wealth, and for practising and seeing the benefit of connecting.

Of course, you might want to dip in and dip out and go back and forth, depending on the context, the relationship, the aims, and so on. This is why familiarizing yourself with the material first and tailoring it to the specific child and your way of interacting is important.

HOW MANY ACTIVITIES TO USE

Another common question posed relates to the activities – for example, are they to be used one at a time, or in a more structured way, as part of an ongoing journey?

For some, there might be a couple of one-off activities, but overall, this book is intended to follow a child on their journey (or for supporting adults to have more of an understanding, sensitivity, and awareness), so that different activities can be done in a more gradual and layered way that meets the child where they are at and provides a springboard for lots of possible meaningful interactions.

Therefore, there might be activities that they do at different stages, ones that they look back on and reflect on, ones that get added to (e.g. their pen portrait or for life story work or conversations), and others that are revisited, and/or done in retrospect. Some might be repeated, because on a different day at a different time with different moods, situations, and feelings, there might be new discoveries and reflections.

As this topic can be emotive, you should choose your time carefully, be led by the child, and go at their pace. They can be gently encouraged and supported in a compassionate and empathetic way, but they should not be forced, bombarded, overwhelmed, or pushed to do any of the activities. Better to do it gradually and respectfully, and drip feed – a bit like in the story, glimmer by glimmer, peek by peek, step by step. And sometimes, they might be more for the adults supporting, to provide a reminder and explanations as well as ideas of how to frame ways to talk to the child.

Some children may benefit from trying one or two of the included activities, while others will most likely benefit from doing the majority of them, in addition to other supplementary tasks and interventions. For this reason, some pages in this book have been designed to be photocopied, so that if you wish, you can select the suitable activities and give them to the child/parent/carer/professional separately or stapled together to make their own personalized book, box, or folder. This also means that the same activity can be used several times to support different situations or stages.

In addition, to accommodate the huge range of children and adults who will be reading this book, I have sometimes intentionally offered different exercises for each activity (e.g. when talking about feelings there is a rainbow, a football, a tortoise, a TV, and many other template choices). This variety, again, is to offer diversity and choice, and to acknowledge the uniqueness of each child.

Together, you and the child you are supporting can choose which exercises are the most appealing and relevant to them. It is overwhelming to do all of the activities, and generally not necessary, so try to take your time, be selective, and tailor them – this is why it is helpful for you to familiarize yourself with the options first. Remember that, throughout, children can skip activities, opt out, or say no – they need clear permissive messages about this and that it is their choice.

It is important to hold in mind that it is about quality, not quantity. It is better to do something meaningfully and in an enriched way, as discussed in the next few sections, than rushing through. The number of activities and time taken will vary depending on the child, the relationship, the task, the setting, the context, what else is being done, and so on. For example, a foster carer looking after a child, or a therapist working alongside the child over a period of time, might use multiple activities, whereas others working more short term in brief interventions might use one or two for psychoeducational purposes.

Using the Taya the Tortoise story

CAN I JUST READ THE STORY WITHOUT THE ACTIVITIES?

Some children will simply find it helpful to read or have read to them the story of Taya the Tortoise as a stand-alone story which can be used as a way to start conversations about feelings, vulnerability, fears, trust, and so forth with an adult. The child may not feel the need or be ready to complete many of the activities, which is absolutely fine. Other children might find it helpful to have a recording of the story or to read it in sections.

WHAT IF THE CHILD DOESN'T WANT THE STORY?

For those who find the story too long or intense, you can also pause and have enriching discussions about the different pages, pictures, words, and concepts throughout. There is no right or wrong way of reading the story, it is about being adaptive and flexible to the child's needs. It is, however, recommended that the adult read the story first themselves so that they are familiar with it and can plan how they might adapt or read it with the child.

Sometimes, the story is helpful in providing the adult with psychoeducation, understanding, ways of framing things, and entry points for discussion.

You can also do the activities without the story. While they have been written to complement and flow together, some children won't like or connect to the story, or will find it too emotive. For others, it might be less relevant – for example, those who are not in alternative care, or who haven't experienced trauma. For those situations, you can use the activities without the story.

The importance of language and offering choices

So why is the language and choice of words and terms used important?

The language, labels, and questions we use can be very powerful, and can shape, influence, expand, or shut down interactions. Think carefully about the language you use (there is more information on this in my book, *A Treasure Box for Creating Trauma-Informed Organizations* (Treisman 2021), and on my online module, and live training on language can be found at www.safehandsthinkingminds.co.uk).

We also need to be mindful of not assuming what word or term the person likes, feels comfortable with, or can be activated by. So many of the words we use can be full of jargon, sound clinical, and be dehumanizing and confusing. So, explaining these in child-friendly ways, not assuming they understand, giving choice, and being led by the child are really important points.

Some examples follow; however, there is no one-size-fits-all and we do not often know how something will land or what might activate someone. We do not have emotional x-rays and we cannot be superhuman or mind readers. Therefore, it is so important to think carefully and intentionally about the language one is using.

Having choice over a word is also important as it can support the child's voice to be heard and honoured, to find something that fits and has more meaning for them and allows them to have more agency – this is crucial given that many children might have felt silenced, 'done to', unheard, and powerless.

We might say things like:

'I just used the word... I am not sure what that means or looks like to you and we can spend some time thinking about that.'

'Can I just check in and ask if there is a word you would prefer me to use, like...or..., or if there is one I should avoid or not use?'

'I might say a word that you don't like or feel comfortable with or that doesn't feel right or fit, so I will check with you or you can let me know by...'

'I can't think of a different word at the moment. I am not sure if this fits or doesn't, what do you think, or do you have one you might use instead?'

'I have just chosen to use the word... Can I just check if that word makes sense or fits or if there is a better word?'

'Some people use the word..., others use the words..., or we could make one up. There is no right or wrong way – which would you prefer?'

'Is there any word we should put in the banish box or bin?' (This is important for stating our intention and where we are coming from, or to name what we are unsure of.)

For a child in foster care, the words they choose to call their different 'family' members, like their 'mum', 'family', 'stepbrother', 'half-brother', 'foster carer', or the people they live with, can be very important. So, we need to give them an opportunity to say which they prefer or feel more comfortable with, and not make assumptions.

This care and sensitivity should also be applied to feeling words; for instance, one child might choose to use the word 'sad' to describe a particular feeling, whereas another might use a term such as 'down', 'upset', 'depressed', 'low', 'wobbly', or 'blue' for a similar feeling. There may also be a whole other array of words, including a term they have made up or find useful, like 'pooey' or 'ouchy'.

Their understanding, history, and experience of the word/feeling, such as 'sad', can be so unique and individual, and we need to respect this and explore this. We need to provide opportunities for emotional nuance, enrichment, and texture, and for them to feel heard. This is even more important in a trauma context, as they might not have had these opportunities and may have experienced emotional poverty.

We could ask the question, 'If "sad" were a colour, what would it be?' To one person it might be 'blue', to another person blue is not sad – it is their favourite or their most peaceful colour. They may associate 'sad' with an animal or a creature. They may choose it to be slow and sluggish like a sloth. But someone with a pet sloth will have much warmer associations with that image. The same will go for songs – even a happy song that creates joy in many can have a sad association for someone, and a sad song can bring back happy memories or sensations.

This is similar for 'sadness' as a sensation in the body, as a texture, a sound, a type of weather, something in nature. For each individual, it might be experienced uniquely.

Attitudes to sadness might also differ. One child might have learned that it is ok to show when or if they are 'sad' and had this modelled and responded to by adults. Another child might have learned it was unsafe to show their feelings or they were positioned as 'a cry-baby' or 'weak', or that 'sadness' to them is seeing their parent clinically depressed, so they have very different associations and memories of the word.

All of these considerations feed into why it is so important to be mindful and to create space for a child to select a word, give feedback, and have options to say or check in if a word is uncomfortable, jarring, unclear, or activating for them. The child must be able to share their understanding of a word or term. This is the reason that, throughout the activities, I have offered a range of choices for words, or prompted people to select their own words and terms.

Another example might be the use of the word 'calm'. One child may like the word 'calm' and find it soothing or helpful; another might not know what it is or hasn't experienced or felt 'calm' as they have been marinated in chaos, fear, stress, unpredictability, and adrenaline buzz. We might need to explore this – or go back to noticing, identifying, and defining what 'calm' looks like or means to them. Another child may have been abused by people using that word in painful ways, such as telling them to 'shut up and be calm', or to 'stay still and calm down', or they may have been told the confusing message of 'calm down' by an adult who themselves is shouting and not modelling 'calm'. There are children for whom 'calm' is unnerving as it represents the 'calm before the storm' or where in the context of 'calm' they have felt alone, not been responded to, or felt things being on edge. In this scenario, the word 'calm' for that child might take them down a memory time hole, a trauma time warp, or a chain of pain, as they have negative associations with the word 'calm'. Such children might prefer to choose a different word, such as 'relax', 'serene', 'peaceful', 'mellow', 'grounded', 'soothed'. This is not about the word 'calm'. The child might really like and resonate with the word – it is just about being curious, giving choice, and not making assumptions.

Similarly, where possible we need to try to use tentative, open, and curious language, especially when talking about feelings or doing these activities. We want to leave room for feedback, expanding on conversations, not shutting the child down or making assumptions. We need to be mindful of not using statements that can be minimizing or invalidating, or those that use toxic positivity, such as 'I know exactly how you feel', 'We are all in the same boat', 'You shouldn't feel...', 'Don't be silly...', 'At least...' Where possible, we need to stay in a curious and wondering position, using statements such as 'I wonder if...', 'I am not sure, but...', 'I am not in your shoes, but I wonder if...', 'I could be wrong, but maybe/might...', 'I don't have an emotional x-ray, so I don't know...'

This care around language also refers to the language used through the Taya story and workbook, for example 'shutting down, clamming-up, retreating, unplugging, disconnecting, psychologically flying away, dissociating', and so on, or metaphors like a 'tidal wave of emotion' or 'spidey senses'. These are used to give some creative and varied ways of expressing experiences and feelings and to avoid the assumption that there is just one option or way of naming something.

Some children will find that these words and phrases really resonate with them, or we can support them to find a new word or saying that can help to frame and name what they might be experiencing. Others will not understand these and might need some further explanation and examples, or they won't resonate with them. For others, it is a springboard for them to discuss and choose something else that fits for them. Often the magic and usefulness are within the curiosity, wondering, and exploring.

Interpretation and making assumptions

Building on the above, we need to be mindful of interpreting or assuming meaning or symbolism. We don't have emotional x-rays and different words will mean different things for different people. There is no one-size-fits-all. Where possible, we need to ask, be curious, and check in. And if it is our opinion or a guess, we need to be careful with that information, stating it in reports or communication with others. For example, someone might choose the colour red, and we might think that red is the colour of anger (in most books, cartoons, posters, and so on, anger is represented as red). However, for a particular child, red might be the colour of love, passion, luck, or their favourite colour. Someone might choose a rainy day, and if we don't like the rain, we may think this is 'sad or negative', but for them it might be their favourite type of weather or their happiest kind of day.

Getting the environment right for engaging with the story and activities

The activities should ideally be tried when the child is in a thinking, comfortable, and learning space, not when they are tired, hungry, cold, hot, distracted, overwhelmed, or distressed. Some of the questions and conversations might be more helpfully interweaved in day-to-day conversations and in less formal ways, rather than sitting down and working through the workbook in a school-type way. The adults can take some of the golden nuggets and find ways to gently bring them into the appropriate moment. Often small bits at a time can work best, like Taya did in the story, glimmer by glimmer, heart print by heart print.

Ideally, the conversations and activities should be done at a time when the child and adult are not going to be rushed, and have the time and energy needed to be present. Think about the practicalities of timing and appropriateness, such as mealtimes, bedtime, bells ringing in school, the child missing their favourite activity to meet with you, about to go into a test, and so on. The child needs to know and feel verbally and non-verbally that they are free and able to share whatever feelings, questions, and thoughts they have, and that their feelings are valid, heard, seen, and important. They also need to be assured, particularly if they don't like art or creative activities, that there is no right or wrong way to do the activities – it doesn't need to be a piece of art, it can be a scribble or a stick drawing, and, if they prefer, they can adapt the activity to a different medium or way to express it, whether that is through music, writing, sport, or whatever. They are just ideas which are intended to be tailored and put into the person's style.

It can be really useful to **integrate movement and to think about the space, the sensory experience, and the environment,** so that the child is as comfortable and grounded as possible. This can make a real difference! (Activities 9–17 provide lots of ideas around this.)

For some people, **sitting still in a chair** and looking directly into someone's eyes can feel intimidating, unfamiliar, overwhelming, exposing, formal, immobilizing, and much more. This is especially the case for those where it possibly sends them down a memory time hole, trauma time warp, or reminds them of other times in their lives where they have felt stuck, trapped, put on the spot, lectured, assessed, out of control, lacking freedom, and so on. So, a powerful antedote to this is being able to move and be freer (although this can also feel scary if someone has coped by being in 'freeze' mode).

This is one of the reasons we often get much more from children (and adults) when we are in the car, on a walk, playing a game, doing an activity, and so on. Lots of people find it easier to talk when moving around, when they are distracted, when they have things to do with their hands, or other things to focus on and anchor to.

Of course, there is no one-size-fits-all, and different people have different sensory profiles and optimal learning spaces and preferences. However, for some people you might like to integrate some movement or regulating items before, during, and after the conversations and activities.

Please see Activities 9–17, and also my *Presley the Pug Relaxation Activity Book* (Treisman 2019), *A Therapeutic Treasure Deck of Grounding, Soothing, Coping and Regulating Cards* (Treisman 2017), and my training on emotional regulation for more on this.

Some examples of movement ideas are shared below (by no means an exhaustive or prescriptive list, and these will vary from child to child):

1. Talking while doing an activity like playing pool, playing a game, doing the washing up, going for a car ride.
2. Talking while the person is moving, pacing up and down, going back and forward on a swing or rocking chair, kicking a football gently back and forth, or throwing a ball or a balloon to and fro.
3. Having something which someone likes and finds regulating (remember, don't make assumptions as each person will have different preferences and choices) in one's hands, such as a stress or squishy ball, play-doh, slime, clay, pipe cleaners, a stretchy, a pop-it, being able to rip or crumple paper, using a maze or a left-right image to follow or trace, colouring in, having things to draw. You could use particular materials or textures which they like to touch, such as silk, bubble wrap, furry or fluffy fabric. As mentioned, there is no one-size-fits-all – one person will love and find velvet comforting and another will get the heebie-jeebies. Another will find it really helpful and focusing to do a crossword or sort a Rubik's cube, another will find these annoying and distracting. So, don't make assumptions; ensure variety, choice, and curiosity.
4. Playing background music – remember to provide different options for this.
5. Integrating some rhythm, drumming, or clapping activities at the beginning, end, or in brain breaks. The repetitive and rhythmic actions can be grounding for some.
6. Having a fragrance or smell which they choose to put on their wrist, on a stress ball, in an infuser, or as a hand cream. As shared before, please be mindful of assumptions. For example, when thinking of a 'calming' smell, people often might select or assume lavender. However, some children might not like lavender, they might be allergic to it, they might be activated or have negative associations with it, or they might already be down-regulated and need something to wake them up, or help them regulate, such as citrus, eucalyptus, or peppermint. It is about being a detective and an explorer and finding what works for that child. This will vary, whether you are trying to pump them up and get them excited or trying to bring peace and calm.
7. Having things to sort, categorize, or organize, such as different coloured or shaped items, a puzzle, paper clips, Lego, a Rubik's cube.
8. Making, creating, and using a sensory, grounding, soothing box, bottles, bag, or jar. This can be optimized with items which the child can see, hear, smell,

taste, which make them feel calm/connected/happy, or whichever feeling and state they are trying to be in and experience. See Activities 9–17.

9. Integrating breathing or grounding exercises which the child has chosen and which they like and you can adapt to suit them.
10. Thinking about temperature, lighting, seating position, timing, hunger level, and so on. These can make a big difference to someone's comfort.
11. Taking brain breaks and/or having a no, an opt out, or pass signal, gesture, button, or communication cards which enable the person to indicate what they need or for the person supporting them to model using them. Use the communication cards in Activity 18. Often it is very helpful for children and adults to have a visual prompt which they can use as a communicator or as a button to express their needs, wants, and thoughts. This can be even more important for children like Taya who often retreat from situations, have been made to feel silenced and unheard, or struggle to express their own needs. Also, when we feel overwhelmed or under pressure, it can be hard to find the words or to say the words. Therefore, having communication cards can be very helpful in these situations. I would suggest only picking a few so it doesn't feel too overwhelming. There are also some blank ones if you or the child want to tailor these and create their own. Sometimes, they might be encouraged to use one, such as 'I need a brain break', or 'My mind is wandering off'. At other times, the adult might model using one themselves or offer one as a suggestion, such as 'I need to move around'. There are also cards to indicate if we asked too difficult a question, for example 'Ouch, that is tender'. If needed and helpful, there are cards where the child can make things simpler, such as yes, no, always, sometimes. These can be used as responses to questions but also to categorize things such as feelings. These cards can also be found on my website at www.safehandsthinkingminds.co.uk.

What else would you add?

Choice and options

Choice can be very helpful and can build strengths. Choice is also super important for those children who, in the context of trauma, have felt 'done to', out of control, unseen, unheard, helpless, and powerless. In the context of abuse, they often couldn't say anything, or it wasn't respected when or if they said 'no'.

We have talked above about the importance of offering choices when it comes to language, but it's also really important to integrate choice, agency, and mastery in all contexts. Levels of choice will naturally vary depending on the situation and for some children too much choice can be overwhelming, but if you start from the position of taking a positive approach to offering choice, and considering the needs of your child, this has potential to lead to more empowered and meaningful engagements. Here are a few ways of trying this:

- *Choice of whether to do an activity in the first place* – and also to be able to pass, skip, say no, or opt out at any time, or for them to be able to tweak, adapt, and put their own flavour onto it. You might show this using a football, but they might want to take the concept and change it to dinosaurs, stars, PlayStation, flowers, and so on. Or you might use colouring pens and paper, but they might want to do a collage, a PowerPoint presentation, or a sculpture.

- *Choice of which activity to do.* Give lots of choices for the same thing or with a similar aim, to encourage individuality and personal expression. Some children might like to do a particular activity multiple times or at different stages and some might be drawn to one activity which particularly resonates or is in line with their interests, such as a rainbow, or a planet. However, as shared above, the activities are intended to provide inspiration, to be a springboard, and to create moments of fun, connection, and joy, so it is important that the child is not forced, coerced, or pushed and can say no, or can put their own spin on it.
- *Choice in materials and mediums.* A child might like to use pens, pencils, crayons, paints, as well as a range of colours, shapes, textures, and so on. But they also might like to work using different mediums and not from the ideas in this book, or they may expand on the ideas in the book in their own way, for example using a PowerPoint presentation, a video, a comic strip, a large piece of paper, a play. This also needs to consider different cultural aspects of their identity, so, for example, different skin tone crayons, papers, stickers, dolls, and different items to represent a range of different experiences.
- *Choice of people and interactions.* The child should be able to choose who they want to be there with them, and who they share or show their work with or to.
- *Choice of language.* The child should be able to choose what words or terms they want to use (see earlier sections on the power of language).
- *Choice of environment.* The child should be able to choose where they sit, their position, and, where possible, the location, items they have with them, and so on (see the earlier section on movement).

What else would you add? What other elements of choice could you integrate into your setting and context?

This care around movement, language, and choice should ideally be interwoven with the ideas below around scaffolding and warming the context.

How can we scaffold and warm the context?

Unless the person using the activities already has a great and connected relationship to use as a springboard (such as in a positive parent/carer/adult-child relationship), it can be useful for other adults building that relationship to scaffold, be gentler, and warm the context, rather than just diving in to ask personal, thorny, and emotive questions, and expect answers. Some people can find it hard understandably to share or put words to their feelings, thoughts, and experiences, for a range of reasons, especially when talking about things that might be emotive, painful, and thorny, or when talking with a stranger or an adult whom they may not trust or feel comfortable with. Examples of this might be meeting with a social worker to talk about foster care, or with a worker to start having life story conversations. And it might be even harder for a child who has been let down, betrayed, or hurt by adults or learned that talking about feelings can be dangerous, scary, lonely, and so on. So, it is important to adapt depending on the situation (there is no one-size-fits-all), but I often use the following steps which I hope might be useful in scaffolding and warming the context. You might need to do one for much longer or go back and forth – this is not a manual or recipe book. For some children, you can move very quickly in minutes through them, but with others the first part might take much longer, and progress can take more time:

- Start with chit chat, something easy, fun, comfortable, and benign for them to talk about which allows ease, flow, and less pressure. This warms the context and sets the scene. It is like creating a bridge. This might also include playing a game or doing a fun activity, and talking about things they like such as dancing, chocolate, football, Harry Potter. This brings in fun and playfulness, but it also can give us an important baseline and a sense of their way of speaking and their body language, tone of voice, facial expressions, and emotional vocabulary when they are not in distress, overwhelmed, or dysregulated. This is helpful, as it gives us an indication of what they might be like when more comfortable and not activated. We can then look out for clues or indications of when or if this might change or when they might be activated. If they are already uncomfortable when talking about easier and more fun things, it is a warning flag to us that we might need to go more gently and spend more time getting to know them, setting the scene and regulating first, before proceeding to deeper, more emotive conversations.

  Additionally, I often use a choice of responses using different props or resources to answer a benign question or to talk about an easier topic. People can feel comfortable in different ways, so often relying on words is too restrictive (see Activities 18–20). So, for example, if we ask about how they feel about football or a TV programme, they might be able to answer with words, but they may prefer to instead draw how they feel and think about it, make a collage, write it down, demonstrate it using feelings or trauma cards/images (Treisman 2018, 2022), use feelings figures/stones/cubes/wheels, or show it as a hashtag, a meme, an emoji, a song, a rhythm, a gif. Some might prefer to use a texture, a colour, a type of weather, or something in nature to express this. The reason I do this around something benign first is because I want them to practise doing it with something they find easier and comfortable before I ask them to answer using resources or props for a more emotive question. It is easier to do this with football, for example, than talking about their childhood or abuse. This also shows me a bit about what their preferred method or item is or if I need to add other options or explore a bit more.

  If they are struggling to do this, then it is clear that we need to go back to basics, slow down, do more relationship building, warm the context, and integrate more movement and regulation.

- If you are unknown to the child or still building a relationship with them, it is of course important to share who you are, why you are there, what is going to happen, and that they can ask you questions. Often children have so many different adults around them, many whom change and who have long and confusing titles and professional names. For children who often are overwhelmed, shut down, and understandably fearful and mistrusting of adults/professionals, this clarity is very important. Often, this needs to be repeated as once is not enough and brains in pain or strained brains can struggle to think or learn or hold information in the same way as other brains.

  In addition to wondering who we are and what we do, they might understandably have all sorts of fears, apprehensions, and worries about what will happen to their information, and the consequences of what they say. This can be exacerbated if they have previously been marinated in discourses such as 'Don't air your dirty laundry', 'What goes on behind closed doors stays behind closed doors', and for those who have learned that sharing can lead to scary or bad things happening, or they haven't been believed. You might, therefore, spend some time going through messages about sharing and confidentiality, and name and acknowledge some of their apprehensions, hopes, and fears. Name key and important messages around feelings, such as how all feelings are valid, and it is ok not to know (see Activity 19).

- Where appropriate, integrate regulating, anchoring, grounding, and movement into the interaction so that the child has things to make them feel more comfortable, including the environment. (See the earlier section on movement and the environment, and Activities 9–17 for a range of ideas and suggestions.)

- It can also be very helpful, where appropriate, to ask them the question from someone else's perspective such as a toy, a friend/teacher/carer/family member, their pet, or a TV, movie, or book character, or a part of them (e.g. their brave part, their funny part, their frustrated part, their critical part). For example, 'If I asked Peppa Pig/Harry Potter/your best friend/your teacher/your dog/your excited part/your frustrated part, what might they say/ask/think/describe/feel/notice?' Sometimes, I might talk about different perspectives and use things like a kaleidoscope or optimal illusions to demonstrate this or give them different scenarios to further explain.

  This can be effective because sometimes externalizing and creating a bit of space and separation can support someone to be able to think a little bit more, to feel less on the spot, and less personal. Similarly, for some children, talking through a puppet, a toy, a pet, a mask, or a character can be easier than feeling put on the spot to talk about themselves. Sometimes, I use different glasses or hats to represent different positions or perspectives, or they can stand in different places in a room. Again, if they are struggling at this (it won't always be appropriate or possible), it might be an indication that they need more relationship building, movement, regulation, scaffolding, or explanation before moving on to something more emotive.

- After laying some of the foundations, you might then ask them the question you are hoping to ask with a pre-warning that it might be thorny or a big question and they can say no, opt out, and take their time. Explain that there is no right or wrong response and they can also use the communication and what I need/want cards, or make their own (see Activity 18). When I ask the question, which might be about a tricky situation, circumstance, or feeling, I give them a choice of how to answer. For example, they might choose to type, write, draw, select music or rhythm, use a hashtag/meme/gif/YouTube clip/emoji, use a visual card or a postcard, use a different prop, show it through a pose or movement.

- And of course, whatever they say, I thank them for sharing. I validate, empathize, and acknowledge what they say. I listen and am alongside their feelings and try to be attuned and compassionate. And if appropriate, I might then explore a bit more about the feeling so that we have a greater understanding of it and then can think what we can do with it.

Responding to silence or shrugs

Often when we ask a question or try to explore someone's opinion or thought and we get a shrug, silence, or an 'I don't know' response, it can lead to a range of feelings within us. We may feel frustrated, irritated, stuck, rejected, tired, annoyed, and much more, especially if we are a parent, carer, or professional pouring our heart, soul, and energy into a child and feeling that we are getting very little back (see the third section of the adult guide on our own wellbeing and anchoring). For example, a professional may have deadlines and pressures to write a report for court, to see other children in an already overstretched 'workload', or to get the answers to feedback at a meeting.

For some adults, having someone say 'I don't know' can send us down a time hole, maybe to a place where we have felt ignored and rejected by other people in the past, and this can stir up those feelings and experiences or push those buttons of feeling not good enough. And because these can be our tender and thorny parts and our emotional relational hotspots, we can feel this more intensely and respond as such.

Here are some tips and tools which might help you to shift things, to be more curious and patient, and to move the conversation forward. These are just ideas and suggestions, they are by no means exhaustive and prescriptive, and they inevitably will need to be tailored to the particular child, context, relationship, and setting. Moreover, there will be others you might like to add or try. Sometimes, a bit like a Rubik's cube, you need to try lots of different combinations to find what fits.

First, it can be useful to be curious about the not knowing. For example, if 'I don't know' could talk, what might it say? What might it be trying to communicate?

What is its story, journey, meaning, and purpose? If they did know, what might happen or what might that mean? What might they have learned about knowing or not knowing? We need to try to understand the why, as without this, we can make assumptions and leap in. There might be different reasons which will lead to different interventions or avenues of support (it is highly recommended to use the worksheets in this section to support you with some of these). Holding these possibilities in mind will support us to tread gently, think creatively about how we might name, respect, and work around these, and to be curious and more patient. This is an important first step, as when you see a behaviour differently, you see a different behaviour, and when you see a person differently, you see a different person.

Second, it also can be helpful to reflect on ourselves and our own responses. Emotions can be contagious, and children can sense if we are irritated, annoyed, and frustrated. This can make them feel forced, rushed, like a failure, not good enough, and it can activate their own survival and protective modes like shutting down, retreating, and clamming-up or even going into fight and battle mode. As Maya Angelou said, 'People will forget what you say and do but will never forget how we make them feel.'

So, it is important to stay as grounded, reflective, and thoughtful as possible, and to try to be the limbic whisperer and calmer (limbic is the emotion and feelings centre of our brain) when they might be in a limbic hijack. We need to try to reflect instead of reacting, and to be curious instead of furious, and if we can't understandably do this in the moment, as it can be very tricky, then we can go back later and apologize, take ownership, reflect, and do relational repair. Reminding ourselves of some of the reasons why they might be saying 'I don't know' and that it is not a personal assault can help us to be more curious, patient, and open. This is also why for many people having micro strategies or rituals which you do before you speak to the child and during, such as 'grounding and calming' tools, as well as wider support avenues such as super vision, thinking spaces, and reflective practice, can be important and helpful.

Building on the above, the following worksheets give us some additional tips which might be helpful to hold in mind to support a child who is bottling-up their feelings or saying 'I don't know'. These further build on the above sections around the relationship, choice, movement, and scaffolding, which can all be very helpful and core aspects of supporting with this. So please do revisit those. And of course, much of this activity book is around supporting this.

BE CURIOUS INSTEAD OF FURIOUS - IF THE 'I DON'T KNOW' OR 'CLAMMING UP' COULD TALK WHAT MIGHT IT SAY & MEAN? WHAT MIGHT BE BEHIND IT OR MIGHT IT REPRESENT? WONDER / POSSIBILITIES / REASONS. INCLUDING POSSIBLE PAST PAINFUL & BLOCKING EXPERIENCES.

REGULATING, SOOTHING & GROUNDING ACTIVITIES & INTEGRATED MOVEMENT (INCLUDING THINKING ABOUT THE ENVIRONMENT, SPACE & SENSORY ASPECTS

OUR OWN RESPONSES, ACTIVATORS, AGENDAS & REACTIONS. WHAT MIGHT IT STIR UP/ RESURFACE/ PUSH FOR US? HOW ARE WE RESPONDING?

SOME POSSIBLE AVENUES FOR SUPPORTING PEOPLE WHEN THEY SAY 'I DON'T KNOW' AND/OR CLAM OR BOTTLE-UP.

WARM THE CONTEXT, NOT DIVING IN - EASING IN & TREADING GENTLY. BENIGN & CHIT CHAT - THINK ABOUT PACING.

NAMING & BEING TRANSPARENT ABOUT ROLE, EXPECTATIONS, WHAT IS GOING TO HAPPEN, NO RIGHT & WRONG. SOME PSYCHOEDUCATION ETC.

(INCLUDING SPACE FOR QUESTIONS & CLARITY)

GENTLY & TENTATIVELY NAME & EXPLORE WHERE APPROPRIATE SOME OF THE POSSIBLE BLOCKS, BARRIERS, APPREHENSIONS, WORRIES, ETC

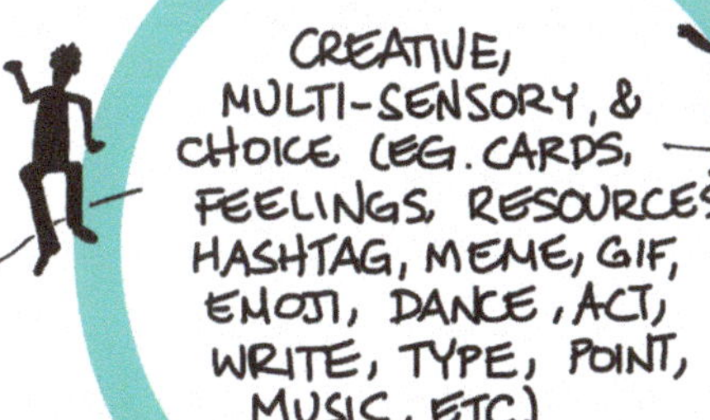

CREATIVE, MULTI-SENSORY, & CHOICE (EG. CARDS, FEELINGS, RESOURCES, HASHTAG, MEME, GIF, EMOJI, DANCE, ACT, WRITE, TYPE, POINT, MUSIC, ETC)

BREAKING IT DOWN...
- "YET"
- GUESS
- WONDER
- IMAGINE
- EXPLORE

ETC

SOME POSSIBLE AVENUES FOR SUPPORTING PEOPLE WHEN THEY SAY 'I DON'T KNOW' AND/OR CLAM OR BOTTLE-UP.

'IF YOU WERE ASKING ME THE QUESTIONS WHAT WOULD YOU ASK OR SAY' OR 'ARE THERE ANY QUESTIONS I SHOULD ASK THAT I HAVEN'T' OR 'ARE THEIR THINGS I COULD DO DIFFERENTLY OR THAT MIGHT HELP OR MAKE YOU FEEL MORE COMFORTABLE' ETC

'IF I DON'T KNOW COULD TALK WHAT MIGHT IT SAY'? OR 'WHAT DOES 'I DON'T KNOW' LOOK LIKE OR FEEL LIKE?' OR 'ARE THERE THINGS YOU DO KNOW ABOUT?' OR WHAT MIGHT IT BE LIKE IF YOU DID KNOW?'

MULTIPLE CHOICE/ CARDS/ WORKSHEETS/ THINGS TO POINT TO ETC.

REWORD OR EXPLAIN THE QUESTION IN DIFFERENT WAYS - CHECK UNDERSTANDING

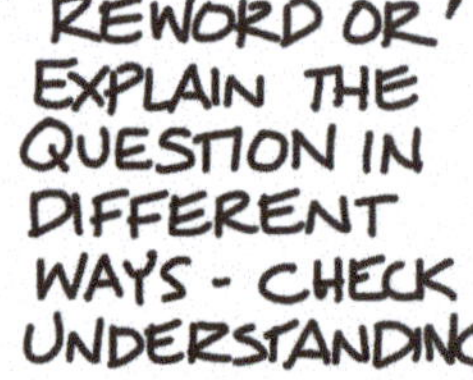

DISTANCING/ OTHER PERSPECTIVES/ EXTERNALIZING, EG CHARACTER / TOY/ FRIEND / FAMILY/ STORY / CLIP ETC

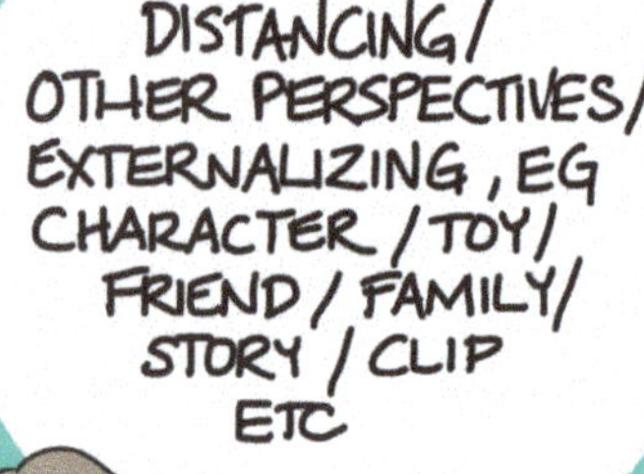

PLANT SEEDS/ GIVE TIME / COME BACK TO/ OPT OUT & PASS

What else ??

VALIDATE, NAME & ACKNOWLEDGE THAT IT IS OKAY NOT TO KNOW OR FEEL HOWEVER THEY FEEL; &/OR TO CHANGE THEIR MIND

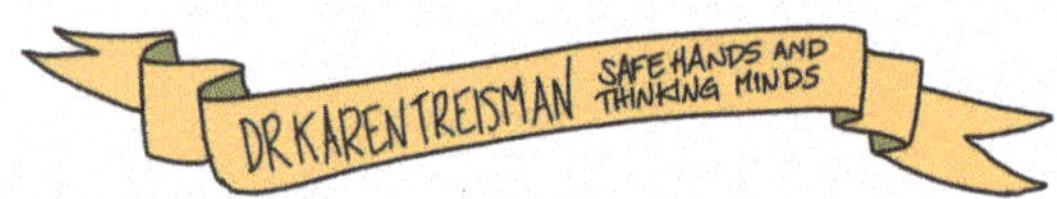

IMAGISTIC.CO.UK

How to make these activities more meaningful

What are some ways to make these activities more than a tick box or words on a paper? How can we explore, expand, enrich, express, and embed the activities and concepts?

As shared previously, this activity book can be more than colouring in and filling in a worksheet. Sometimes, that is sufficient, and all that the child can manage at that time, and that is absolutely fine and is an entry point. However, overall, this book encourages conversations that are more meaningful, layered, and relationally rich, which is why the magic can be in how we explore, enrich, expand, and embed them. Of course, this will vary depending on the child, the purpose, our role and timing, and the overall relationship. There is no set or prescriptive way to do this and there are many other approaches and models. However, I often use as a guide my 7 E's model: exhale, expand, explore, enrich, embody, embed, and express (Treisman 2017); as well as some of the below questions and avenues of discovery. The 7 E's can make the exercises and conversations far more than a piece of paper, or a tick-box exercise.

The first E, *Exhaling*, in essence means slowing down, soaking it in, pausing, thinking, and reflecting. It also means not rushing or focusing on quantity over quality but doing something in a more thoughtful, paced, and meaningful way. It also refers to how, before jumping in or going too fast, sometimes we need to go back to basics, take our time, and set the scene. Before we ask someone how they feel, they might need to be supported to identify and widen their emotional vocabulary or have messages around feelings that will be discussed. We might need to co-regulate a child in distress or build a rapport with them first, or explain our role, or warm the context before diving in. As the adult, we often need to exhale, pause, reflect, and get ourselves in a place to be present, attuned, connected, regulated, and grounded. This might include being our own or others' limbic whisperer and calmer. This can be an important but tricky step when we have deadlines, pressures, want to make quick changes, and can see what needs to be done. However, we want our conversations to be the opposite of the child's previous experience, which often was a shock, and felt rushed, pressured, forced, and unprocessed. So, sometimes we need to go slower to go faster in the end. Exhaling allows us to be more attuned, intentional, planned, and reflective.

The second, third, and fourth E's, *Expanding*, *Exploring*, and *Enriching*, mean taking the word or the concept and really exploring it, appreciating it, and finding ways to learn more about it by layering, expanding, and enriching it – this might include thinking about what it means, looks like, how it shows itself, and so on. It is about adding meaning and texture to it (some sample questions and examples of ways to enrich and expand follow shortly).

The fifth E, *Embodying*, refers not just to talking the talk and being a word wizard but walking the walk and modelling the model. It is about how we make the child feel and how we embody and convey what we are trying to show or teach. It is like the invisible force or energy a child picks up on, is enveloped and marinated in. If the space or relationship could talk, what might it say or how might it make the child feel? It is about how the child or person feels seen, connected with, attuned to, and how we respond with active listening, compassion, empathy, validation, acceptance, and more. It is the felt and sensed experience – the being with.

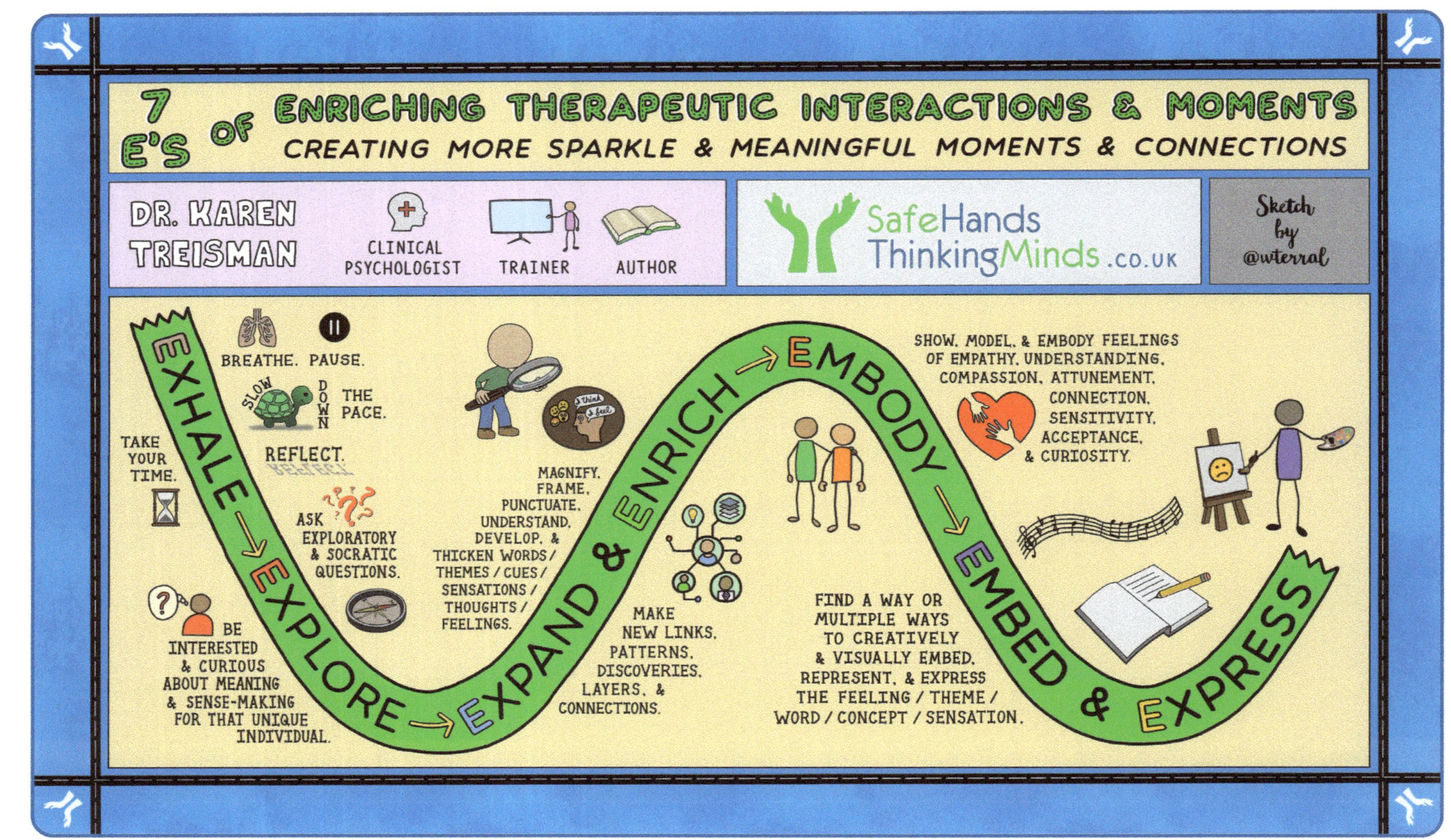
7 E'S OF ENRICHING THERAPEUTIC INTERACTIONS & MOMENTS
CREATING MORE SPARKLE & MEANINGFUL MOMENTS & CONNECTIONS
DR. KAREN TREISMAN
CLINICAL PSYCHOLOGIST
TRAINER
AUTHOR
SafeHands ThinkingMinds .co.uk
Sketch by @wterral
EXHALE → EXPLORE → EXPAND & ENRICH → EMBODY → EMBED & EXPRESS
TAKE YOUR TIME.
BREATHE. PAUSE.
SLOW DOWN THE PACE.
REFLECT.
BE INTERESTED & CURIOUS ABOUT MEANING & SENSE-MAKING FOR THAT UNIQUE INDIVIDUAL.
ASK EXPLORATORY & SOCRATIC QUESTIONS.
MAGNIFY. FRAME. PUNCTUATE. UNDERSTAND. DEVELOP. & THICKEN WORDS / THEMES / CUES / SENSATIONS / THOUGHTS / FEELINGS.
MAKE NEW LINKS. PATTERNS. DISCOVERIES. LAYERS. & CONNECTIONS.
SHOW. MODEL. & EMBODY FEELINGS OF EMPATHY. UNDERSTANDING. COMPASSION. ATTUNEMENT. CONNECTION. SENSITIVITY. ACCEPTANCE. & CURIOSITY.
FIND A WAY OR MULTIPLE WAYS TO CREATIVELY & VISUALLY EMBED. REPRESENT. & EXPRESS THE FEELING / THEME / WORD / CONCEPT / SENSATION.

The sixth and seventh E's, *Expressing* and *Embedding*, refer to the usefulness and power of not just relying on words and cognitive expressions. This is because feelings and experiences can be somatic, felt, embodied, and multi-sensory, and so often it can be helpful to find creative, verbal, sensory, and body-based ways to process, understand, communicate, and integrate the word, concept, or feeling. Once is often not enough, as we sometimes need to express, feel, or hear things multiple times in different ways over time to take our brain to the gym, have a different experience of something, and for it to start sinking in or going into our muscle memory. So, repetition and revisiting through embedding can be important. It can also be helpful to have tangible or visible reminders that the child can carry with them or have in their day-to-day life, especially as often they are not always with us physically. We can bring some of the conversations and take-home messages into their everyday experience, for example on a pencil case, in a transitional object, on a keyring.

Some examples of some aspects of the E's follow – these give a flavour of how you can use this model and apply it to a range of the activities in this workbook.

AN EXAMPLE USING OUR IMPORTANT PEOPLE/LIFE CHEERLEADERS

The child may be able to say who their team of supporters and life cheerleaders are (such as in Activity 59). These can be real, imagined, alive, dead, parts, bits, or qualities of people, creatures, pets, and so on. First, in line with exhaling, this might have taken a while for the child to think of and you might have had to explain, come back to, or scaffold before they were even able to list or name a person, people, or qualities. They might have started with one person or done it for someone else, like Taya including Tristan and the other characters. They might have first had to exhale and put other stepping stones in place before this exercise felt appropriate or suitable.

It is then not just about saying or quickly writing a list of these people or their qualities on a piece of paper and moving on to the next activity. It is about taking time to explore and enrich this activity, and about how each of these people/creatures/beings/qualities is discussed.

For example, 'What is it that the child likes/admires/appreciates/values about this "person" or part or quality of them?', 'How do they make the child feel?', 'What advice, tips, suggestions, or messages might or do they give?', 'What parts or qualities would they like to borrow/have/soak in/connect with/share/learn?', 'When might this part or quality visit or be helpful, or has shown itself?', 'When might they like to draw and anchor on to these people or parts?' There are endless possibilities and avenues for exploration and wonder.

We might also use this to explore the concept of how we might be physically alone, but we are emotionally and relationally together and connected. We might talk about feeling held, supported, believed in. We might talk about our team of life or our life orchestra. We might relate this to community or collective care or to relational strength and riches (such as in Activities 43–57).

Then, in line with the expressing and embedding from the 7 E's, they might talk about, practise, revisit, and infuse into their daily routine the life cheerleading activity (perhaps before bed, before going to school, before doing a presentation, when feeling lonely or overwhelmed) and then find ways to creatively represent this cheerleading team that suit and resonate with the child. This means they have something tangible, but not only do they have a visual reminder but hopefully the experience of making or creating the piece also holds positive memories and experiences within them. (See Activity 59 for loads of ideas, including things like photos of the important people on a collage, hexagons representing the different people on a football, drawings of the people, or symbols which represent them, or sayings they might say on a cape, or segments on a caterpillar representing different people or parts of people.)

And, of course, this activity can be revisited, added to, and changed so it is an evolving process and journey. It might also be that the adult also does one themselves for their own wellbeing and reflection, as well as modelling the model. We can also add to this as time goes on and we meet or are inspired by new people or parts of people.

A FEELING EXAMPLE USING THE 7 E'S AND A SENTENCE COMPLETION STRENGTHS EXAMPLE

If, for example, a child shares that they are worried, you could exhale and take your time to validate and acknowledge this. Then you might expand, explore, and enrich it, to try to find out a bit more and to get more of their meaning-making, and to increase their and your understanding and the emotional texture. You could, for example, gently ask about or explore their worry – not in a bombarding manner, but in a thoughtful, paced, well-timed way.

These are just a few suggestions of enriching questions:

- 'What would you call or name the feeling (e.g. the worries, the anxiety, the fear, the wobbles, the jelly)?'
- 'If the worry (or whatever name they chose) could talk, what might it say or tell us?'
- 'What might it look or sound like?'
- 'What people/places/situations/smells/sounds/sensations/tastes/experiences make the worries bigger, more intense, stronger, and visit more?'
- 'What people/places/situations/smells/sounds/sensations/tastes/experiences make the worries smaller, shrink, and visit less?'
- 'Where do the worries visit in your body, and what does this look or feel like?'
- 'If the worries were a colour/shape/texture/pose or movement/animal/something in nature/item or object/type of weather/sound or song/rhythm, what might they be?'
- 'When did the worries first visit, and what has been your relationship and history with the worries?'
- 'If the worries packed their bags and left tomorrow, what might you miss and what might look or feel different?'
- 'What is the opposite to the worries?'
- 'On a scale from 0 to 5, where would you put...? What does that mean and look like to you? Describe..., and what is keeping you from being a..., what might help you move to..., and where you would like to be. What do you

think your (another person) would say if we asked them? What might it be on a different day?

Then, for example, if the child said the worries were like flutterflies or butterflies, you could do a whole range of tangible, expressive, and creative activities around the flutterflies or butterflies, such as naming them, drawing them, changing their influence. Some examples are seen in the photos below.

This can also be applied to when a child makes a statement or shares a feeling or completes a sentence completion activity (Activity 47); for example, if a child says 'When I feel happy, I smile'. Of course, we need to be mindful of toxic positivity and the possible hazards around this, but the person supporting them might gently ask enriching, exploring, and expanding questions where appropriate, such as 'Wow, ok, so what things make you smile?', 'How does your body feel when you smile?', 'When was the last time you smiled?', 'Who makes you smile the most?', 'What puts a smile on your face?', 'What makes your smile visit the most?', 'If you could play one moment over and over again, what would you play?' The child can then be supported to embed this further by thinking about, and anchoring on to, the different thoughts, feelings, and body sensations which they had about that special moment. They might name and describe these.

Subsequent creative activities can then follow in order to enrich these responses, such as drawing, sculpting, writing about, making a collage, or depicting in a sand tray their responses. Every time they smile, they could also add to a sparkle moments jar, their treasure box, a what makes me smile poster, or their time capsule (Activities 48–56).

PUSHING MY BUTTONS EXAMPLES USING THE 7 E'S

Another example of enriching and expanding and making the activities more meaningful when appropriate and within the person's skill set and aims is using Activity 32, What Pushes My Different Buttons? There are no right or wrong answers, and multiple possibilities. However, this might start with lots of normalizing and validating conversations around how all of us will have things that bug us or push our buttons. We might give examples from our own lives, from the Taya story, and from elsewhere. We might think about why it is important to learn about these things. We might talk about warning signs. We then might gently start to talk about what smells, sounds, sights, tastes, people, places, situations, and so on might push the 'worry' button, or the 'overwhelm' or 'anger' button. We might do this for ourselves or others. We might describe what this looks like or feels like, in a non-blaming and non-shaming way. We might also think about the opposite: what pushes our happy/calm/joyful/confident/proud buttons? We might talk about ways we can notice this and what we can do when it happens. We might then make a creative version such as using a TV control or clothes buttons to express this. We might add to this and take our brain to the gym and notice when these buttons might be pushed. For those using this book in a more therapeutic way, this gives a sense of how to deepen and expand on the activities.

Understanding Trauma, Dissociation, and Retreating Behaviours

In this second part, I will introduce clamming-up, retreating, disconnecting, and dissociation, and provide some psychoeducation. It will primarily focus on when this happens in a trauma and abuse context.

These responses are multi-layered, dynamic, and nuanced

Please note, I will use different words interchangeably throughout, such as retreating, withdrawing, avoiding, clamming-up, bottling-up feelings, disconnecting. This is intentional, as different words will resonate with different people.

This activity book is primarily focused on children who have coped and survived by retreating, numbing, blocking, clamming-up, retreating, and disconnecting.

And some will also have survived and adapted to painful experiences by dissociating (please note that there are many different types of dissociation: somatic dissociation, dissociative amnesia, depersonalization, derealization, dissociative identities, etc.). It is important to acknowledge that dissociating, avoiding, withdrawing, and other related ways of adapting are not one dimensional, but are often ever evolving, dynamic, and multi-layered. They do not occur in a vacuum and are shaped and influenced by the wider culture, context, and relationships. Within this, it is important to recognize that this activity book is zooming in on withdrawing, disconnecting, and dissociating responses from a trauma lens. However, a holistic lens is crucial as there are often many other co-occurring and interacting needs, including additional learning needs, neurodiversity, other survival responses, health needs, the impact of drugs and alcohol, and the ripple effects of poverty, which are less attended to in this specific activity book.

Additionally, the intensity, severity, impact, and how children present are often on a continuum and will understandably look differently for different children at different times and in different contexts. We know that the level of impact can massively vary and is important in terms of the level and intensity of support needed. For example, in relation to dissociation, if someone is driving or listening to music and their mind wanders off, this is understandably different from someone who has large chunks of their life or day missing and those for whom it is impacting their ability to make connections or be present at school. For clarity, it is important to also mention that this activity book is not suggesting that every child who experiences trauma or withdraws or is quiet dissociates; however, it is a fairly common and understandable survival and protective response in the context of trauma and chronic stress.

The next few sections explore some of the reasons and ways that this disconnecting, withdrawing, and dissociating can occur, in order to increase our understanding and awareness of it.

What happens when children adapt and cope by retreating and disconnecting?

In the context of trauma, violence, terror, and abuse, children can feel overwhelmed, flooded, terrified, betrayed, violated, powerless, helpless, trapped, stuck, scared, alone, and many other feelings and sensations. They have had their dignity, humanity, safety, integrity, and boundaries violated. They often have experienced this within their relationships. They may have been left alone without a safe or trusted adult or the much-needed co-regulation of an adult, and trapped in toxic stress, fear, terror, and that emotional ouch and stingy feeling, without help or a way out.

Some children have experienced relational and emotional poverty. They were in relationship and emotional deserts, a place of loneliness, emptiness, and deprivation, with a galaxy of missed opportunities and unmet needs. Often, they might have felt or been silenced, felt unseen, ignored, abandoned, misunderstood, and more. Some children may have had a parent physically there, but not emotionally or relationally present, attuned, or available. They might have watched, seen, or felt their parent or carer avoid them, withdraw, cut-off, block, and retreat, and they have often been on the receiving end of this without understanding why.

Some children when marinated in these experiences will sadly but understandably conclude that it is their fault and that they are to blame or are too much for their parents. Often in the trauma world, we can focus on things that happen to a child, for example in the context of sexual abuse or physical abuse, but it is also important to think about what didn't happen that should have happened – the absence of things, the missed opportunities, the deprivation, whether that be tummy time and skin-to-skin contact, or their emotions being attended to and them feeling loved.

Within this, they might have not had an adult helping them to make sense of their experiences, feelings, and surroundings, and to understand, name, and attend to their inner and outer emotional worlds. Their experiences (often scary, overwhelming, and painful) have been left without explanation or a cognitive framework to anchor on to, or support as to how to respond or navigate them. This is one of the many reasons why supporting children's emotional experiences and their emotional vocabulary is so important and a key feature of the activities in this book.

Moreover, they often didn't have the developmentally complex skills or the time to process some of their experiences, as they had to survive, the trauma was ongoing, and they didn't have any adult support or a safe place to access. So, their experiences have often been and are still unresolved, unformulated, unprocessed, disconnected. This is why their experiences can come out as fragments, pieces missing, things not being integrated, flashbacks and nightmares, or dissociation, among many other possible ways they can manifest.

Relationships for them might not have offered a retreat, relief, or opportunities to be soothed; instead, they might have been the source of fear, pain, disappointment, hurt; and so the messages they might have been marinated in and therefore learned about relationships, adults, and other people are that relationships or other people are scary, unpredictable, painful, not reciprocal. So with this view that 'relationships are scary', 'relationships hurt me', 'relationships let me down', it makes sense that some children fear and are unsure, mistrusting, worried about adults and want to withdraw, disconnect, and protect themselves from relationships, expecting all relationships to be the same as previous ones. Children can become understandably relationship wary. As Valerie Sinason, a psychotherapist, said at a conference, 'We pattern the world from the shapes we have been used to.'

Many of these children have had numerous and ongoing misattuned, out of sync, and unresponsive experiences within their relationships. This is often misunderstood as people can think that trauma is a one-off incident, an isolated memory, or an identifiable single event that can be recalled and pinpointed. However, in the context of relational, developmental, attachment, and betrayal trauma, this is generally a cumulative dosing and layering of experiences that has happened over time. The child (their brain, gut, nervous system, immune system, regulating system, and reflexes) has often had to absorb, be shaped by, and marinated in repeated and ongoing experiences of trauma, fear, stress, loss, suffering, and wounding. They have often been on a steady and prolonged diet of this pain, rejection, and overwhelm. And if this is their early or in-utero experience, then it is all they have known and is key to how their identity has been formed and programmed.

Let's look at what some of these experiences might have included:

- Children might have had experiences where they were embarrassed, blamed, humiliated, dehumanized, shamed, and more. The range of this could be vast but some examples include responses to spilling the milk, crying, asking for help, wetting the bed, making a mistake, looking a particular way. Some may have been told or felt it was their fault, for example, for being hurt, or that they were 'bad', 'unlovable', 'worthless', or 'not good enough'.
- Some children may have had their feelings minimized, invalidated, or weaponized against them. For example, they may be told they are silly, stupid, need to 'grow up' or 'toughen up', they should not make a big deal and should get over things, move on, or that it was in their head, and they are exaggerating. Some might have been laughed at, mocked, or disbelieved.
- Other children might have learned that their feelings are too big, too much, and too messy for the adults around them, and that for a range of reasons their parents/carers couldn't contain, tolerate, or respond to them.
- Some children have learned that their feelings led to something catastrophic or scary happening or to further pain or hurt. Examples of this include being

removed and put in foster care, police being called, someone being hurt, domestic violence, a parent drinking, a parent leaving, severe punishment.
- Some children have found that their feelings and needs were not met, understood, or responded to (see the still face experiment by Ed Tronick available on YouTube).
- Some children have learned to hold in their feelings or to not show or express them, or to respond to them themselves rather than sharing them in a relationship and feeling them together. They may have learned to fear their inner experiences of feeling anything because feelings have been scary, unprocessed, too much.
- Some children have felt alone or lonely within their feelings and had to hold or feel them or experience them without adult validation, understanding, or support.
- Some children have also had very confusing and conflicting experiences. For example, they might have had to survive by attaching to their parent/caregiver. However, this can also be painful and wounding, so they might survive by suppressing, disconnecting, separating from, or blocking some parts of this. For example, 'I love you, but I hurt you. I'm scared of you, but I need you.' Holding both of these feelings can be too much, and so some children cope by disconnecting, splitting, or separating from one of these parts of themselves.

There are many other examples, this is just a small flavour. What else would you add?

Box 1: Thinking space questions

- In the context of the child's experiences and history, why might relationships be more difficult for them? (You might find my parenting patchwork and trauma cards useful here – there are also online modules available via www.safehandsthinkingminds.co.uk to help you optimize their use.)
- What have the child's relational and connecting experiences, styles, prototypes, and templates been?
- What fears, expectations, assumptions, and hopes might the child have around relationships as a result of these experiences?
- What might relationships and connections mean to the child?
- What might they have learned about relationships, trust, closeness, relinquishing control, and intimacy?

How do some children adapt and survive within these traumatic interpersonal and relationship experiences?

With the above in mind, children understandably cope, survive, and respond in many different ways – sometimes, multiple different ways at the same time. As said previously, this activity book focuses on those children who cope by retreating, disconnecting, and withdrawing. For other ways children respond and survive, see my other resources on relational and developmental trauma, including my Cleo the Crocodile activity book (Treisman 2019).

Children have had to evolve and adapt to often unimaginable, overwhelming, and intolerable experiences. They have been pushed out of their window of tolerance and staying present or connecting has been too painful, or impossible. In the context of trauma, if the child didn't have a relational anchor and someone to protect them, it makes sense that they might need to have developed other protective shields, blocks, locks, fences, or barriers to survive, and cope, and to protect themselves from further pain.

Children often cannot physically fight or overpower an adult hurting them, they cannot physically leave or escape the situation. Yet it can be very hard, scary, and overwhelming to be present in their bodies and minds, to be on the receiving end of repeatedly reaching out to an adult and being ignored, silenced, let down, disappointed, blocked, and rejected. Dan Siegel (2013, p.385) shares that 'the retreat into isolation can sometimes feel more controllable than being flooded with a sense of needing another person for comfort and connection'. So understandably, if the child can't fight and they can't leave, they often survive and adapt to these experiences by psychologically leaving, flying away in their minds. They might disconnect, detach, or seal off from experiences, feelings, sensations, and memories. Dissociation, retreating, and blocking off can be like an anaesthetic to the body and mind. It is too painful to connect to the abuse, so they need to suppress what is happening and find ways to disconnect from it.

Importantly, we need to respect, honour, and acknowledge that the retreating/blocking/clamming-up (whatever term used) kept the child as safe and protected as possible. They might have adapted and learned that it is better to:

- numb than to feel
- reject than to be rejected
- control than to be controlled
- protect than to connect
- psychologically fly away or to find ways to check out or exit than to be present
- retreat than to feel or be faced with the hurt
- not feel or know than to face unimaginable pain, hurt, and knowing.

Taya learned that the outside world and people can be scary, dangerous, painful, unpredictable, and so staying in her shell made her feel more protected – it makes sense to try to find a place, sometimes an inside place, that is less overwhelming and where there are fewer threats.

When this move to protect and survive happens, it is generally not conscious. For little children, it is often pre-verbal, encoded, and imprinted in their body. Their brain, nervous systems, body, mind, and gut have had to adapt and respond over and over again to the environments they are in, and so they have had a lot of practice. These survival and protective responses have been used, repeated, and activated multiple times, and have been embedded and learned. They have become habituated, like a reflex and an automatic activation. So sometimes, even when the child is not in a dangerous situation or around a threat, it can still feel to them like a threat (their spidey senses pick it up as a threat). As they are used to protecting themselves in a particular way, their response can still spring into action. The child is often not aware of when it happens, or that they may have zoned out, disconnected, or psychologically floated away.

There are many varied ways a child might adapt or survive. For example, some might become more like chameleons and be who the people around them need them to be; or they appear to have a fragile sense of self, as if there is an absence or they are going through the motions. The worksheets that follow share some of the ways that a child who withdraws retreats, clams-up, disconnects, and sometimes dissociates. (This is just a flavour and is by no means exhaustive or a checklist. They can vary for different people and in different contexts.) Some reflective questions and ideas for use will follow after the images.

When I/we feel overwhelmed, threatened, unsafe, scared

Here are some of the ways that I/we might withdraw, retreat, clam-up, disconnect, and/or dissociate to protect, shield, adapt, and survive. (These are just a flavour and by no means exhaustive or a checklist. They can really vary for different people and in different contexts; they are dynamic and nuanced and can be on a continuum).

We might also see these showing up through many different physical/health, relationship patterns, and behavioural, or sensory expressions; and/or through play/ drawings etc.

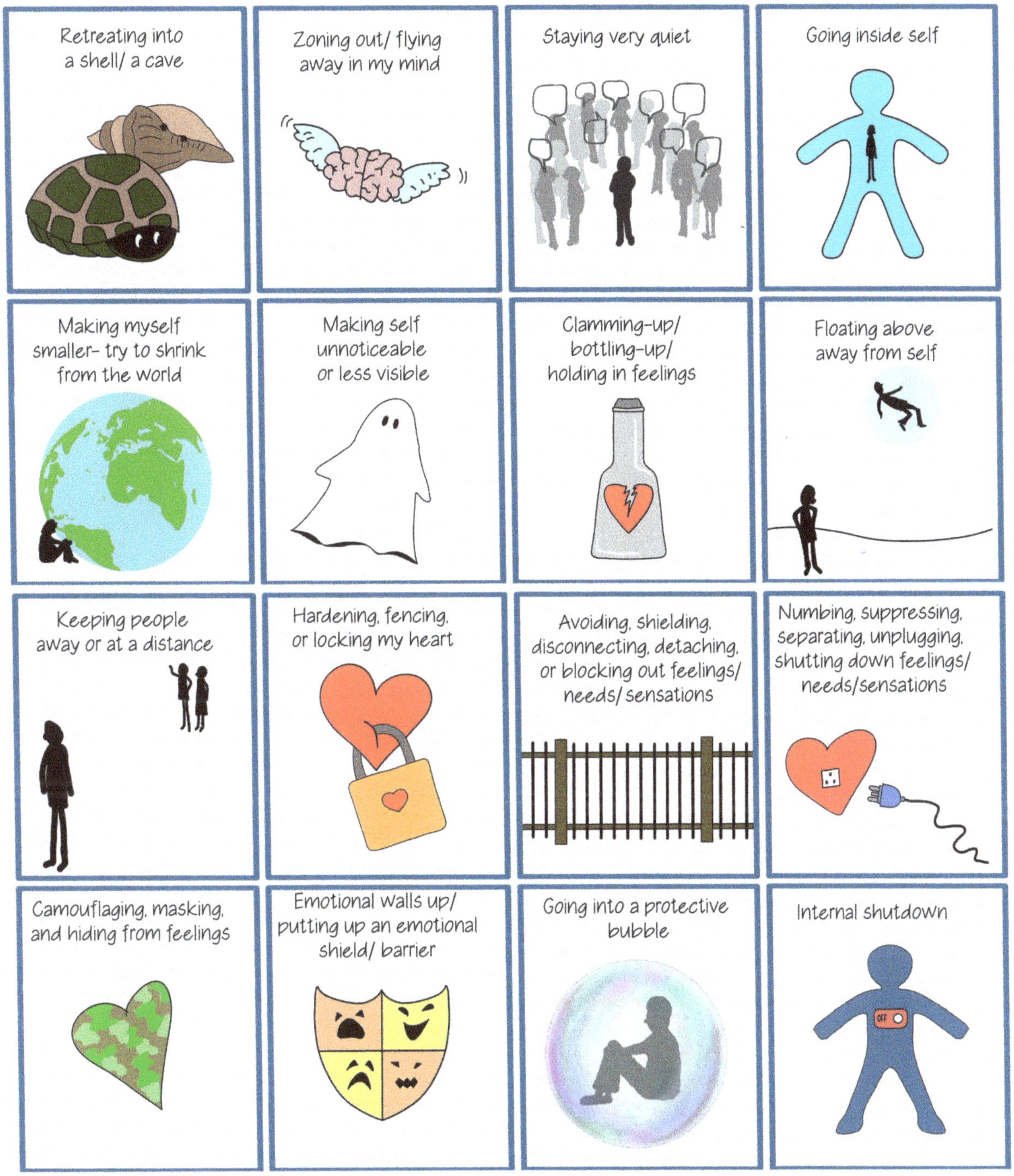

Retreating into a shell/ a cave	Zoning out/ flying away in my mind	Staying very quiet	Going inside self
Making myself smaller- try to shrink from the world	Making self unnoticeable or less visible	Clamming-up/ bottling-up/ holding in feelings	Floating above away from self
Keeping people away or at a distance	Hardening, fencing, or locking my heart	Avoiding, shielding, disconnecting, detaching, or blocking out feelings/ needs/ sensations	Numbing, suppressing, separating, unplugging, shutting down feelings/ needs/sensations
Camouflaging, masking, and hiding from feelings	Emotional walls up/ putting up an emotional shield/ barrier	Going into a protective bubble	Internal shutdown

What else would you add?

When I/we feel overwhelmed, threatened, unsafe, scared This can also look and feel like:

Daydreaming staring into space

Like life is happening to someone else or watching a film of it

Glazed, empty, and hollow look/ looking through people

Like I am on a different planet

Things around us or in the world might feel unreal, moving, blurry, or distorted

Stop reaching out asking for help/ showing needs

Can appear in another world/ go blank/vacant/ empty

Going through the motions/ autopilot/robotic

Less reachable/ more distanced/ less responsive

Things can feel distant, floaty, fuzzy, or foggy

Disconnected/ unplugged/dazed

Tired/low in energy

Hard to feel, notice, or connect with sensations or signals in body

Feel like I'm not in my body or like my body isn't mine

Feel like I am disappearing, or I am not really there

Hard to feel, notice, or connect with feelings/ emotionally numb

Struggling to track conversations

Struggling to remember/ concentrate/ pay attention/ forgetful

Memory lapses/ gaps in time/ missing memories

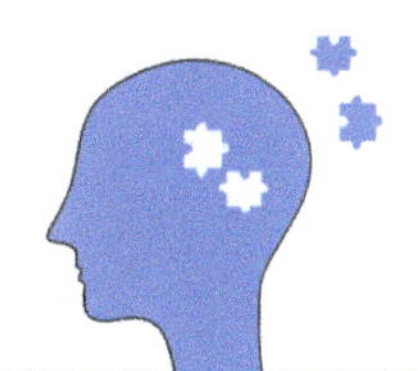

Incongruence and mismatch between the feelings, the word, and the affect

Baby talk/ regress

Might talk in the third person or say 'we' or 'they' when talking about self

Time goes too fast/ too slow

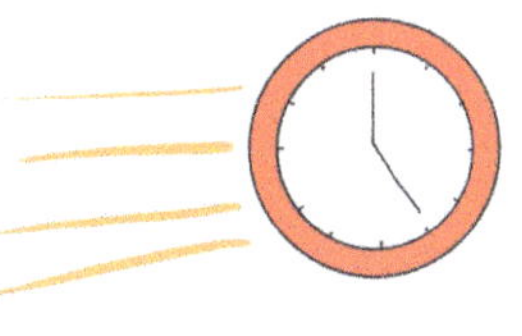

Distracted/ preoccupied

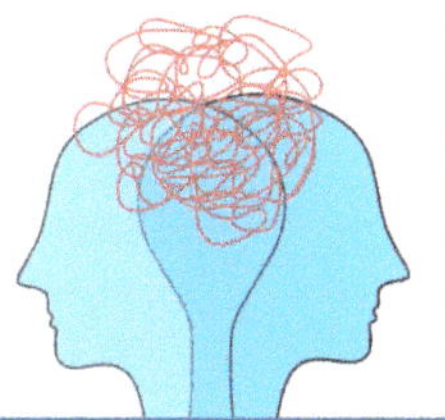

Can appear 'colder/ disinterested/ aloof'

Might appear frozen/still/ immobilised

Might find it hard, unsafe, painful, or overwhelming to find the words, and to express self/needs

Less joy/enjoyment/ spark from things

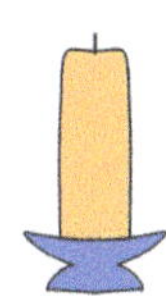

Might shrug, say I don't know, I don't care, I don't remember, I'm not sure...

Swallowing/holding in feelings and words

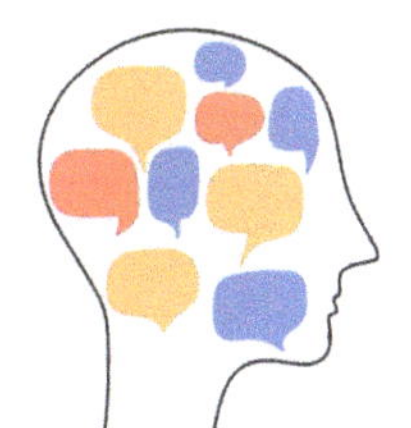

Sensory seeking or sensory withdrawal/avoidance

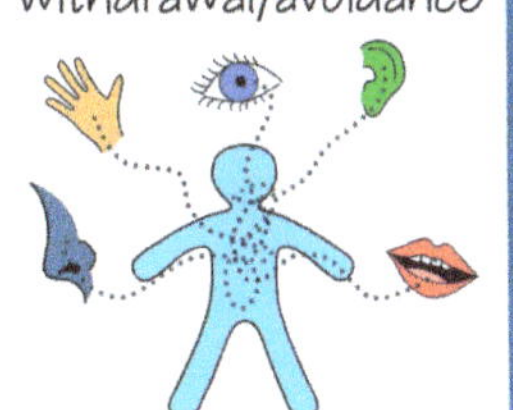

Different voices or different personas/ parts/aspects of self

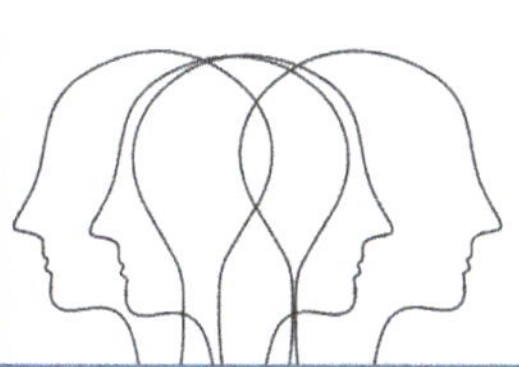

Reminder/memory voices

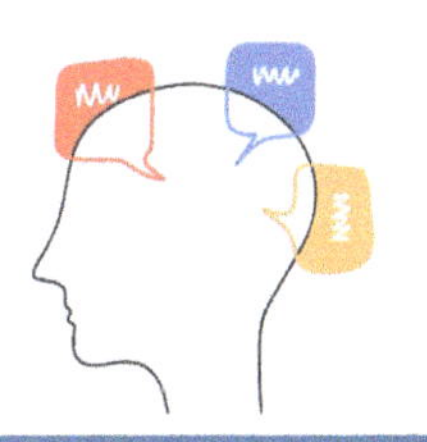

Physically there but not emotionally or relationally there or present

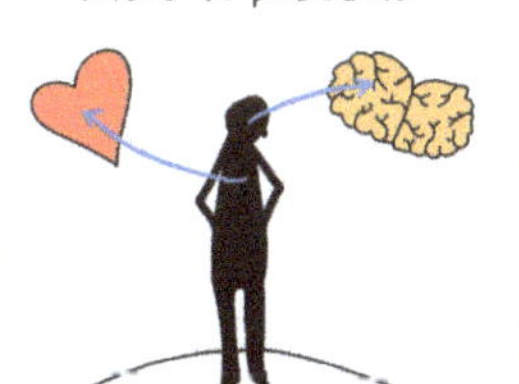

Rapid shift in mood

What else?

IMAGISTIC.CO.UK

Box 2: How to use these worksheets

These worksheets can be useful to increase understanding, awareness, and sensitivity to the person and what they might be experiencing. They can support people to feel validated and to have their experiences normalized and recognized. They can support us to have some more empathy and compassion. They can give us some ideas, words, metaphors, and analogies to discuss or interweave into psychoeducation. They can also be used as a springboard for exploring and enriching further, such as thinking about what this means or feels like to the person, specific examples of when they have experienced them, the impact of them, what makes them more intense or visit less.

They can provide an opportunity to think about which ones they may or may not experience, which visit the most, which they do not recognize, which they find distressing, which they find comforting, and so on (you can also incorporate the communication cards in Activity 18 with these questions, such as always, never, sometimes).

Additionally, if appropriate, they can be used as a whole worksheet directly with the child or certain squares can be cut out and creatively used; or they might be helpful to show and share with surrounding adults to increase their understanding. If it is too much for the child, try it with some distance, asking them which might apply to Taya the Tortoise or a character in a movie, or someone else they know.

The 'what else?' is an important part of all the worksheets, so that the child can add other ones, or say which they would change or think are missing. It also provides a springboard for the child to choose their own words, terms, symbols, images, and metaphors.

Here are some questions to use with the worksheets:

- Which of the images from the worksheets feel familiar and resonate?
- Which are surprising or interesting?
- Which would you add? Which are we missing?
- What might it be like to experience some of these?
- Do they make a bit more sense having read the other sections around why they might occur or why a child might survive in this way?
- What might be some of the impacts and consequences of these? How might they show themselves?
- How might it feel to be on the receiving end of these?
- How can these be misunderstood?
- These can also be due to other factors and reasons, not always trauma – what else would you consider?
- How might you gently and age-appropriately name, share, or teach these to children and others around them, such as teachers?
- How can you honour and respect these, rather than pathologizing or medicalizing understandable responses to unimaginable situations?

A little note on talking about the word 'parts'

We know that for some people this term 'parts' can evoke a strong reaction or have certain connotations or associations with certain diagnoses, especially as some of these concepts have been sensationalized or poorly represented in the media and in some clinical settings, and therefore can often be misunderstood. These parts (could be referred to as layers, facets, aspects, different bits, littleies/littlelys, or many other terms) can look and feel very different in each person. The aim here is not to pathologize or diagnose at all, that is the opposite intention of this activity book. In this context, I am talking in a very normalizing and validating way about how each of us can have different parts of our identity, needs, experiences, and personality. Whether it is a protective part, a brave part, a scared part, or a five-year-old part, it makes sense that some people might become or have different versions of themselves when it is too overwhelming to be themselves, or when they haven't had the opportunity to integrate and process their different experiences. Some parts might have been unprocessed or stuck. So often, children haven't learned that all of them – all of their parts – can be loved, welcomed, and accepted. They have often been shamed, blamed, humiliated, and felt unlovable for certain parts of themselves, or had to cope in terrifying situations by splintering-off certain parts, or other parts have had to step up to support them or confront or navigate that particular stage of their life.

It makes sense that if a child's experiences (often scary, overwhelming, painful ones) have been left without explanation or support, or they haven't had the developmentally complex skills or time to process some of their experiences because the trauma is ongoing, this has left them feeling fragmented, disjointed, and disconnected.

This is why supporting children and all of their parts and experiences to feel truly accepted is so important. And why they need, where appropriate, to start weaving together and integrating their experiences and being able to show and express their different parts and for these to be welcomed, respected, honoured, and understood. We want to support them in moving to a felt sense of wholeness.

Some of the advantages and disadvantages of withdrawing, disconnecting, retreating, and dissociating

So, building on the above, the retreating, shutting away, locking away, dissociating were needed and at times helpful, protective, and shielding. Some powerful questions around this and around being curious and understanding the response and behaviour more are shared in Box 7 in the third section of this adult guide.

Positively, coping and responding by withdrawing and retreating can sometimes support the child to detach from the pain, to escape and create some distance, protection, or sealing-off from their difficult experiences. However, the other side of this is that while it often stops or reduces the painful, thorny, and stingy bits coming in and from being felt, it also means that the reverse can happen – it can reduce or stop the magic, joy, beauty, connection, laughter, and fun from coming in and being felt (see Activities 38, 39, and 43). For example, as in Taya the Tortoise, a child might shut down, dim, or block themselves from painful and thorny feelings, but this can also mean that they shut out, dim, or block the warm, colourful, and feel-good feelings and the richer and more textured aspects of life and relationships.

Similarly, while they might block themselves from relationships that can hurt, harm, and let them down, they can apply that to all relationships and people and so it can block connections that show them love, care, trust, safety, and opportunities for relational healing and repair (Activities 43–59). In addition, if a child is harder to connect with or feels less reachable or present, it can make others like teachers, friends, parents, carers, and professionals distance themselves more, and so the child experiences even fewer reciprocal interactions.

Sometimes holding feelings and needs in or pushing them down or away can be tiring and leave less energy and space for other things, such as learning, engaging in activities, taking in the fun. When we bottle-up our feelings, it doesn't necessarily mean that they go away or disappear – often they can get bigger, linger, or remain unprocessed, and they can spill or be transferred in other ways (e.g. through our emotions, body, health, sensations, experiences like nightmares or flashbacks) (see Activity 38). Equally, some children have to block, numb, or disconnect from their bodies and from their bodily sensations (see later sections on the body and trauma).

Additionally, if children are less able to be in the moment, have lapses in memory, are in their metaphorical tortoise shells, or just going through the motions, they might also have fewer opportunities for creating more integrated and connected memories and narratives. They might be less emotionally engaged and connected, as well as possibly having fewer opportunities to process, and life can pass them by. They might miss the joy, the fun, the good times.

Hiding in a cave, waiting for the storm to pass, or retreating into a shell makes sense when there is threat, a storm, and danger, but if you stay in that cave or shell for prolonged periods, there will be things that you miss out on and you won't learn that parts of being outside can be ok, helpful, and advantageous.

So, this story and activity book is about acknowledging and respecting why this way of coping and supporting all of the parts and layers was needed, and being kind to their parts and responses, but also supporting children to find ways to open their hearts (when safe to do so) and to reconnect to relationships that can heal, and to opportunities for joy and connection. It's also to support them to integrate and connect the different parts of themselves, their lives, and their experiences.

Why does the child continue surviving in this way even when they are no longer in danger?

If a child has had to cope and survive in this way, often they continue to navigate the world like this. Even if the threat or danger is removed or changed, and they might be in a new home or in a different situation, they might perpetually be in survive mode. Just because they might *be safe* does not mean they *feel safe* – there is a difference between being and feeling safe.

This is for a range of reasons, including that often this way of coping and surviving has become a reflex, an automatic activation. It is generally not conscious. They have had to cope and survive in this way over time (their brain, body, mind, gut has been taken to the gym over and over again). It has become patterned, activated, and repeated multiple times, and so it has become learned and embedded, and often habituated, so even when not in a situation of danger they can still understandably respond as if they are.

Their spidey senses and danger antennae might still be on high alert and attuned to picking up signals and cues, even sometimes when they are not needed (e.g. an alarm can go off for burnt toast, but it does not require the same attention as a fire). The fear of letting those antennae down or putting their spidey senses away is often big – they have had repeated and learned experiences that they are needed and helpful and it is safer to retain them.

Understandably, they might still hear and feel the person or echoes of the person or people who hurt them, perhaps through voices, memories, flashbacks, nightmares, or inner dialogues, or when they look in the mirror they might see the person or parts of these people. For some, these voices and inner dialogue can be encouraging, supportive, and protective; for others, they can be threatening, scary, and hurtful, and reinforce self-loathing. And, of course, it can be a combination of both, and can also change.

The child might have things that activate, tap into, or stir-up past emotions, sensations, and memories. This means that these emotions, sensations, and memories can spill out, as if they are the ripples, debris, legacy, and echoes of the trauma or parts of it. It's a bit like an emotional hangover, emotional lingering, and ghosts of the past. Often in the trauma world, we talk about how the 'here and now' can get entangled with the 'there and then', which can further keep the trauma alive and present, because unprocessed and unresolved trauma often doesn't have a time stamp. For example, there are certain situations, people, sensations, smells, sounds, textures, and feelings which people can experience in the present but which are reminiscent of past experiences that have been memory banked or encoded. And at these times, when activated, it can send them down a memory time hole, a trauma time warp, or a chain of pain to the 'there and then'. These experiences can be like an emotional landmine, or a tsunami of emotions, memories, or sensations, or a jellyfish zap moment. (I've intentionally given lots of different metaphors as often these can be helpfully interwoven into psychoeducation.)

Sometimes it is easy to make the link between these experiences and sensations and the trauma, like smelling the perfume of the person who abused them, or someone being called the same name as the person who hurt them, a teacher raising their voice, a certain song, or the sound of glass breaking or of footsteps entering, feeling powerless or trapped, being put on the spot or criticized. At other times, they can be cryptic, subtle, harder to decode, or difficult to articulate or remember, but can still lead to a response, a sensation, or a feeling. It can be scary and confusing, even more so when the child doesn't understand or can't make sense of what is happening, or why. Often the child won't have a clear memory or conscious understanding of what happened or be able to explain it, because they were too young, it was pre-verbal or in the in-utero period. Because it is encoded and imprinted on a sensory level, it is wordless, and they have put it in their internal memory black box, and often they didn't have an adult explanation or support at the time and afterwards to name and understand it.

So, as adults we often see the reaction or the response but not the layers, the trauma ripples, or the survival response and reflex underneath. For example, a child is told by a group of kids at school that they can't play football with them, and the child has a big emotional response to the word 'no', and the feeling of rejection lands on them like emotional dynamite. For the child, it signifies so much more than being told no to playing football; it taps into a wound and a history of painful feelings and experiences. The child has had repeated and layered experiences of feeling rejected, excluded, and not good enough, so being told no to football can, without the child necessarily having a conscious awareness of it, or being able to name it, resurface a chain of pain and send him down a trauma time hole to the many layers and entanglements of being rejected and not feeling good enough. It feels more intense and heated, and what others see is the response to that.

We can see this happening with lots of other emotional and relational hotspots, such as feeling ignored, embarrassed, blamed, shamed, silenced, criticized, forgotten, controlled, a sense of unfairness and injustice. When these feelings are activated in the 'here and now', the present, but represent something painful (often not consciously remembered) from the 'there and then', they can be felt deeply and the response to them is often interwoven with all those other experiences. These can also be autobiographical or sensory, such as the time of year, something on TV, a subject in school, a theme in a book, a smell, a sound, a taste, a temperature, a movement.

Another reason why our survival responses can continue to respond even when not in the trauma situation is because our brains are amazing, and they are shaped and patterned by our experiences. They try to generalize and predict what will happen based on our previous experiences. They remember what previously happened, and then layer onto the present what has happened in the past. So, if, for example, a child has learned that they are unlovable, or that relationships hurt them and are not to be trusted, understandably they often will apply this lens to new experiences and relationships. They shape our expectations, predictions, and assumptions. A child might view their foster carer based on their learned experiences that relationships are scary, hurtful, conditional, not to be trusted. When someone looks at them blankly, this might be felt in a way that is activating and makes them feel ignored, silenced, othered, and emotionally alone, as it is reminiscent of previous blank faces and how those faces made them feel. So, while the situation might be different, the echoes and ripples can continue through perception of our self, our world, and our relationships.

For many children, the threat, pain, and hurt are ongoing and not in the past. They live on through their memories and sensations, or through further experiences which can exacerbate and reinforce these feelings, such as having multiple moves within foster care, being excluded from school, being bullied (school-based abuse), experiencing discrimination and persecution, feeling unloved, powerless, misunderstood, rejected, not good enough.

And sometimes we also do things to protect us, which is important, but can also stop or reduce opportunities for new learning. So for example with Taya the Tortoise, she protects herself by retreating and staying a lot of the time in her shell, which is understandable; however, this means that she not only is missing out on some aspects but is not then having the opportunity to test out and learn that the outside can be ok. So sometimes, the fear of this builds and can become even bigger.

There are many more reasons why children continue to survive in a certain way – which others would you add?

A spotlight on trauma and the body and our sensory world – why we need to have multi-sensory interventions

This section has been adapted and shortened from my book on trauma-informed healthcare (Treisman 2024) – please see that book for a more detailed explanation and focus on these areas.

I want to touch on this area briefly to shed some light on the impact trauma can have on the body and why throughout this activity book we discuss the importance of multi-sensory approaches, of the environment, of integrating movement, anchoring, and regulating approaches, and aspects such as temperature, hunger, sleep, and hydration. This book has also stressed the importance of touch, facial expressions, tone of voice, proximity, positive experiences, and using more than language, cognitive frameworks, and words, and the potential healing nature of having reparative and feel-good experiences with one's body, with movement, and with touch.

In the context of abuse and certain types of traumas, the trauma can permeate and pierce through layers and really get under one's skin. This has been aptly described as the 'body keeps the score' (Van der Kolk 2014), 'the body remembers' (Rothschild 2000), and 'our bodies are apt to be our autobiographies' (Frank Gillette Burgess). Our body is our container, the thing we are born and die with, which travels with us through all of our experiences and our life. People might have experienced too much or too little touching, for example skin-to-skin, physical affection, changing nappies, being soothed, teeth brushing, toileting, how hurts were attended to, and so on. Children's bodies in the context of trauma have often been ignored, violated, neglected, hurt, injured, trapped, dehumanized, and so on. Children have also often felt stuck within their bodies, immobilized, powerless.

Trauma is a multi-sensory experience that can have a multi-sensory impact, therefore our interventions and approaches need to be multi-sensory. For example, think of the multi-sensory whole body and nervous system experience of domestic violence (with its many nuances and variations), and what the child and their immune system, regulatory system, sensory integration and processing systems, and arousal systems have to absorb. There is seeing (visual) with their eyes certain facial expressions, items, blood, bruises, the violence itself, flashing blue lights, darkness; there is hearing with their ears (auditory) the sound of their own breathing, the clock ticking, certain music, doors locking or banging, footsteps, keys jangling; there is smelling with their noses (olfactory), bleach, fabric conditioner, alcohol, cooking aromas, perfume, flowers. And then there are the body's responses such as feeling hot/cold, wet, tense muscles, hungry, dry mouth, stomach in knots, headache, numb or nothingness; and the emotions such as feeling overwhelmed, trapped, shocked, scared. These are multi-sensory experiences encoded at many different layers and therefore our approaches and interventions need to consider and actively support at a multi-sensory level. (For a powerful interactive experiential exercise of this please see my book on trauma-informed healthcare (Treisman 2020).)

Moreover, the child might have experienced or received very conflicting messages during the trauma, and at times had to switch off, tune out, or disconnect from their bodies. For some, this can mean that they struggle to feel anything in their bodies or recognize their body's needs (e.g. like in somatic dissociation). These children may say 'I don't know' or 'I am not sure' when we ask them to notice or feel things in their bodies such as emotions. Other children can struggle to identify certain body sensations or be quite disconnected from their bodies, for example around needing the toilet, identifying or knowing their temperature, or recognizing when they are hungry. Other children only feel things when it is an intense sensation, such as through self-harming or big intense sensations. And others can be the opposite and might struggle to notice or respond to threat or risk in certain ways, or might miss signals of danger, as they are numbed and shut off to them.

I often say, 'If your body could talk what would it say? If your body could show you a map of what it has been through, what would we see and learn?'

Often when trauma or highly charged emotional experiences occur, they are encoded and embedded in the limbic system, so come out as sensory, somatic, and emotional memories. And this is layered by trauma experienced by children often when they are pre-verbal or in-utero. Therefore, trauma can show itself not with a clear verbal narrative or cognitive framework but rather in unintegrated and unprocessed vivid images, fragments, memories, and sensations, and reliving experiences in nightmares, flashbacks, and activating experiences. This can make remembering and putting internal experiences into words more difficult. It is often difficult for children to find the words, to be able to name or articulate their experience, or to access their expressive language or emotional dictionary, to explain what has happened, especially at heightened, emotional, and activated times, for example when they feel attacked, punished, shamed, interrogated, not believed.

This also means that trauma is often embedded or stored in our bodies, and can be re-experienced or re-lived through our bodily sensations (e.g. headaches, stomach aches, rashes, heart palpitations, skin flare-ups, tense muscles, nightmares, poor sleep, strange eating habits and relationships to food, wetting the bed) and of course our immune system. In essence, the body may remember what the mind wants to forget. Some children become more sensitized to sensory reminders and can be easily activated, or the body has numerous false alarms; others might cope by shutting-off or disconnecting from their bodies (somatic dissociation). We know this can impact people's relationship to their body, sensory world, feelings, sensations, and more, and can also show itself in people being more sensory seeking, or sensory avoidant, and many shades in between.

This really emphasizes the importance of integrating movement and regulation (Part 1 of the activity book), and why giving people different experiences within and around their bodies and their environments is so important, and why we need to use more than words!

Having explored so many of the contexts and experiences children might have lived through and adapted to, we can now look at the reasons why some children (and adults) might retreat, clam-up, and shut down.

Why might children clam-up, retreat, withdraw, and say 'I don't know'?

The following worksheets are intended to help us understand a little bit more so that we can be more curious, empathetic, patient, and compassionate towards the child, and less judgemental or frustrated. I hope you can use them to find more creative and relational ways to be alongside them and support them on this journey. Some strategies and practical ideas for how to support children who clam-up were shared in the first section of this adult guide and of course are peppered throughout this activity book.

SOME REASONS WHY WE MIGHT SAY 'I DON'T KNOW' 'I'M NOT SURE', RETREAT, CLAM UP, BE SILENT, ETC

- It might be too painful, emotionally charged, embarrassing, humiliating, hurtful, scary or hard to talk about or revisit

- We might feel overwhelmed or full-up, and have too many other things going on (too many thinking tabs open)
- The power dynamic between us

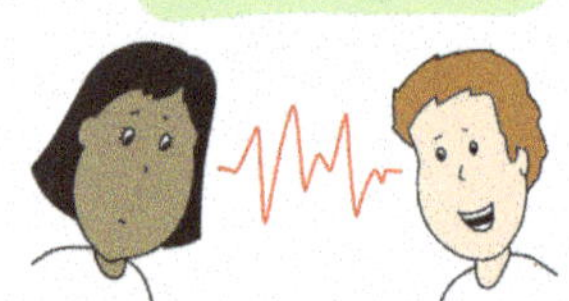

- We might generally not know

We need to try to be curious instead of furious and reflect on if the behaviour could talk what might it say or be trying to express to us - this is a flavour and not an exhaustive or prescriptive list - we do not have emotional x-rays or mind readers) (PAGE 193)

- We might struggle to understand the question or what is being asked or expected. The question might also be unclear, poorly worded, too big, etc
- We might have been told that knowing is dangerous or scary
- We might have had past experiences of painful responses from people (eg. not being believed, misunderstood, shamed, blamed, silenced, minimised, weaponised, uncaring, cold, betrayed, etc)
- We might have had to have coped, survived, or navigated by retreating, clamming-up, shutting down, shrinking etc
- We might fear the consequences, ripples, and possible repercussions of answering, including what might happen or how might the information be received
- We might be worried that if we put things into words, it might make it real and/or we won't be able to take them back

SOME REASONS WHY WE MIGHT SAY 'I DON'T KNOW' 'I'M NOT SURE', RETREAT, CLAM UP, BE SILENT, ETC

PAGE 2 OF 3

- We might have been told or threatened not to talk or share

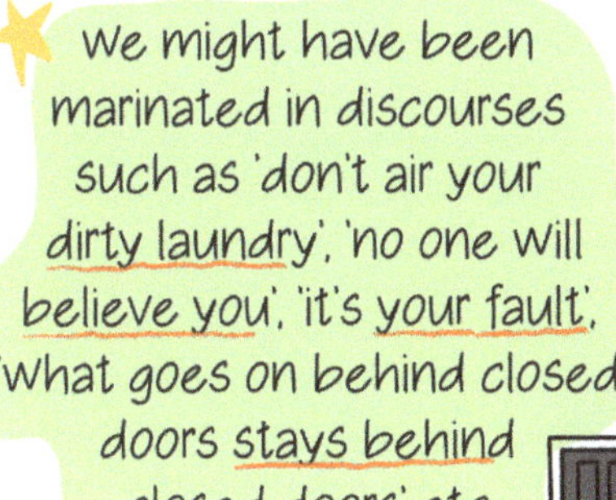

- We might have been marinated in discourses such as 'don't air your dirty laundry', 'no one will believe you', 'it's your fault', 'what goes on behind closed doors stays behind closed doors' etc

- We might feel on the spot, stuck, pressurized and exposed
- We might want to finish, stop, or end the conversation or avoid further questions
- We might not know, trust, or feel comfortable with the person

- We might have had to repeat and retell things so many times to so many different people

Dr Karen Treisman
SafeHands ThinkingMinds

- We might not feel ready or in a place to answer

- It might be hard to be still in the chair and/or struggle with eye contact

- We might find it hard to explain, describe, or put into words; or might not have the words (including the emotional vocabulary and dictionary) – it might also be an image or sensation etc
- Brains in pain/strained brains can struggle sometimes to think/talk/express/articulate etc (eg. including what can happen in the broca's part of the brain)
- We might fear that others might hear what we are saying /might get into trouble

- We might feel that there isn't enough time or space to share, process, explain etc

IMAGISTIC.CO.UK

SOME REASONS WHY WE MIGHT SAY 'I DON'T KNOW' 'I'M NOT SURE', RETREAT, CLAM UP, BE SILENT, ETC

PAGE 3 OF 3

- We might worry about confidentiality

- We might find it hard to pay attention, concentrate, or remember for a range of reasons
- We might be worried that if we say things we will then spill and leak out – an emotional tsunami or tornado
- We might be worried about upsetting the other person or trying to protect them

- We might be a quieter or less talkative person

- We might be communicating through non-speaking ways

Dr Karen Treisman
SafeHands ThinkingMinds

- We might be hungry, tired, cold, fed up, distracted etc
- We might have had difficult experiences with people, adults, services, professionals etc
- We might have been made to feel that we are not important, or that we don't have anything to say or have been made to feel unseen, not listened to, or our opinion unvalued etc

- We might struggle to connect or identify to feelings and could have coped by numbing, dissociation, etc

- We might be seeing and 'assessing' what the other person might do and how they might react
- The physical environment or space might not feel 'safe' or supportive

- What else would you add?

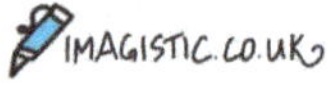

Some of the fears, worries, and experiences people might have around sharing their feelings and talking

If I show how I feel something scary or bad might happen

If I feel it will spill out

If I am not seen, I can't be hurt

If I don't feel I can't be hurt

If I talk, people won't like me/they will laugh at me/ leave me out

If I talk people won't listen/understand

If I talk people will get mad

I don't have the words

If I talk, I might say the wrong thing

I don't like feelings. I wish they would go away

I don't feel anything I feel numb

If I show how I feel I will be ignored, silenced/not believed/ blamed/shamed /shut down/humiliated/ embarrassed/misunderstood/ minimised/weaponised against me etc.

What else?

If my mind is blank, I don't need to think about what happened/is happening

Box 3: Some reflective questions and ways to use these worksheets

Take your time to look at the above worksheets. Some strategies and ideas for how to respond are also shared in the second part of this adult guide and of course throughout this activity book. It might be helpful to revisit them.

- Which resonate for you? Which do you recognize or might fit?
- Which would you add or change?
- If these are experienced, how might they contribute to someone clamming-up, being unsure, bottling-up their feelings, saying 'I don't know', being quiet?
- How does holding these in mind make you feel? Would you approach the person differently?
- If you hold these in mind, how could you use these to creatively be alongside and support the person experiencing these?
- How might these help you to take this less as a personal assault?
- How might these help you to be more curious instead of furious?
- How might these help you to see or view the behaviour differently? Remember, see a person differently and you see a different person, see a behaviour differently and you see a different behaviour.
- How might you gently honour or name these, or try to find ways to support them to have a different, healing, and reparative experience?

These worksheets can be useful to increase understanding, awareness, and sensitivity to what the person might be experiencing. They can support people to feel validated and to have their experiences normalized and recognized. They can support you to have more empathy and compassion. They can give you some ideas, words, metaphors, and analogies to name, discuss, or interweave into psychoeducation. They can also be used as a springboard for exploring and enriching further, such as thinking about what this means or feels like to the person, specific examples of when they have experienced them, the impact of them, what makes them more intense or visit less.

They can also provide an opportunity to think about which ones they may or may not experience, which visit the most, which they do not recognize, which they find distressing, which they find comforting, and so on. (You can also incorporate the communication cards in Activity 18 with these questions, such as always, never, sometimes.)

Additionally, they can be used as a whole worksheet directly with the child or certain squares can be cut out and creatively used, or they might be helpful to show and share for other adults to increase their understanding. If it is too much for the child, try it with some distance, asking them which might apply to Taya the Tortoise or a character in a movie, or someone else they know.

The 'what else?' is an important part of all the worksheets, so that the child can add other ones, or say which they would change or think are missing. It also provides a springboard for the child to choose their own words, terms, symbols, images, and metaphors.

Therapeutic Re-parenting Skills, Tools, and Ways of Being

Having explored some of the practicalities and ways of enriching the activities in the first section of the adult guide, and the psychoeducation and aspects around retreating and disconnected in this section, our final part of the adult guide is centred around therapeutic re-parenting skills, tools, and ways of being.

I wanted to write a poem to capture some of the concepts in the story and throughout the activity book. Rhythm and melody can be very healing and helpful and so I wanted to honour this through a poem style.

Box 4: Taya the Tortoise Poem

There was a tortoise named Taya who lived in Ethiopia, a beautiful, lush land,
Who roamed slowly and gracefully through the trees and the grainy yellow sand,

When she was scared, she would retreat and make herself teeny and small,
And when she was happy, she would stretch herself and look so very tall,

She had a hard shell which also protected her heart,
She would tuck her head and neck in and hide as a start,

When other animals approached her, she could be very shy,
Her mind could travel somewhere else like clouds moving in the sky,

Taya had some lovely friends who wanted her to be able to be herself and to have more fun,
To dance, to play, to laugh, and to have adventures and bask in the sun,

Sometimes when unsure and things felt too much in her shell she would stay,
She sometimes worried if she spoke up what would others think, do, or say,

When in her shell, it could be hard to connect, laugh, have fun, or to feel the joy and the light,
She had learned to sometimes protect herself and her mind would just take flight,

When things felt too hard, she would split, fragment, and her mind would fly away,
Sometimes, this was easier than staying in the present and/or what might happen if she would stay,

When things got too much to revisit, live in, or face,
She could fly away in her mind and go to a different space and place,

At times, she had to cope by shielding, clamming, and shrinking from the world and had to disappear,
If you saw inside her or had an emotional x-ray, you might have seen a river of many a hurt tear,

When this happened her mind sometimes felt like it was muddy, full up, or foggy,
And it could be hard to remember things and so she could feel out of sync and groggy,

Her thoughts, memories, and fears could whirl around swishing and whizzing,
And other times there was little there and there were chunks, gaps, and bits missing,

Sometimes she felt misunderstood, some people thought she was cold or didn't care,
She could seem empty, disconnected, switched off, and just stare,

She could be talking to people but not hearing what they said and could respond with a glazed look,
Her life could feel like it wasn't hers or that she was watching it happen to someone else like a character in a film or in the pages of a book,

Sometimes, she had to camouflage how she felt, shield, or put on a mask,
To protect, to stop further hurt, to create some distance of further pain that was her task,

Sometimes, her brain had been in so much pressure and strain,
And things could happen that stirred past things up and sent her down a memory time hole and chain of pain,

At times, she felt alone or feared that she would get in trouble and so life could be an emotional odyssey and a struggle,

So, she learned to survive by putting up emotional armour and a strong protective bubble,

Her heart had been hurt and so she had to harden it and keep people out with an invisible lock,
And to find ways to push people away, keep them at a distance, and to put up a block,

Taya needs others to be patient with her through all the ups and downs and twists and turns,
For her brain to feel safer and through repeated experiences that things can be ok it learns,

Her spidey senses with time and new experiences will learn that scary things don't always happen,
With patience, time, joy, and people beside her she will start to learn a new relational pattern,

Sometimes, it is tricky to talk about things and she can feel very little and numb,
But we need to help her, believe in her that there are better times and that this is something that she can navigate through and overcome,

She needs someone to show her that she is more than enough and can be accepted – all her thorny bits, shapes, and parts,
To integrate and bring together those different threads of her so the healing journey starts,

It has been hard to open up and to reach out and to learn how to trust,
But bit by bit her brain, body, nervous system, and gut will learn how to absorb the magic and to adjust,

Cheerleading her on and believing in her, heart print by heart print being there for her, peek by peek,
And showing her, we see her, we hear her, and we want to hear her when she speaks.

The benefits of therapeutic re-parenting

Why is therapeutic re-parenting, healing-infused, enriched, attachment, and trauma-informed parenting/caring so important and such a key part of supporting children who have been hurt? Why is love not enough?

Children who have been hurt, let down, and rejected, among other difficult and distressing relationship experiences, have sadly often learned that relationships – the ones that should offer them comfort, relief, love, and protection – are sources of threat and pain. They have learned that relationships might signal danger, and can be things to be feared, avoided, controlled, and not to be relied on or trusted.

These children need to be shown by adults to learn new and transformative ways of being in relationships, and what to expect from relationships. It makes sense that because the trauma and suffering occurred within these relationships, the meaningful way to heal and recover is through relationships and connections. Put simply, relational trauma, suffering, and wounding require relational repair and healing (Treisman 2016). We want to increase their capacity to absorb, feel, and be in reparative relationships. In the context of relational poverty, they often have felt invisible and misunderstood, and had relationships that might have been disconnected and distanced, for example. They often haven't had a much needed emotional and relational feast and sustenance. To remedy this they need to feel valued, appreciated, seen, understood, and held in relationships that are attuned, present, and connected.

They need to – over a long period of time and on a regular basis – experience, sense, feel, and internalize new, safer, and healthier types of relationships. This will be through millions and millions of repetitive and healing moments (taking their brain to the positive relationship gym, over and over again). This repetition is important, as change happens through activated, patterned, and repeated experiences. They are having to re-train their brains and nervous systems to go against what they have previously learned, been programmed, and had to adapt to. And often within this, children need to grieve for the loss or deprivation from previous relationships, or for the relationships which they longed for.

This relational repair is more than traditional parenting or showing the child love. Because they are children who have been hurt and who have had different early foundations, it requires a lot of time, energy, dedication, patience, and extra therapeutic parenting tools. This type of parenting and support includes holding the hope for the child, and for the overall situation (easier said than done!), and having that persistence and sticking power, like Tristan and Tillie with Taya. It is about having radical acceptance and compassion for the child and keeping on leaving heart prints, being able to have a trauma lens, and to be curious instead of furious. It is about being multi-sensory. It is about meeting the child where they are at and finding ways to support them to start experiencing things and learning new skills that they might not have previously had. This is not about their chronological age but meeting them where they might be at socially, emotionally, and developmentally – and this is not a static or fixed age or stage. It is dynamic and can shift and change at different times and in different contexts. Some therapeutic re-parenting tools and qualities will be introduced briefly in the following sections. They are the underpinnings from which to hang so many of the activities and concepts of this activity book on.

Our own wellbeing, care, anchoring, and regulation

Building on the above, we need to fill children's life treasure boxes up on numerous occasions on a daily basis (these can be seemingly tiny moments), so that children are continually being filled with relationship gems, treasures, experiences, and key developmental and life skills. This is crucial, as for many of these children, their earlier life treasure boxes were not richly filled, treasured, or handled with care. In order to do this, we must respect, appreciate, and acknowledge our own treasure boxes and keep them replenished and nourished. This is essential, so that we can continue to have gems to give to the children; it is virtually impossible to consistently keep on giving from an empty box. To use a different metaphor, we have to put our own oxygen mask on first.

Before presenting some of the key parenting positions, let's focus some attention on our own wellbeing, anchoring, and regulation. This is intentionally given priority in this section of the adults guide, as we are our greatest tool and strategy, and the main vehicle for change. We need to feed and sustain ourselves in order to be those safe hands, thinking minds, and regulating bodies (Treisman 2016) for the children. Therefore, although thorny to do and loaded with unhelpful societal, family, and individual messages, we need to prioritize our own emotional wellbeing and regulation, particularly as we need the energy, motivation, and fuel to keep going through some very difficult situations. Our own wellbeing shouldn't be viewed as a luxury, or seen as an add-on feature, or as selfish – it should be seen as essential, as expected, as routine, in the same way as something like brushing our teeth is viewed.

Parenting or supporting a child who is hurt and who has experienced relational, betrayal, and developmental trauma can have a multi-layered emotional, physical, social, financial, spiritual, and cognitive impact on those around the child. This is particularly so when caring for children who, like Taya, disconnect, withdraw, clam-up, shut down, retreat, and put up their emotional barriers, which can feel rejecting. Being on the receiving end of these behaviours and feelings, especially when it is in your home (supposedly your safe haven) on a regular basis, can be extremely difficult, exhausting, and frustrating, and subsequently can activate a whole host of other thorny feelings and stingy emotions. These trauma-based responses can push our own buttons, hotspots, and prickly parts (we are all human, so we all have some of these). This fits with the powerful saying, 'The expectation that we can be immersed in suffering and loss daily and not be touched by it is as unrealistic as expecting to be able to walk through water and not get wet' (Remen 1996). There is a cost of caring, bearing witness, and being alongside others' hurt, distress, and suffering.

These trauma-based responses can sometimes make us feel similar to how the child is feeling inside – hopeless, helpless, out of control, powerless, shocked, shamed, blamed, heavy, sad, angry, worthless, rejected, exhausted, not good enough, and much more. We can feel as if it is relentless, as if we are banging our heads against a brick wall, at a loss for what to do. This emotional heavy lifting can also be added to by a lack of reciprocity within the relationship or not having those sparkle moments or feel-good connecting moments. If a child is not particularly responsive or reactive, or doesn't feel present or engaged, we not only have the tricky bits of feeling rejected or excluded, but also cannot experience the bits of parenting or human interactions which light us up or provide the motivation to keep going. It can understandably be harder to keep bringing the energy and sustained interest when interacting with someone who isn't as present or isn't bringing the same energy.

Moreover, being faced with these trauma-based responses can also make us feel as if we are an elastic band being stretched until we are close to snapping, or we actually do snap. At these times, it is likely – because we ourselves are in survival mode (regularly firefighting and operating in crisis mode) and being in a place of exhaustion and feeling stuck – that this will restrict our clarity of thinking, and we can find it much harder to be our best selves. We may even be experiencing what is often referred to as secondary trauma, vicarious trauma, compassionate fatigue, moral injury, caregiver strain/stress, emotional saturation and exhaustion, burnout, and blocked care (a helpful concept from dyadic developmental psychotherapy).

As with the children who have experienced trauma, when we are feeling depleted and full up, our reactions and responses tend to be more emotionally driven and heightened. Our window of tolerance or our emotional bandwidth can be impacted, and so in these moments we can feel more negatively about situations, and about the child, and we can also be harsher towards and more critical of ourselves, the child, and others. We might also overreact, blow things out of proportion, snap more easily, or take things more personally. It can be harder to keep our hearts open and to be holders of hope. We can also go the other way (or all of the shades and swings in between), for example, by distancing ourselves, switching-off, putting walls up, blocking things out, pulling away, retreating into our own shell. Our own emotional health can cascade down to the child.

Therefore, with all this in mind, although extremely difficult, and with the acknowledgement that we are all human, we need to find ways to stay regulated, calm, reflective, and grounded ourselves, and to not get pulled in as deeply, as often, or as quickly into the emotional quicksand, or an emotional cyclone. Having some tools and processes for doing this is so important, as children are like sponges; they are impressionable, and their spidey senses and antennae pick up the mood, the energy, how we feel about them, and what we bring into the space. To be a relational co-regulator or their or our own limbic whisperer we need to be mindful of our own body language, tone of voice, and facial expressions.

For practical ways of supporting your own wellbeing, while acknowledging that there is no right way, and that everyone is different, and it is a personal thing, please see my books *A Therapeutic Treasure Box for Working with Children and Adolescents with Developmental Trauma: Creative Techniques and Tools* (Treisman 2017) for additional ideas, and *A Therapeutic Treasure Deck of Grounding, Soothing, Coping, and Regulating Cards* (Treisman 2017) for some illustrated strategies. I also run trainings around this. You might also find several of the activities in this activity book helpful for you too such as Activities 9–17, 28–56, 59, 62.

Box 5: Reflective exercise on wellbeing

This is ongoing and evolving, and you can notice, explore, revisit, add to, or change your answers. It isn't a one-off. Also, you can write, draw, sculpt, make a collage, or use any way you like to express and further expand on your responses.

- What does wellness, your own emotional regulation, and wellbeing mean, feel, and look like to you? Why is this so important and beneficial (physically, emotionally, financially, socially, relationally, organizationally etc.)? What are the costs, consequences, ripple effects, and hazards of not attending to your wellbeing?
- What do you look like, feel like, and act like when you are your 'best and happiest' self? How do others know when this is the case? What do you and others do, feel, say, show, notice? What personal and professional factors contribute to this?
- What are some of the physical, emotional, spiritual, and relational hazards of cumulative stacked-up stress? What do you know about the role of stress on health, wellbeing, cognitive abilities, decision making, and so on?
- What do you look like, feel like, and act like when you are stressed or depleted at work and at home? How do others know when this is the case? What do you and others do, feel, say, show, notice? What personal and professional factors contribute to this?
- What do you see, hear, smell, taste, feel, touch that make the anxiety/fear/frustration/doubt (whatever feeling you want to explore) visit? What makes the calm/happiness/joy/hope (whatever feeling you want to explore) visit?
- If the feeling, behaviour, or sensation could talk, what might it say (e.g. the self-doubt, the guilt, the overwhelm, the headaches, the rash, the butterflies in tummy, the drinking, the lack of sleep, the hope, the motivation)?
- How does your body communicate, show, or share with you when it is full up, overwhelmed, exhausted, stressed, calm?
- What advice would you give to your loved ones/those you advise at work around wellness and wellbeing? How would it be if you transferred this message to yourself? (See Activities 40 and 41.)
- How did/does it feel to care for yourself? Do you experience any guilt over taking time to care for yourself?
- What blocks and barriers are there for you taking this time? (Some of these can be entangled with your own history, experiences, and relationship to wellbeing, in your childhood, parenting experience, school, and work, as well as within societal, community, and social media messages, discourses, and narratives.)
- If you keep filling children's glasses up with water, or their bowl up with fruit, how is yours going to get replenished, and by whom? What can you offer to others, if your water or fruit is depleted or gone? What do they say on an aeroplane about putting your own oxygen mask on before putting on a child's mask?

- How can you be there for others, without leaving yourself behind? How can you light a child's fire, if yours is burned out? A car or phone needs to be refuelled/charged – what do you or could you do to refuel and charge?

What else would you add?

We are only human, making and embracing 'mistakes' and showing that we are sorry

As with all of these tools, ways of being, and techniques, it is important to remember that we are all human, and it is inevitable, useful, and healthy to make mistakes. There are going to be misunderstandings, discomfort, missteps, back and forward progress and change. So please try to be kind, forgiving, accepting, and compassionate to yourself, and to others, and to give yourself grace, as this can be a frustrating and trying journey. It is helpful and necessary for children to learn, and to see that mistakes do happen, and that they are a normal, expected, and a useful part of life, and equally that they can be short-lived, moved on from, embraced, and learned from.

The most important bit, which further supports the strengthening of the relationship, is the magic part that comes afterwards, where, as the adult, we can acknowledge, model, own, and say that we are sorry and then work to reconnect with the child and repair the relationship. The way we model and respond to mistakes feels especially important in a trauma and disrupted attachment context, where children may have learned that 'mistakes' can have catastrophic consequences, and where these children often already have poor self-belief, self-confidence, and self-esteem and high levels of shame, humiliation, and blame. This might have been from how someone reacted to them wetting the bed, spilling milk, making a noise, getting into trouble at school. They might have been hurt and harmed but not had someone meaningfully apologize or acknowledge the pain that has been caused, or apologies were given after the pain, but they were not actioned or did not feel genuine.

But how can we expect a child to be able to say or show that they are sorry if as adults we aren't able to model and teach this? We need to lead by example and show that when things happen, we can work through it and come back together. We can say, text, write, show, send a card/postcard saying that we are sorry, or that we are changing or learning from things. We might use statements like 'If I could go back in a time machine', 'If I could have a do-over', 'If I could rewind...', 'Having had some time to think and reflect, I wish I could start again and I would...', 'Some of the things I want to improve and work on are...' This models the model, and also fits with the saying by educational philosopher John Dewey, 'We don't learn from experiences, we learn from reflecting on experiences.'

Showing, not just telling or lecturing about feelings and being safe

As we have discussed, so much of therapeutic re-parenting or supporting children who have been hurt is not just lecturing or telling them, or expecting them to believe or trust us. To them, trusting is often scary, dangerous, overwhelming, even alien and too much. Some children have learned that adults are not to be relied on or that adults did not keep them safe, and they will understandably often judge or generalize new experiences based on their past experience. So, if this is their learned experiences over time, we need to start reteaching and retraining children's brains, bodies, nervous systems. Trust must be earned, and there is a difference between being told you are safe and feeling that you are safe, being told you are loved and feeling loved, being told you can trust someone, and feeling you can trust them. They might have been told these things in the past, but it didn't match with what they experienced. So, words are not enough.

This is why it isn't fair to expect children to relinquish control or to trust us. We wouldn't expect them to not swim when drowning or to come out from a cave if there is danger. We need to gradually, drip by drip, heart print by heart print, show them with repeated, patterned, consistent, and predictable experiences that they are safe, that they can come to us if they are sad, hungry, or stuck, or have made a 'mistake'. We are trying to power-up their magnet, fill their memory bank with new experiences, and retrain their brains. We want them to absorb the outside, to move into the inside and understand that those strategies and survival and protective responses that were used there and then were valid, important, and needed, but aren't needed all the time in the here and now. We need to help them recognize, hold on to, and notice these experiences (Activities 43–57).

This is why, wherever possible, our words need to match our actions and our actions match our words. Children learn through their experiences – what they see and feel. You can tell a child they are safe, but they need more than words to feel and believe that. This will take time and energy and relearning.

Box 6: An example of a 'safety' tour at lunchtime at school

It's essential to try to see the world from the child's perspective and sensory experience, to get alongside them and truly show them over time. The example here illustrates this (of course, it will vary and look different to different children in different situations).

At school, a young girl pushed and shoved to get to the front of the queue, and sometimes hurt other children to get to her food. There could have been a number of reasons for this:

- The canteen created sensory overload – the smells, sounds, sights, lights, temperature, and so on. It could be overwhelming and unpredictable.
- The child was separated from her attachment figure and then surrounded by other kids, big kids, strangers, groups, cliques.
- There was a lack of structure and predictability in the canteen and a whole bunch of different expectations and rules.

- It might have tapped into her relationship to eating, her weight, body image, teeth.
- It might have been difficult because there were aspects around friendship, peers, and other people, who to sit with, being teased, being watched, and much more.
- The child had to wait, stand in a queue, and trust the adults that there would be enough food.
- And many others...

For this particular child, layering on to the previous points, she had past experiences of being deprived, malnourished, and starving. Food for her was about survival. Therefore, when she walked into the canteen, she had a physiological feeling of hunger, and this took her down a chain of pain and back to all the trauma times where she was starved and hadn't had her needs met. When she entered the canteen, she was activated and in the grip of trauma.

The school knew about some of her experiences with food and were kind and supportive, understanding some of why she was responding in the way that she was. They told her that they were sorry that in the past she didn't have access to food and they promised her that she would be able to have food and they would make sure that she got to eat and would not be left hungry.

But did she believe them? NO! Being told something and feeling and believing it are very different things. She had often been let down and hurt by adults, so understandably didn't trust them, and had a whole memory bank of experiences where she hadn't been looked after, so this overrode what the teachers were saying.

When I came to work with her, I needed to show her and give her brain and her nervous system a different experience, so it was more than words and lecturing to her, or just telling her she was 'safe'. She needed to actually experience, see, and feel it for herself. First, I had to get key people at the school on board with my idea and do some psychoeducation, because I needed them to support the process. Second, I needed the child to eat before doing the 'safety' tour because if she was hungry when we were doing our exploring, she would be overwhelmed and activated and it wouldn't work. So, she came out of class early to eat, so that she was full and not preoccupied by thinking about food.

And then she and I put on our chef's hats and jackets. We had fun and were playful, we took photos and posed in the outfits. And with her buy-in, and the school support, we went around with a camera phone, and started our discovering and experimenting. We met the food delivery van, and we looked inside and took pictures and videos of all the bags and boxes. We helped carry the bags of food into the kitchen. We looked at the huge amounts of food. We looked in the fridges, freezers, and cupboards at all the food. We interviewed the chef about how he calculated the quantities and what he did to ensure that there was enough for the number of staff and students.

With each part of the process we asked questions, we explored, we took photos or videos, and I validated and listened to her perspective and responses. On a different day, we watched the lunch and saw how many leftovers there were. On another day, we did an experiment and asked one class to ask for second helpings of food and observed how there was still enough food. On another day, we got two classes to ask for second helpings of food, and then when they got to the last few people and ran out of food, we looked at how quickly the chef could make a sandwich or find an alternative from the fridge. We did this on several days, over several weeks. So, as shared previously, it wasn't a one-off exercise, as we learn from repeated, activated, and patterned experiences. It was muscle memory brain training, over and over again, and it was all done together relationally and in validating and regulating ways.

From a range of options, the child chose to turn the photos she had taken into a collage and a photo story book, so she could look at these as a reminder when the self-doubt or fear visited. After this, of course there was the odd bump in the road, and we continued to work on her experience and relationship to food using deeper therapeutic strategies (so this was not standalone but part of a wider package of support). In the meantime, with these new experiences and some sensory strategies to use in the queue, and with some signals from the people serving the food when they saw her, she was fine in the canteen. And when the voice and sensation of 'I am going to starve' visited her, she had all these other contradicting experiences that she could use to anchor on to and use to help restore her balance and ability to navigate the situation.

This example demonstrates the difference between showing and doing over time, and not just saying.

Shifting our thinking

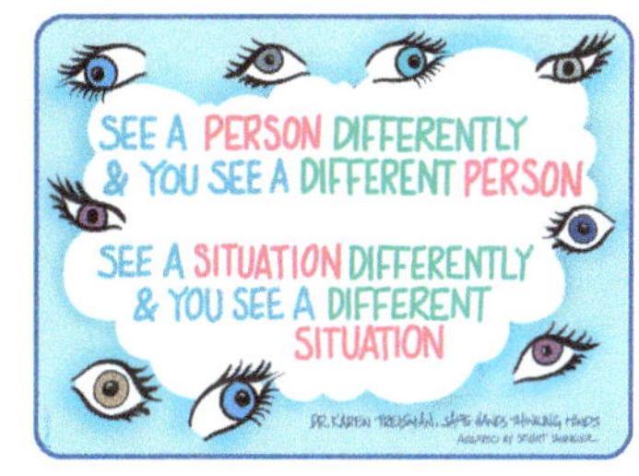

The more we connect with and acknowledge the pain and hurt a child has experienced, and respect and try to understand why the child's walls have been put up in the first place, **the more curious we can become instead of furious**. It can also make the behaviour or response feel less personal, confusing, or overwhelming. **And if we can see a child differently, we see a different child**. *We can make that trauma-informed shift from 'What is wrong with you and what is the matter with you?' to 'What has happened to you, and who was there with you when it happened or who is with you now? Who are you? What matters to you? What is your story and your experiences? What are you trying to tell us?'*

It is also about recognizing, acknowledging, and trying to connect with all the different layers and parts of the child. This is often likened to an iceberg, where often we can only see the tip and the surface levels of the iceberg, but underneath and less visible are all of the other hidden levels of the iceberg. Similarly, this can be likened to a set of nesting dolls, where we see the large outer nesting doll, but can be unaware of all of the other smaller dolls which lie within the big doll.

The more we understand the behaviour, the more we can support the child to feel understood, noticed, valued, connected, and empathized with, and we can help them to understand their own responses and reactions. However, we need to tread gently, as taking down walls, or even a brick at a time, can be scary, exposing, and painful, so this needs to be done with care and we need to be supportive and honour why the wall was there in the first place.

Additionally, understanding behaviours is also important, as the way we interpret, feel, and make sense of the behaviour can have a big impact on how we respond to it. This might depend on our mood, on the particular time of day, on our coping resources at the time, and also on our own experiences, relationships, and history to the particular behaviour or the common theme of the behaviour. Imagine how differently you will respond to a child when feeling exhausted/after having a horrible day at work/if the behaviour activates you, or reminds you of something or someone else.

Box 7: Some powerful questions and positions to reflect on

These questions can be asked gently, explored, and added to over time. You might find the second section of this adult guide, specifically the worksheets, very helpful here.

1. How has the blocking/numbing/retreating/dissociation helped the child to survive, navigate, cope, be protected?

2. When was this blocking/numbing/retreating/dissociation needed/helpful and been their friend/helper/protector?

3. What would have happened if the blocking/numbing/retreating/dissociation wasn't there or wasn't possible?

4. If the blocking/numbing/retreating/dissociation packed its bag and vanished, what might the child miss, long for, have to face? What might it look like/feel like (advantages and disadvantages) if the blocking/retreating/bottling-up/clamming-up disappeared or was absent?

5. What function/meaning/purpose might the blocking/retreating/bottling-up/clamming-up be communicating to the child about their relationships and their coping, and why? What might the story, needs, and messages be behind it?

6. If the blocking/retreating/bottling-up/clamming-up could talk/had a voice, what do you think it might say and sound like? What would it tell/explain to us?

7. Why might they have learned (and it be understandable to have done so)

that it is better to reject than be rejected? Better to numb than to feel? Better to protect than connect? Better to psychologically fly away and exit than to be present? What lessons and experiences might have contributed to children coping and surviving in these ways?

8. When might the blocking/numbing/retreating/dissociation be a hazard/get in the way/stop something from happening?

9. Who is the child behind the blocking/numbing/retreating/dissociation? What makes them light up, tick, sparkle, laugh, connect? What are their other interests, passions, parts, qualities?

10. What is the child's relationship with the blocking/retreating/bottling-up/clamming-up? What role might it have played in their life? Where might they have seen it, learned it from, developed it, needed it? What has the history of it been? Why might it have started and developed at the time?

11. Where does the blocking/retreating/bottling-up/clamming-up occur? Are there differences depending on the context?

12. What other variables and factors do you think might influence and impact the blocking/retreating/bottling-up/clamming-up? Are there particular patterns or themes of the blocking/retreating/bottling-up/clamming-up?

13. What factors (e.g. environmental, sensory, autobiographical, physical, cognitive, relational, emotional, and contextual) make the blocking/retreating/bottling-up/clamming-up bigger, more intense, smaller, absent, present? What fuels/amplifies/changes/calms the blocking/retreating/bottling-up/clamming-up?

14. What happens when these activating factors occur? What do they look like? What is the impact of them? Are there ways in which the child and others could reduce or respond to these?

15. What happens in the times when the blocking/retreating/bottling-up/clamming-up is absent or less? What is different and why? How can these times be noticed, increased, and celebrated?

16. What is the impact of the blocking/retreating/bottling-up/clamming-up on the child and on those around them? For example, on their sleep, eating, mood, school life, relationships, friendships, learning, hobbies, daily living skills, and self-esteem. What is the blocking/retreating/bottling-up/clamming-up making trickier or stopping the child/adults from doing?

17. What different responses, reactions, and feelings does the blocking/retreating/bottling-up/clamming-up evoke in different people? What does the way

we feel when at the receiving end of the blocking/retreating/bottling-up/clamming-up tell us about the child's feelings and inner world?

18. If the blocking/retreating/bottling-up/clamming-up was a puzzle or a patchwork, what pieces do you think it might be made up of, and what picture might it form when put together?

19. What, if any, is the child's sense-making, attributions, explanations about the blocking/retreating/bottling-up/clamming-up? How are these similar to or different from other surrounding people's conceptualizations of it? How stressful is the blocking/retreating/bottling-up/clamming-up to the child and the team around the child?

20. What strategies/interventions have been tried already? What bits of these were helpful or less helpful, and why? What responses from others has the child had when showing the blocking/retreating/bottling-up/clamming-up?

21. How does knowing a bit more about what the blocking/retreating/bottling-up/clamming-up might be communicating shape your feelings/thoughts/conceptualizations/descriptions about the child? How does the blocking/retreating/bottling-up/clamming-up change when viewed from a different angle and lens? How might this lens impact your way of understanding, responding, and supporting change?

22. Is there a particular part of the blocking/retreating/bottling-up/clamming-up that really pushes your buttons, or gets under your skin, or worries you? (We all have some!) What is your story of, experience of, and relationship to that difficulty/theme/feeling? Which of your values/beliefs/hopes/expectations are being challenged by the blocking/retreating/bottling-up/clamming-up? What, if anything, is being tapped into, stirred up, resurfaced, pushed in you/others when on the receiving end of the blocking/retreating/bottling-up/clamming-up?

23. What are some of your own and others' emotional, cognitive, sensory, and physical responses to the blocking/retreating/bottling-up/clamming-up?

24. Which of your own stories, values, beliefs, hopes, fears, and experiences are influencing your meaning-making of the behaviour and your response to it?

What else would you add?

Teaching and showing new ways of being in a relationship

As shared throughout this workbook, Taya had learned that relationships were scary, overwhelming, and not to be trusted. She had learned to protect herself instead of connecting to others, often withdrawing, disconnecting from, and retreating from relationships and experiences. What this meant was that she protected herself from further pain and hurt but she also missed out on some of the magic, helpful, joyful, important, and beautiful parts of relationships and connections (see Activities 43–57).

So ideally, we want to honour and respect why children retreat, when this can be helpful, and why it can be hard to peek out or come out, while also gradually and gently showing them the benefits of relationships when they are trusting, helpful, and caring. We want to fill up their positive treasure box and power up their positive magnet.

Here are some of the ways to do this:

- Being a role model.
- Spending positive quality time together.
- Being playful and playing.
- Identifying and naming feelings and how we respond to them. (See Activities 19–38, as well as the first section of the adult guide where it talks about feelings.)
- Being consistent and predictable.
- Having sticking power and being gently persistent.
- Holding hope.
- Learning about, witnessing, experiencing, and seeing healthy and not harmful relationships, and interpersonal interactions. This includes how they are modelled and navigated, and how they can be beneficial. (Activities 43–57 are focused on this.)

There are many more ways, which are shared throughout this section and the activity book.

We want to show the child that when they do peek out, they will have a positive experience and they can start to experience and absorb some of the wonderful aspects of life. We want them to start learning that they can show all of their colours, textures, parts, and layers, and that they are with someone who won't hurt them and who they can let in or rely on or go to for help. This is also about changing over time their lens and template, shifting from the view that 'relationships are scary, unpredictable, painful' to 'relationships can be scary, unpredictable, painful, but they also can be loving, caring, consistent, kind, and reliable'. We want them to have new experiences that almost contradict their past experiences, and which give them new territory to explore and new ways of seeing things. It is retraining the brain and nervous system to pay attention and select different information.

Of course, this is also not always about rainbows and fairies, and there will be the ups and downs, and twists and turns, that relationships can go through, including the thorny and stingy bits. Sometimes, I creatively explore this through metaphors or activities such as snakes and ladders, twists and turns, the labyrinth or maze of relationships, the rollercoaster of relationships.

Believing in the potential to heal and recover, and the power of fun, playfulness, and hope

Children who have experienced relational and developmental trauma (and other life experiences) have often been marinated in toxic stress, adrenaline, and cortisol; their relationships are often characterized by fear, control, and rejection-based interactions. They often have not experienced as many opportunities for play, fun, and joy. The stress, fear, and trauma can overwhelm, restrict, or crush the playfulness and joy. Therefore, we want children to experience a different type of relationship and to increase their capacity for joy, play, fun, and connection – relationships that are kind, authentic, compassionate, fun, playful, joyful, gentle, warm, loving, nurturing, and so on. Ideally (and we know it can be really tricky), adults should provide children with genuine hope, support, and encouragement. This conveys important messages to the child, such as:

- 'I am for you and not against you.'
- 'I hope to show you over time and through experiences that you can trust me, but I need to earn that and I get that it is difficult and different from what you have previously experienced.'
- 'I will believe in you, even if you don't believe in yourself.'
- 'I see the best in you.'
- 'I want the best for you.'
- 'I will be there with you.'
- 'We are in this together.'
- 'I am rooting for you.'

It can be powerful to write these down or express them to the child in a manifesto or commitment.

We must maximize opportunities for children's success and cultivate their skills, gifts, and strengths. Using the word 'yet' can be helpful (see Activity 42). When children or adults are feeling stuck and frustrated, we can talk about 'yet' and hold on to how we are always evolving, absorbing, learning, growing, and changing – that it is part of being alive. In a gentle (not a toxic positivity) way, we can celebrate their effort.

Moreover, a key part of therapeutic re-parenting and enriched parenting is about being healing and recovery infused and centred, and being a hopeful bearer, sharer, and holder. This can be really hard when we feel as if our wheels are spinning and change isn't happening, or we go one step forward and five back, and we see little progress. So, we need to find ways to convey that healing is possible, and to continually remind ourselves and others that if relationships and environments can harm, this means that equally they can heal and help. If our brains can be impacted and shaped by trauma and stress, they also can be impacted and shaped by connection, love, fun, play, relearning. Due its neuroplasticity, the brain has the ability to adapt, adjust, grow, and change following new experiences. Finding ways to anchor on to the little shifts, changes, and sparkle moments (as the small things can often be the big things) can help with this. (See Activities 48–56 and 62.)

Building on this, playful interactions, fun, joy, and laughter can also stimulate production of important feel-good chemicals (e.g. dopamine and opioids) in the body, which can also act as a stress buffer and diffuser. Similarly, being fun and playful can be key for diffusing power battles, as well as pushing on parents/carers and children's feel-good reward buttons and increasing overall positive and reciprocal interactions. This can also fill the child's memory bank and create a stronger foundation and treasure box of experiences to anchor on to when things feel thorny. The child can feel seen, heard, that they matter, that the person enjoys spending time with them, that they are important. In the context of trauma, children have often felt heaviness and hurt, so one of the remedies for this is lightness, fun, and joy.

Here are some examples of nurturing and playful interactions (of course, they will vary child to child and there is no one-size-fits-all):

Each time Andrea hurt herself, Sarah would give her a getting-better ritual, which included three big breaths, three kisses, three puffs of magic dust, some healing cream, and a special plaster.

Kwame found touch and intimacy difficult and activating, so instead his foster carer made him a blanket of love which she could wrap around him with permission and consent, and a doodle-bear filled with loving messages.

Patrick brought in a slug from the garden. Instead of saying 'Get that dirty thing out now!', his adoptive mother Leila said, 'Oh my goodness, look at that! What is the slug's name?' Patrick answered, 'Mr Slimy.' So, while setting limits, but being mindful of Patrick's perspective, and of the power of playful parenting, Leila said, 'Great name, shall we go play outside with Mr Slimy? That's where slugs are happiest, they need to live outdoors, near the ground and the trees. They don't like being inside houses. After that maybe we could draw a picture of Mr Slimy and take some photos of him. How does that sound?'

Sofia found getting dressed in the morning difficult, and often would be late for school because of this. So, with support, her mother made and recorded her a fun song about getting dressed in the morning that, in a playful rhythmic way, went through all the different steps of getting dressed.

Ravi did not enjoy his walk to school, so his mum added in games such as racing to different points on the way, doing silly animal walks, and playing I-spy.

Games and activities can be wonderful ways to increase, enhance, and strengthen adult-child relationships and to find ways to practise and develop key skills such as trust, sharing, reciprocity. They also create more positive memories and moments to anchor on to. Please visit the link here for a list of some suggested games and activities which you might like to incorporate or add to: www.safehandsthinkingminds.co.uk/wp-content/uploads/2024/11/Some-games-and-activities-to-strengthen-and-enhance-adult.pdf.

Regulating, anchoring, and grounding – relational regulation and co-regulation

This is a huge area and one which I can't do justice to in a few paragraphs; however, I do have numerous other resources and trainings on this topic. But to give a bit of an overview, a big part of supporting children who clam-up, retreat, disconnect, and so on involves regulation and anchoring. We need to have and provide children with tools and strategies to support them to soothe their nervous systems, to restore some balance and find their new homeostasis, to increase their capacity for joy, and to have some things to help them navigate through life. We want to support the child to feel seen, heard, and attuned with, and for them to find ways to be in the present and to stay connected and engaged in relationships and the world around them (when it is safe to do so).

A child shouldn't have to do this alone; they cannot learn key life skills without being shown. After all, we would struggle hugely to read if we hadn't first started learning the alphabet. It is the same with regulation and finding ways to soothe our nervous systems or understand our feelings – we need to do it within a safe and trusted relationship, alongside someone, before we can internalize these skills, place them in our memory banks, and use them when we require them. Co-regulation is the precursor of self-regulation. These skills are meant to be learned within the relationship.

So, we want to support children to find ways to sit with their feelings and to not suppress or push them away, and for their feelings to be validated. This can be done in hundreds of ways and there is no one-size-fits-all (some will be within a professional context such as in therapy or from a sensory perspective with an occupational therapist). However, here are some ways we can support these children and their feelings:

- Using consistent and predictable parenting/caring/adult responses.
- Communicating what is happening and being an interpreter and guide. Children should have a general sense as to what their parents/carers/adults expect from them (sometimes this is referred to as pre-teaching). This feels even more important in the context of trauma, where so many children have experienced inconsistency, unavailability, unpredictability, chaos, and broken promises. They might not have known what was going to happen or when it was going to happen, or been in situations where they felt powerless, helpless, shocked, and more. We can help by communicating things like when the routine is about to change, when we are about to do something such as reach for an item (often a child will flinch), or when we are going to make a loud noise (like turning the hoover on).
- Having structure to provide children with some consistent anchors, predictability, and certainty in the day, so that they have more head space for focusing on other things, like learning and playing, rather than worrying about what's coming next and the day-to-day routine.
- Practising and preparing situations and scenarios together. We can talk through with the child what might happen, what they can do, what to expect.

For some children, doing this through role playing, showing it through dolls and puppets, or social stories, or video clips, or using book or TV characters as examples can be very helpful.

- Identifying and naming feelings and how we respond to them. (The first section of this adult guide, the paragraphs below on feelings, and Activities 19–34 can support you with this.)
- Noticing when your child is withdrawing, disconnecting, or dissociating, and gently and gradually bringing them back into the present. Sometimes this might be with words, other times it might be with gentle touch, calling their name softly, sitting next to them, playing a particular song, using a particular scent, doing some rhythm or tapping, and so on.
- Identifying and noticing different things, smells, sounds, sensations, textures, sights, and movements that soothe, anchor, ground, and regulate the child. This might be things that up-regulate (wake up, alert, energize them) and things that down-regulate (bring calm and peace). We can then find ways to integrate and infuse these into their day-to-day and when they might need them or benefit from them. (See Activities 9–17.)
- Integrating movement and micro-movement strategies together; doing anchoring activities together like the 'calm place' or 'life cheerleader' exercises. (See Activities 9–17, and 59.)
- Ensuring that their physical needs are met and they are not too hot, too cold, hungry, sleepy, and so on.
- Thinking about our own responses and regulation, particularly when something has gone wrong or is worrying. This includes what our face, body language, non-speaking, tone of voice, words are conveying and expressing.
- Showing and exploring, not just telling, as in the 'safety' tour canteen example in Box 6.
- Finding ways to show the child that they can positively bring about change, and that their opinion is important, listened to, and valued. This is crucial, given that many children in the context of trauma, like Taya, have often been in situations where they felt powerless, ignored, and out of control. Their voice has most likely been silenced, misinterpreted, or minimized, and they may have been left with a sense of things being 'done to' them. Therefore, supporting children to have a sense of autonomy (at a level which is right for them, including their age and stage), to be in the driving seat, and to be the author of their own story, can be transformative. We need to make sure, where possible, that they have a sense of agency, choice, and options.

Identifying, acknowledging, naming, and responding to feelings

An important part of therapeutic re-parenting, to give them a gradual and creative reparative and healing experience, is supporting them gently to expand on their feelings vocabulary and their understanding of feelings. This includes the wide repertoire of feelings such as pride, joy, excitement, fun, as well as hurt, pain, sadness, and so on. We'll look here at just how we name and model our feelings or infuse feelings conversations in everyday interactions about our day, or a TV programme, or when reading a story, on the school pick-up, before bed, playing a game, and so on. We want feelings talk to become more normalized and common, so that it isn't just reserved for when something has gone wrong, or someone is in trouble, or you're having a big formal conversation. We want children to increase their feelings awareness and dictionary by having feelings conversations drip fed, little and often.

And also, of course it can be useful to hold these ideas in mind if we are having thorny conversations too, or navigating activities in this book that might be emotive or activating. As shared in the first section of the Guide for Adults, we are not forcing, bombarding, or pressurizing children to talk about or name their feelings, we are going at their pace, just gently being alongside them and cultivating the conditions to share feelings.

This is particularly important in the context of trauma, where children have often not had the same experiences to learn how to identify, process, and respond to feelings. Most likely they have had their feelings magnified, ignored, minimized, silenced, shut down, humiliated, misinterpreted, and so on. Children like Taya might have learned to clam-up, numb themselves, disconnect from, or bottle-up their feelings; the feelings that are felt inside need to be kept locked away or hidden. There can be a real mismatch between what we see on the outside of the 'shell' and what is on the inside. They might be thinking, 'If I show my feelings what will happen? Is it ok? Is it dangerous? What response will I get?'

There are so many ways of expressing our feelings – it doesn't need to be talking or words. Some children will express themselves through sensations and body messages, or through art, music, drawing, drumming, movement, masks, puppets, poetry. And as shared in Activities 19 and 20, some children might not be able to express their feelings for a range of reasons, but they might be able to listen to a story read by someone else about feelings, or they might be able to show them using feelings cards, cubes, stones, lollipop sticks, Jenga, miniatures, and so on. And they might express that feeling using a type of weather, an animal, a texture, something in nature, a rhythm, a song, a gif/emoji/meme/clip/hashtag (see Activity 20 for more on this).

It might also be tricky for children to identify their own feelings as that can feel more personal and exposing, so it can be easier to notice them in other people, or someone on TV, in a book, in their toys, on cards. This can provide a bit of distance. It might be harder to identify feelings in general, but more possible if it is about something specific like a certain lesson in school, or a particular situation. The adult tentatively wondering about different possible feelings, or naming their own, while acknowledging these might be different from the child's feeling, can also be helpful.

Sometimes how we respond can make a big difference to how someone might feel seen, heard, and listened to. As adults, we need to be able to identify, name, and validate the child's wide range of feelings as much as possible (without overwhelming or flooding them), and to offer them connection, reflection, empathy, acceptance, curiosity, and understanding around these feelings, rather than telling them how to feel or minimizing their feelings or trying to erase or make it better (e.g. 'At least...', 'Don't be silly', 'You've got nothing to be worried about', 'Dwelling doesn't help'). We need to be as emotionally open as possible to feelings and experiences, for the child not only to learn about feelings but also to feel them and to start to understand that it is ok to feel how they feel, and that they are not alone. They need to start experiencing that if they show their feelings, we will listen to them; in essence that they are having reparative and healing experiences around feelings. Then it is about how we support them to sit with these feelings and understand them a bit better; and we can introduce some strategies or tools to navigate through them.

We want our responses to convey that we hear them and are listening to them (e.g. 'I am sorry you are feeling...', 'It makes sense that you might be feeling...', 'I get that you are feeling...because...', 'I'm so sorry that you learned that...but in this house, we do... We know it will take time, but we are going to work together to...', 'When I corrected your homework, you might have thought that I thought you were stupid or that you couldn't do it. No wonder you might feel angry and frustrated, I'm so sorry, that wasn't my intention. From now on I will try to...').

Building on the above, it is useful to remember Daniel Siegel's phrase (Siegel & Bryson 2015) which supports the idea of naming and acknowledging feelings first. You have to 'name it to tame it'. Often, once we put a name to something, it can take some of the air out of it and can make it feel less overwhelming and scary. To do this tentatively and carefully (we don't want to tell someone how they are feeling, because we don't know how they are feeling, but we can be curious), we can use statements such as 'I wonder if you are feeling...', 'I don't have an emotional x-ray but I wonder if...', 'I would also feel...if...', 'I'm not surprised you are feeling... when...', 'When my heart is beating fast like a drum, it often is telling me... I'm not sure if you think yours is telling you something similar?', 'If the feeling could talk, I wonder what it might say?' It can be helpful to sometimes support children in organizing their feelings; for example, 'You look a bit scared. I'm sorry the door was loud, I know that sometimes loud noises can be scary...', 'I noticed you might have floated off somewhere in your mind just then. I wonder if that's because... I know that might feel scary for you. It makes sense that you might feel scared because of that. I'm so sorry...were so scary for you.'

Also important to how we discuss the activities and children's responses towards them is that sometimes we make assumptions about feelings. For example, we might use a common message around feelings such as 'sharing is caring', but many children, like Taya, have learned that sharing is not caring and instead for them it has led to hurt or pain or embarrassment. Or we might say that all feelings are valid and important, but for many children this doesn't ring true, as they haven't had that experience. So, we often dive in without understanding where someone is at or what a big question 'How are you feeling?' is to some people. Adults also all have their own relationships to, history with, and experience of feelings.

So, it is important to take some time to think about what we need to start teaching, exploring, and expanding on around the theme of feelings. Are there assumptions we are making about feelings, or expectations about them? What has the child learned about feelings and why might we need to tread gently and re-teach them? Why might talking about feelings be tricky? What might the feeling be trying to tell us?

Sometimes, we need to walk before we can run, and to go back to the basics. Activity 19 shares some of the key messages around feelings that I often explore with children, parents, and carers. It might be a case of drip-feeding and infusing these into conversations or into the activities. However, I would recommend spending some time reflecting on them, practising them, and thinking about them before sharing them with the child. Take your time to have a read and think about which resonate, which might be similar to or different from other people, what you might add, and what might the consequences be of having these or not having them. For some people, it might be useful to send a brochure or video of some of these before you meet the parent/carer/child or in between sessions to help to scaffold and warm the context. You might want to name and share some of them before diving into feelings talk, and to use them as a springboard for further conversations. It might be that we hold in our minds some of these messages, so that we can tread more gently, be more patient, and make fewer assumptions. At this stage you might want to reread certain passages from the first section of the adult guide: 'Getting the environment right for engaging with the story and activities', 'How can we scaffold and warm the context?', 'Responding to silence or shrugs' and 'How to make these activities more meaningful'. These provide lots of tips and ideas for how to scaffold conversations, integrate movement, and enrich feelings conversations.

As is also shared in the first section of this adult guide we need to support children to learn words and terms that resonate for them. While they might say 'sad', they could also use down/upset/depressed/blue/low/heavy, and so on, as well as a word which they choose like 'pooey', 'oohy', 'mucky'. And there might be words or terms that are missing in the images or conversations which they might want to add, such as misunderstood, heartbroken, weird.

Mixed, blended, entangled, and fused feelings

A hugely important part of exploring, normalizing, and validating feelings is around the acceptance of mixed, blended, entangled, and fused feelings. In society, so often we are polarized, split, binary, and othering; we try to put things in boxes or make them fit or to simplify or make them one-dimensional. For example, when a child starts nursery we might excitedly exclaim, 'You must be so happy and excited to be a big girl and starting nursery', but while many children might be excited, they might also be a bit worried or apprehensive. It is ok to have co-occurring feelings. We can have multiple feelings at the same time, and one doesn't cancel or take away from the other. It is so important in life that we acknowledge that feelings can be confusing, jarring, conflicting, puzzling, and also multi-dimensional, with many textures.

This is even more crucial in the context of trauma. Children have often been blamed or shamed for their feelings, told how they should feel or react, or have had to camouflage or mask their feelings. They might have had to cut-off from their feelings. Often their feelings have been disjointed and not integrated. With trauma and abuse, it is common to have mixed feelings. For example, I might be scared of my parent who hurt me, and at the same time love them and feel loyalty towards them; I might fear them and long for them at the same time. My body might have felt hurt, intruded on, controlled, and in pain, and also special and have responded with pleasure. We can integrate and hold these feelings at the same time. We might be proud and also have regrets and doubts. We might be in a place of trauma and also be able to connect with survivorship and have hope. We might be smiling and also be sad or struggling. We might be overwhelmed and also feel capable. We might be kind and still set boundaries, and so on. It is really important that we either name and explain this to children and model it ourselves, or when we ask or talk about feelings we leave space for all the different textures and colours in between so that they don't feel that there is a right or wrong, good or bad way to feel and they have a sense that all feelings and aspects of them are valid and important. This extends to us – we are likely to have mixed, blended, entangled feelings about ourselves, situations, the child, our relationship. These messages are shared in Activity 19.

Keeping the child in your mind

It is important to show the child that they are valued, noticed, and truly seen, and that you keep them in your mind, and in your heart. Again, especially important in the context of trauma, where children might feel forgotten, like a burden, unimportant, abandoned, ignored, lost, and had their needs, thoughts, and feelings minimized or denied. There are lots of different ways to show them that they have been kept in mind:

- Having regular check-ins and touching base.
- Spending quality time together.
- Showing them that you are truly listening (with your whole mind and body), and that their thoughts, feelings, perspective, and opinions matter.
- Remembering things that they said to you, things they want and like, things they are interested in. This is like being their memory bank; for example, 'I was thinking of you because...', 'You were on my mind when...', 'I know you said...so I made/bought...', 'That reminded me of when you said...'
- Noticing, naming, and supporting them when they are absent or don't seem like themselves. This includes being tuned into their mood and signals, naming their feelings, and responding sensitively to them.
- Trying to see things from their perspective or through their eyes.
- Using symbols and items to convey the message that they are on your mind, such as giving them some string or a golden thread to represent that you are always connected and tied together, or a mini brain to show that they are always on your mind. Other ideas include writing loving post-it notes and putting them in the child's school box, sticking them on their mirror or sending them a 'Hug' or a 'Thinking of you' in the post, or having an item of theirs, a photo, or a piece of jewellery that they made, that you carry with you or wear.

It is also important to reflect on what your and the child's hopes, dreams, and wishes are for yourselves, for each other, and for the overall relationship. This can be expanded on and made more child friendly and creative by using props like a genie, a wishing well, or a wand, or drawing/making something like a bridge or a magic gateway for getting to that future place.

A parting message

We have covered a huge number of ideas, concepts, tips, and tools. There is too much to absorb and for each one we could sink deeper and go into the layers of it, so please give yourself time to think and reflect. Different things will resonate for different people at different times and in different roles. Remember, it is better to focus on quality over quantity and that 'every interaction can be an intervention' (Treisman 2017) – the small things can be the big things. You will already be doing lots of this and so some of you will be just enriching and tweaking current practice; others of you will be trying to integrate lots of these ideas into your life. You will all be at different stages of your journey. I hope you find this a rich resource and are able to take away lots of golden nuggets and find a way to make them suit you and the child you are supporting, and to blend them with the other things that you are doing, and that already work well for you. I look forward to hearing from you.

I will be here cheering you on and hope you can keep leaving heart prints!

Resources

References

Perry, B.D. (2014). The Neurosequential Model of Therapeutics in Young Children. In K. Brandt, P.D. Perry, S. Seligman & E. Tronick (eds) *Infant and Early Childhood Mental Health* (pp.21–47). New York, NY: American Psychiatric Press.

Remen, R.N. (1996). *Kitchen Table Wisdom: Stories that Heal*. New York, NY: Riverhead Books.

Rothschild, B. (2000). *The Body Remembers*. New York, NY: W.W. Norton.

Siegel, D.J. (2013). *Parenting from the Inside Out: How a Deeper Self-Understanding Can Help You Raise Children Who Thrive*. New York, NY: Tarcher Perigee.

Siegel, D.J. & Bryson, T. (2015). *The Whole-Brain Child Workbook: Practical Exercises, Worksheets and Activities to Nurture Developing Minds*. Eau Claire, WI: PESI Publications.

Van der Kolk, B. (2014). *The Body Keeps the Score*. New York, NY: Viking.

My other cards

Treisman, K. (2017). A *Therapeutic Treasure Deck of Grounding, Soothing, Coping and Regulating Cards*. London: Jessica Kingsley Publishers.

Treisman, K. (2017). *A Therapeutic Treasure Deck of Sentence-Completion and Feeling Cards*. London: Jessica Kingsley Publishers.

Treisman, K. (2020). *The Parenting Patchwork Treasure Deck. A Creative Tool for Assessments, Interventions, and Strengthening Relationships with Parents, Carers, and Children*. London: Jessica Kingsley Publishers.

Treisman, K. (2022). *The Trauma Deck. A Creative Tool for Assessments, Interventions, and Learning for Work with Adversity and Stress in Children and Adults*. London: Jessica Kingsley Publishers.

My other books

Treisman, K. (2016). *Working with Relational and Developmental Trauma in Children and Adolescents*. London: Routledge.

Treisman, K. (2017). *A Therapeutic Treasure Box for Working with Children and*

Adolescents with Developmental Trauma: Creative Techniques and Activities. London: Jessica Kingsley Publishers.

Treisman, K. (2018). *Neon the Ninja Activity Book for Children who Struggle with Sleep and Nightmares: A Therapeutic Story with Creative Activities for Children Aged 5–10*. London: Jessica Kingsley Publishers.

Treisman, K. (2018). *Gilly the Giraffe Self-Esteem Activity Book: A Therapeutic Story with Creative Activities for Children Aged 5–10*. London: Jessica Kingsley Publishers.

Treisman, K. (2019). *Binnie the Baboon Anxiety and Stress Activity Book: A Therapeutic Story with Creative and CBT Activities to Help Children Aged 5–10 Who Worry*. London: Jessica Kingsley Publishers.

Treisman, K. (2019). *Presley the Pug Relaxation Activity Book: A Therapeutic Story with Creative Activities to Help Children Aged 5–10 to Regulate Their Emotions and to Find Calm*. London: Jessica Kingsley Publishers.

Treisman, K. (2019). *Cleo the Crocodile Activity Book for Children Who Are Afraid to Get Close: A Therapeutic Story with Creative Activities about Trust, Anger, and Relationships to Help Children Aged 5–10*. London: Jessica Kingsley Publishers.

Treisman, K. (2021). *Ollie the Octopus Loss and Bereavement Activity Book: A Therapeutic Story with Activities for Children Aged 5–10*. London: Jessica Kingsley Publishers.

Treisman, K. (2021). *A Treasure Box for Creating Trauma-Informed Organizations: A Ready-to-Use Resource for Trauma, Adversity, and Culturally Informed, Infused, and Responsive Systems*. London: Jessica Kingsley Publishers.

Treisman, K. (2024). *Trauma-Informed Health Care: A Reflective Guide for Improving Care and Services*. London: Jessica Kingsley Publishers.

Websites and links

Please visit www.safehandsthinkingminds.co.uk for an array of useful websites, podcasts, links, and online resources around attachment, trauma, and therapeutic re-parenting (regularly updated).

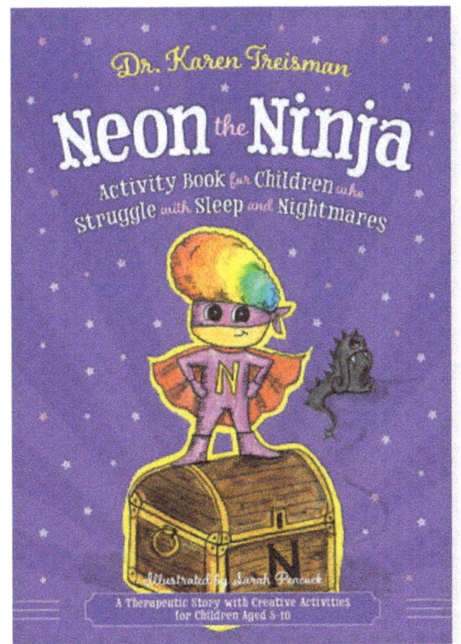

Neon the Ninja Activity Book for Children who Struggle with Sleep and Nightmares

A Therapeutic Story with Creative Activities for Children Aged 5–10

Dr. Karen Treisman

128PP | PAPERBACK | ISBN: 978 1 78592 550 4 | EISBN: 978 1 78775 002 9

Neon the Ninja has a very special job. He looks after anyone who finds the night time scary. Lots of us have nightmares, but Neon loves nothing more than using his special ninja powers to keep the nightmares and worries far away, and to keep the magical dreams and positive thoughts close by.

It combines a fun illustrated story to show children how Neon the Ninja can reduce their nightmares and night worries with fun activities and therapeutic worksheets to make night times feel safer and more relaxed. This workbook contains a treasure trove of explanations, advice, and practical strategies for parents, carers and professionals. Based on creative, narrative, sensory and CBT techniques, it is full of tried and tested exercises, tips and techniques to aid and alleviate nightmares and sleeping difficulties. This is a must-have for those working and living with children aged 5–10 who experience nightmares or other sleep-related problems.

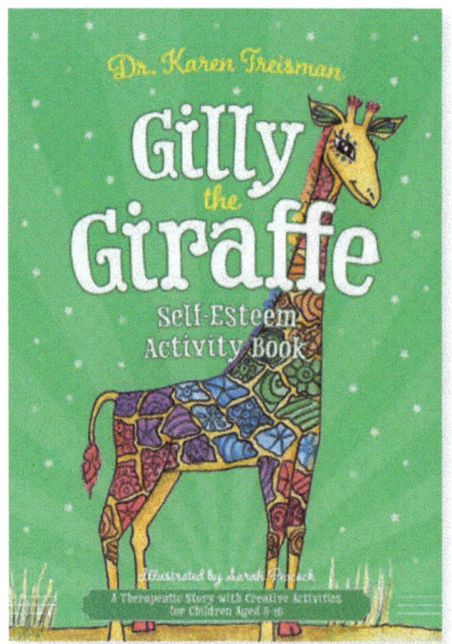

Gilly the Giraffe Self-Esteem Activity Book

A Therapeutic Story with Creative Activities for Children Aged 5–10

Dr. Karen Treisman

144PP | PAPERBACK | ISBN: 978 1 78592 552 8 | EISBN: 978 1 78775 003 6

Even though Gilly the Giraffe has many wonderful things in her life, she sometimes lacks confidence. Why does she have to stand out so much with her long neck, her long black tongue and her mosaic patches? Why do some of the other animals point and laugh at her? Can it be possible to be different and to be cool?

This activity book developed by expert child psychologist Dr. Karen Treisman combines a colourfully illustrated therapeutic story about Gilly the Giraffe to help start conversations, which is followed by a wealth of creative activities for children to explore and build upon some of the ideas raised in the story, and beyond!

The activities are accompanied by extensive advice and practical strategies for parents, carers and professionals on how to help children aged 5–10 boost their self-esteem and confidence.

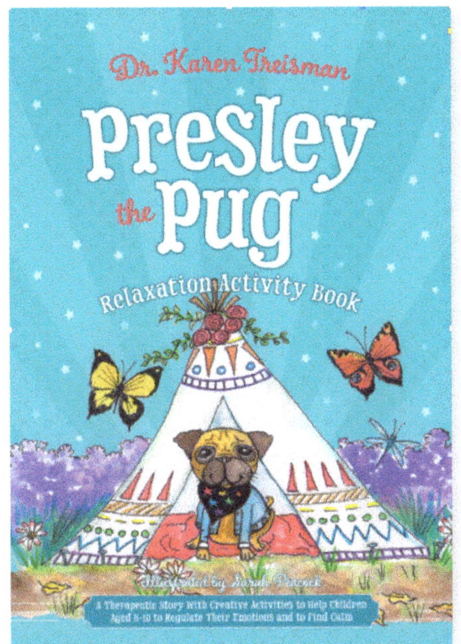

Presley the Pug Relaxation Activity Book

A Therapeutic Story With Creative Activities to Help Children Aged 5–10 to Regulate Their Emotions and to Find Calm

Dr. Karen Treisman

144PP | PAPERBACK | ISBN: 978 1 78592 553 5 | EISBN: 978 1 78775 110 1

Like all dogs, Presley the Pug loves to play, run, and snuggle up under his warm blanket. But sometimes, Presley gets so excited that his feelings take over.

Sometimes it's anger, sometimes stress, sometimes worry. He doesn't know how to calm down! What can Presley do when he feels like this? Luckily Presley's canine friends are nearby with some wise words and they share some of the tricks that have worked for them!

This therapeutic activity book was developed by expert child psychologist Dr. Karen Treisman. It features a colourful therapeutic story designed to help start conversations about coping with big feelings and how to find calm. It explains how Presley (and the reader!) is able to create a 'mind retreat' – an imaginary safe space where he can relax.

The activity book is also packed with creative activities and photocopiable worksheets to help children to explore the ideas raised in the story, including regulating and coping tools like sensory boxes, relaxation exercises and easy yoga poses. It also features advice and practical strategies for parents, carers and professionals supporting children aged 5–10.

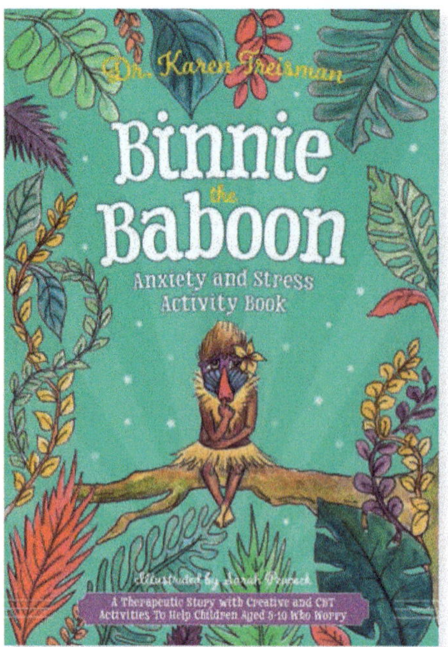

Binnie the Baboon Anxiety and Stress Activity Book

A Therapeutic Story with Creative and CBT Activities to Help Children Aged 5–10 Who Worry

Dr. Karen Treisman

144PP | PAPERBACK | ISBN: 978 1 78592 554 2 | EISBN: 978 1 78775 002 9

Binnie is a creative and energetic baboon, who bounces around the lush green mountains of Rwanda in East Africa. But like many of us, Binnie often feels worried and stressed and these worries often get in her way! What if she gets lost in the jungle, or if her family get sick? What if no one likes her? Sometimes she even worries about the fact she's worried; and if she isn't worried, well why not?!

This activity book has been developed by expert child psychologist Dr. Karen Treisman. The first part of the book is a colourful illustrated therapeutic story about Binnie the Baboon, with a focus on worry and anxiety. This is followed by a wealth of creative activities and photocopiable worksheets for children to explore issues relating to anxiety, worry, fears and stress, and how to find ways to understand and overcome them.

The final section of the book is full of advice and practical strategies for parents, carers and professionals on how to help children aged 5–10 to start to understand why they experience feelings of anxiety, and what they can do to help reduce and navigate it.

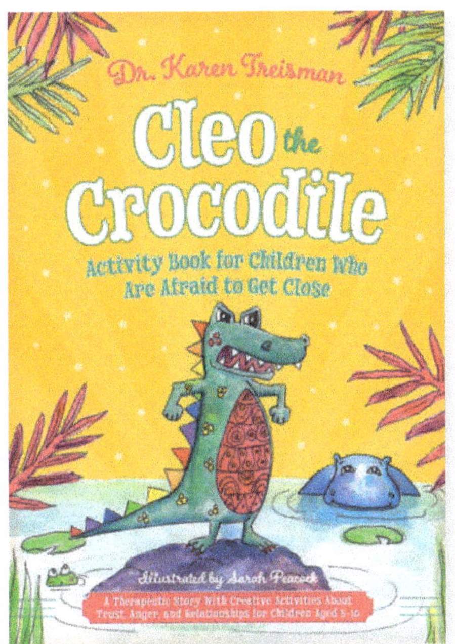

Cleo the Crocodile Activity Book for Children who are Afraid to Get Close

A Therapeutic Story with Creative Activities About Trust, Anger and Relationships for Children Aged 5–10

Dr. Karen Treisman

160PP | PAPERBACK | ISBN: 978 1 78592 551 1 | EISBN: 978 1 78775 078 4

Amongst the beauty of the Okavango delta in Botswana, Cleo the Crocodile loved having fun with all of his animal friends. That is, until one day Hogan the Hippo, who was supposed to look after Cleo, started to act mean and hurt him. Cleo has to leave the swamp to find a safe new home – he's scared and puts his prickles up for protection, so all the other animals are afraid of him. How can Cleo find a new safe home? How can he make new friends when he doesn't know who he can trust?

This activity book developed by expert child psychologist Dr. Karen Treisman combines a colourfully illustrated therapeutic story about Cleo the Crocodile to help start and enrich conversations, which is followed by a wealth of creative activities and photocopiable worksheets for children to explore issues relating to attachment, relationships, rejection, anger, trust and much more.

The activities are accompanied by extensive advice and practical strategies for parents, carers and professionals on how to help children aged 5–10 to start to name their tricky feelings. It will help children to understand their own prickles, to trust others and begin to invest in relationships so they can let others close again.

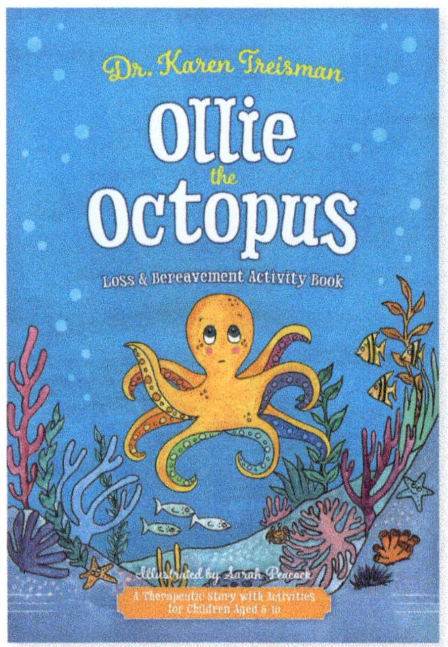

Ollie the Octopus Loss and Bereavement Activity Book

A Therapeutic Story with Activities for Children Aged 5–10

Dr. Karen Treisman

256PP | PAPERBACK | ISBN: 978 1 78775 766 0 | EISBN: 978 1 78775 767 7

In a magical underwater forest lived a colourful and loveable Octopus called Ollie, who loved swimming with his friends and spending time with his mum and dad, Orla and Orson the Octopuses.

Until one day, Orla started to get very sick. The doctors did everything they could to help her, but very sadly, Orla died. Ollie had so many thoughts and feelings spinning around in his head, and his heart was hurting.

This activity book has been developed by expert child Psychologist and bestselling author Dr. Karen Treisman. The first part of the book is a colourful illustrated therapeutic story about Ollie the Octopus, with a focus on Ollie making sense of and processing the loss of his mum, Orla. This is followed by a wealth of creative activities and colourful photocopiable worksheets for children and the people supporting them to explore aspects of loss, grief, death, and bereavement, and how to find ways to understand and cope with them.

The final section of the book is full of advice and practical strategies for parents, carers, and professionals on how to help children aged 5-10 to begin to understand the complex and multi-layered feelings surrounding loss and bereavement, and what they can do to help navigate them through their grief journey.